ANCIENT INDIAN LEGAL PHILOSOPHY

ITS RELEVANCE TO CONTEMPORARY JURISPRUDENTIAL THOUGHT

ANCIENT INDIAN LEGAL PHILOSOPHY

ITS RELEVANCE TO CONTEMPORARY JURISPRUDENTIAL THOUGHT

S.K. PUROHIT
Former Associate Professor of Law,
University of Jodhpur, Jodhpur

DEEP & DEEP PUBLICATIONS PVT. LTD.
F-159, RAJOURI GARDEN, NEW DELHI-110 027

First Edition : 1994
Reprint : 2001

ISBN 81-7100-583-7

Laser Typeset by Laser Graphics, 78, Rajouri Apartment,
(Opp. G.O.I. Press, Mayapuri, Rajouri Garden, New Delhi-64, Ph : 5441435

Printed at Efficient Offset Printers,
Plot 215, Shahzada Bagh Industrial Area-II, Delhi

Published by DEEP & DEEP PUBLICATIONS PVT. LTD.,
F-159, Rajouri Garden, New Delhi-110 027
Phones : 5435369, 5440916.

Contents

Some Thoughts

The Aryan is a Juridical Race. The Aryan race has always had a true conception of law and political life. The greatest juridical monuments of antiquity, the Indian books, the Roman law, and the Germanic law belong to this race, which tends to reconcile the authority of State with freedom of the individual. Among Aryan peoples, there has never arisen that all-controlling despotism which blots out man, as in Egypt, Babylon, China, among the Mussulmans and the tartar tribes--or if it has appeared it has not been of long duration.

—LUIGI MIRAGLIA
(Comparative Legal Philosophy
Applied to Legal Institutions,
p.120, World's Legal Philosophy
Series, Vol. III)

*   *   *

Closely connected with the religious and philosophical views on Aryans are certain fundamental positions in regard to the philosophy of law, which in turn became the antecedents of later legal and ethical developments among the Greeks and Romans. Foremost among these philosophical conception is 'rita' which is at once the organising principle of the universe and divine ordering of earthly life.

—PROF. BEROLZHEIMER
(World's Legal Philosophers'
Modern Legal Philosophy
Series, Vol. II, pp. 37-38)

*   *   *

We may recall that to the Vedic Aryans the central philosophic conception of organised nature was 'rita', which included the natural and human order. A closely related conception was 'dharma'. The Greeks, by emphasizing the creative energy, made of 'rita', Øusis and of 'dhama'. ØEUIS. The Romans, through the Greeks, derived from 'rit', their central conception 'ratum', 'ratio', 'naturalis ratio'; and Augustine Christianized 'rita' and 'Pax'. Order is the universal bond that holds the world together; order assigns a place to all created things; it is a directive and distributive justice.

–PROF. BEROLZHEIMER
(World's Legal Philosophy Series,
Worlds Legal Philosophers, Vol. II,
pp. 831-97)

* * *

Dharma is that which holds society together. It is the honey that binds together all human beings, all creations. It is, therefore, the basis of the wide universe. It, therefore, regulates all life, all activity. Indeed, it is the property of things animate and inanimate. Its scope and implication are unlimited. It denotes, justice, duty, rights, law, code of honour, moral obligation and several virtues, a life of Dharma is a life of faith, discipline, dedication and harmony. Thus, it furnishes the proper perspective, for life and culture. Dharma is the Constitution of the Hindu Society.

–CHIDAMBARA KULKARNI
–Hindu Dharma

* * *

Law is the King of Kings, far more powerful and rigid than they; nothing can be mightier than law, by whose aid as by that of the highest monarch, even the weak may prevail over the strong–*The Vedas*.

–(Satapath Brahman 14.4, 2.23
Bradaranyaka Upanisad 1-4-14)

Custom is transcendental dharma.

–(MANU SMRITI-I–*108 to 110*)

*   *   *

Justice and mercy, reward and punishment, are not to be indiscriminately exercised by kings at their whims and fancies (17-30)

–(KISHKINDHA KANDAM–*Ramayana*)

*   *   *

This wise and the great are able to discern the right and the wrong by their reasoning power and logic.

–VALMIKI *(Aranyakandan–66-16)*

*   *   *

The Laws of Dharma are inconceivable and transcend the human power of imagination. All-pervading God who dwells in the hearts of all knows what is right and wrong.

–VALMIKI–*Ramayana*
(Kiskindandha Kand–18-5)

*   *   *

Acknowledgements

I have no words to express my gratitude to my reverend Guru, Professor S.C. Thanvi under whose guidance I have been able to complete my book on the subject like the present one.

Professor Thanvi is one of the foremost pioneers of Legal Education and is known throughout the country for his knowledge, teaching and integrity. As a student, and later as a member of his staff, I have admired and respected him. So, once in the course of some informal discussion when he expressed his grave concern for the dearth of research in legal theory of our ancients and consequential misunderstanding, ignorance, indifference and, at times, hostility of jurists about our legal theory, instantly I made up my mind to undertake a study in that direction and was blessed with his guidance. Without his personal interest, encouragement and illuminating discussion, constructive suggestions and correctives, this book would not have seen the light of the day.

I am also thankful to my lawyer-father Shri Bhim Raj Purohit for his encouragement and valuable suggestions on some legal problems with which he comes face to face every day, in the law courts.

How earnestly I wish that there could be more appropriate a word than, "thanks" to express my special regards to the present Dean and Head of the Department of Law, Dr. D.C. Jain who has been of immense help to me in so many ways and has always encouraged me in my work.

I have received all the co-operation from my colleagues. I am thankful to Servashri P.B. Bhattacharya, R.C. Chhangani, O.P. Parmar and A.K. Mathur, with whom I had fruitful discussions.

I have taken the benefit of the services of the staff and officials of the Law Faculty Library, Jodhpur University, the Rajasthan High Court Library, and the Library of the Indian Law Institute, New Delhi.

I am indebted to them for their services and assistance. My special thanks are due to Shri R.K. Bohra, Librarian (Law) and Shri Ghanshyam, Librarian, Rajasthan High Court Library who had always and ungrudgingly helped me in every way.

Jodhpur SHANTI KUMAR PUROHIT

Prologue

The Ancient Indian Legal Philosophy is a treasure house containing peerless gems in the form of legal concepts and jurisprudential theories, and it is a pity that no attempt has ever been made to make use of them in moulding or shaping the prevalent theories adumbrated by Western thinkers to suit our genius and culture. Some of them (Western theories) are inappropriate to our genius, culture, and tradition and have thus failed to achieve the desired objective of securing the welfare of the people but have definitely made our lives a conglomeration of values, which, in a large part, are alien to our culture and tradition. The effect of such borrowing from the West has not been salutary and we still seem to grope in the dark. Our country which is a Republic and is wedded to achieve a Socialistic Pattern of Society but little do we realise that in Ancient India, the Dharmashastra had for its objective the everlasting welfare of mankind, as an integral part of cosmic existence. Human welfare, at that time, consisted in the attainment of eternal peace and harmony. The mind of man has to be peaceful, harmonious and contented, and his body to act, in ''harmony and rhythm, with the acts of others.'' In the 'Rig-Vedic' thought which is the sheet anchor of Indian culture and civilisation, the Indian mind lies embedded in all its potency, vitality and simplicity. And to this mind we should turn because this mind may still be considered the sub-stratum for legal Engineering of the present Indian life. We are striving hard to make people's lives happier but happiness, it is thought, merely consists in providing them more of material comforts. This, in the view of this author is an antinomy. One has only to look at the more, nay, highly advanced (in the present day understanding) and affluent societies inhabiting the globe and the untruth will be soon out. The more the materially affluent the societies the greater is the unrest in the minds of the people comprising them. The more are the people agitated, the greater the need to bring them under controlled by legislation. This vicious circle goes on creating more problems than we can solve and man's happiness remains a 'Chimera'. India, which became free only in 1947, started with a legal system that it inherited from the British who looked upon Indian thought (including Jurisprudence) as "dotages of Brahmnical superstition". Historically, the first blow was delivered by the Muslim invaders, and the final by the British rulers who never encouraged any development of Indian Jurisprudence. More shocking has been the attitude of legal thinkers in this country who considered themselves learned if they could speak the names of some Western jurists. This has been the bane of Indian legal thought. Persons learned in the study of the Vedas and sacred scriptures are today dubbed as, in the mildest of terms, as amusingly simple.

During my studies in Indian Legal Philosophy, I discovered legal precepts and practices strikingly appropriate which, if modified to an extent as would take notice of the changing circumstances and the social milieu, will definitely help us to achieve not only the ideal of a Socialistic Pattern of Society but would make our lives happier. This author does not plead to revert to that Philosophy in toto because he is conscious that there are many things in the Indian Legal Philosophy which are obsolete and out of date due to changes brought about by Science and Technology. But such of the precepts, practices and the theories which are useful and suitable to Indian genius and tradition can, hopefully, be built into our legal system. A complete neglect of all that is Indian is neither wise nor desirable and has the consequence of ill-equipping the lawyer of today who is incomplete in his education. If Indian Jurisprudence is made the foundation of legal studies the whole panorama will be brighter than what we find today.

The present book is, therefore, devoted to the task of gleaning out of the Dharamshastras and the scriptures those precious and pearless precepts which, if used as a basis of our Jurisprudence, will usher in the emergence of a Science of Jurisprudence that will be our own and will be unique in itself having no rival on the broad spectrum-glistening with all the colours and the consequent glory. Indian Jurisprudence originated in a theory of sovereignty which could boldly be asserted as the earliest of its kind based on social contract, a form of government, republican in the truest sense of the term, where the people had the unquestionable right to revolt against a tyrannical

King. In Kautilya's Arthshastra, mention has been made of a unique example of a King paying a fine for doing injustice. This secular example emerges from the notion that the King was the fountain of justice and that all Dharma emerged from the King. The King was the emblem of law as if law was deified in the King. To some extent, in a limited sense, the English maxim that the King could do no wrong did not find applicability with the Kautilyan King. The Ancient Indian Jurisprudence recognized no rights of a King to govern which is disclosed by the following :

> Jaṭa sa dushtha-prakritish chaturanto-pyanatmavan
> Hanyate va prakritibhir yati va divashtam Vasham.

A King of evil nature and of vicious habits will, though an emperor, either be killed by his own subjects or subdued by his enemies. These provisions indicate two things. First, the King's right to govern was subject to good conduct; he had no absolute rights or powers. Secondly, they imply that sovereignty was founded on the principle of social contract. If the King violated the traditional pact he forfeited his Kingship.[1] The modern Jurists are making frantic efforts to find out the rightfulness and wrongfulness of an act and to construct such theories of punishment which may help them in checking the growing criminality all over the world. The writers of 'Dharmashastras' considered this fully and we find that wrong in the early Vedic thought is a disorder or deviation from a straight (right) course. Whatever is evil is an evil of deviation and the duty towards law is the ideal of life, or 'Dharma'. A discussion of this important topic finds a place in this thesis. Equally important is the question relating to 'order'. It is said that it is the duty of the State to maintain law and order which it does through the means of law. This all-pervading question takes us to a discussion of the concept of '*Rit*' which has been considered fully in Chapter 3 as meaning 'Order' in its generic sense; as 'legal order' in juristic thought. The concept of 'Danda', as preservation of order, in a political society, was the main principle which the ancients used with advantage. This has been put succinctly as : 'Rit' orders life by nature, 'dharma' by imposing duty and 'danda' by exerting force, i.e., by awarding punishment.

The oft-debated question of the difference between legal positivism and natural law which has not yet been solved, has been discussed and it can, after the study of the Ancient Legal Philosophy, be said that both approaches study law as an expression of order. Natural law treats law as some moral order whereas legal positivism considers it as some logical order. The concept of *'Rit'* in its extensive form meant to the ancient sages as 'universal order' and the idea of one world was understood first by the Indian jurists of the Ancient. Juridical theory of ancient India did not lose its equilibrium nor did it swing from one extreme to another and yet maintained its critical awareness of life and its problems without making law a segregated body. Indian thought was a synthesis, in its best form, of culture and progress of human personality.

There has been, in recent years, a controversy regarding the relation between law and morals. For a resolution of this controversy one has only to look into the Dharmashastra where Wrong (Adharma) is categorized as (a) *Aparadha* (Crime), (b) *Pataka* (wrong which amounts to an immoral act). In both of these the idea of wrongfulness is present and a discussion of this important subject finds a place in this book. The whole legal theory of ancient India has its axis as 'Dharma' which was considered by the ancient thinkers as a righteous conduct for all. In its juridical meaning, as has been fully explained in Chapter 4, Dharma is law, is custom, is authority, is reason, is conscience, and a King rules over this subjects because of this Dharma. In this connection a full discussion as to the meaning of law in the Western legal theory became necessary and in the light of that discussion certain conclusions relating to the true nature of law and its theoretical basis manifested by the various schools of Jurisprudence have been arrived at the end of Chapter 4.

As has been pointed above Dharma consisted in a righteous conduct which in its turn must impose a duty to do or to forbear. This idea of duty or obligation finds emphasis in ancient Indian Jurisprudence which to many, today, must appear something strange. Though rights and duties are co-related in both the systems, in Indian Jurisprudence the duty is primary and rights are only the corrollaries of duties. The social institution of marriage in Ancient Indian Law was considered to be a sacred duty to be performed but in Western Jurisprudence it has become a contract which could be broken at will, if certain conditions exist or are made to exist leading to innumerable cases of divorces and consequent broken homes resulting in unhappiness and misery.

The Indian Law has never been static as has been made to appear by some of the Western jurists, chief among them being Sir

Henry Maine, who characterized it as of a static character and under priestly domination. But he forgot to see that "throughout the Middle Ages, the study and development or law in Europe was the exclusive privilege of the clergy".[2] Roscoe Pound contradicts, in his book 'Jurisprudence' (Vol. III, p. 445), the study advanced by Maine and maintains that growth of law is still possible if it is expounded by sages in sacred or quasi-sacred writings as was done in India. Where Hindu writers fashioned usage or the texts to their idea of 'Right'. Manu the great law giver has said:

'Veda is the foundation of all law, then Smriti: then the code of conduct of good men of the time; lastly, one's own conscience'. This quotation is replete with the idea that from stage to stage the development of law was considerable. Late Dr. Ganga Nath Jha believed that the Indian Law was never static and this author cannot resist the temptation of quoting the relevant passage. (Source of Hindu Law by Ganga Nath Jha, pp. 11-12).

"From the above it is clear that the centre of gravity of authority, which originally rested entirely in the Shruti, gradually shifted from Shruti to Smriti, from Smriti to Custom; and finally to the writings of a few learned and very modern authors, all this points to the fact that in the domain of law, there has all along been a progressive spirit at work. That this is not a mere conjecture, but a fact recognized in the highest circles of society in this country is proved by the declaration of Parashara to the effect that the dharmas for men in Sathayuga are other than those in Treta and the Dvapara and in the Kaliyuga also they are different--the Dharma of each Yuga being in keeping with the distinctive character of that age.

.....This actual adaptation of the law to changing conditions went on effectively so long as there was present in the country a temporal authority sufficiently interested and strong enough to lend to the changes its support and thereby supply the necessary driving force."[3]

It is, therefore, clear that ancient law-makers, including Manu and Parashar had accepted the concept of 'Yugdharma' (law according to age) which implied that law must change in a changing society.

The cornerstone of a democratic form of Government is the Rule of Law. The British Constitution is founded on the twin-principles of the Rules of Law and Parliamentary Sovereignty. The Rule of Law, in England, is zealously protected by the Courts and the whole Constitution of England revolves round this axis. The Indian

Constitution, likewise, has adopted the principle and its (constitution's) various articles have incorporated it and the Courts have unflinchingly enforced this principle. How interesting, then, it is to find, that the theory of State in the ancient Indian Legal Philosophy was based on the principle of the 'Rule of Law' from which even the King could not escape. *The law of 'Dharma' is considered as the ruler of 'Rulers'.* To do one's duty is right. This implied harmony or Samanvaya. Judicial trials are inquiries into truth–what actually happened in a particular case. The law was social habit and resided distinctly in Society. In the Varna system of the ancient, we have the functional distribution of duties and division of labour which resulted in social interdependence. In Duguit's social solidarity we have an echo of this very social cohesion. The law of 'Dharma' goes beyond social interdependence even and merges with the ideal of human existence itself. It directs the survival and perfection of human beings and ultimately the progress of the society.

A few pages earlier, a reference has been made to the ideal of the Indian Republic which is that of a welfare state. A study of the Dharmashastras, the Mahabharat and other scriptures would reveal that the concept of a welfare state was present in Ancient India and it is a travesty of truth to claim that it is a discovery by Western thinkers. Security and protection were provided by the ancients to Anathan (the Orphans), Vriddhan (the old), Vyadhitan (the sick) and this duty had to be performed under a comprehensive mechanism to aid the needy.

In modern jurisprudence of the West the sources of law occupy a prominent place and they have been described almost unanimously as custom, precedent and legislation. Some writers add equity and agreement also. How interesting to note that in ancient India "*Swadha*" played a very important part in supplying material to the formulation of principles of Law. Custom is the socio-physical material of 'Rit' containing within it the notion of rights as well as law. A study into the development and growth of "Swadha" amply demonstrates that the doctrines of 'living law' propounded by Ehrlich is the modern Western counter-part of the old Indian "Swadha" which as realising itself into a pattern following habit of men becomes the "habitual obedience" of Austinian Theory of law and "Volksgeist" of savigny, it being the corporate consciousness of the people. Proceeding further into the question of the sources of law which have been dealt with in Chapter 6 we find that Smritikars laid down the four legs of law-Dharma, Vyavahara (rules of conduct), Charitra (history) and edicts of the Kings raja sasana (edicts of the King) and how one preceded the other and their relationship inter se. It has been alleged and truly, that law was entangled with religious rituals and observances but at a later stage, in the Kautilyan law of 'Arthshastra' the concept of secular law emerges. Barring a few instances, the 'Arthashastra' abounds in secular laws. In 'Vyavahara' we have a compendium of directions how justice would be administered by the judges and we can thus safely characterize 'Vyavahara' as having all the concepts of a developed legal system. In the matter of the administration of criminal justice, the King is directed not to be either a tyrant or be weak. He is ordained to seek the motive of the crime, the capacity of the criminal to endure penalty and age and gender of the criminal. Thus 'Vyavahara' is the search for truth and a manifestation of impersonal, objective, and eternal dharma. It is the modern equivalent of 'law in action' but unlike the American realism, it does not project the judge as an egocentric individual swayed by extra-legal considerations nor does it depict him (the judge) as a dreamer having a pseudo-crusading spirit of judicial review. In a word, he is not a Narcissist and so much the better for him as otherwise ancient India may have witnessed the pulls recently felt by the country between the judiciary and the parliament. *The Vyavahara, or the judicial process* as it may be called today, was not cut-off from the people but was saturated with human values. The greatness of the Indian juristic mind as reflected in the ancient legal philosophy and 'concepts', lies in its realization that reality with all its multifarious forms is one and the same. This reality consists in 'Dharma' which, on the metaphysical level, is the mystic force which holds together the whole world and this it does by permeating through all the concepts and doings of law and harmonises them. Even if that reality cannot be conceptualized in toto, it still, in its inarticulateness, has the power and dynamism to solve the problems of law. What is needed is faith in such an inarticulate spirit, be it only a working faith, and we can hope, without asking for a Utopia, a solution of the modern problems of law. Hopefully, therefore, we can depend upon this mind to solve our present problems in the way in which the ancients tackled their problems successfully. We cannot do any thing else than this.

Absolute sovereignty, in the Austinian sense, was not conceived of by the Indian thinkers, as has already been adverted to earlier. The King was under the authority of 'Dharma' which is nothing but an ancient assertion of the modern 'rule of law'. The function of the King is " प्रजापरिपालन " i.e. protection of the subjects from the twin-dangers the external and the internal. How he performs these two functions is dealt with in Chapter 7 entitled : Law as an administrative device. The rule of the King was termed as 'Raja-Sasana'. A study, in depth, of this aspect of ancient legal philosophy has revealed to this author the efficiency with which the king was kept under check in administering his executive power, solely on the concept of 'Dharma', which permitted him, sometimes, to create governmental agencies to maintain law and order or to work for the security of the State. Recently, we witnessed a period of emergency in order to quell internal disturbance. In ancient India, power distribution was so balanced that there was no need to take recourse to extra-ordinary means. The King never felt helpless and 'dharma' not so dogmatic not to allow the King to protect the people, the government and the State.

The Chapter on 'Mimansa'–the interpretation of law, as incorporated in this thesis, exhibits the ingenuity of the ancients in showing that 'Mimansa' is not merely didactic (upedesha Sastra) but comprises of a reasoned enquiry into truth. Thus, the rules that were to be used for creating Vedic injunctions of a ritualistic nature were transplanted for the interpretation of legal codes. How this could be done has been illustrated in the Chapter aforesaid with valuable observations of Colebrooke. The disquisitions of 'Mimansa' have a closeness to what we call 'Judicial questions' and abound with sparkling logic. The logic of 'Mimansa' is the logic of the law which, in other words, consisted of rules of interpretation of civil and religious Ordinances. Principles are collected from the examination and decisions of cases. Mimansa, thus created a true juridical science. An eminent writer Lingat R., likens Mimansa to the Roman law-method of interpretation where the opinions of jurisconsults were freely considered and relied upon as solutions to various disputes. The ancients understood the significance of interpretation and wisely and discreetly exercised their choice between alternative views placed before them. Truth was the norm, the 'ought' or 'dharma' which was the task of the interpreter to determine. The ancients thought of rules of interpretation as the rules of good sense. The striking feature of 'Mimansa' was, as has been said above, its logic by which it endeavoured to give rational solutions. These solutions passed as rules, and to a great extent, they fulfilled the needs of the times. Interpretation made its way from the immutable texts of Smritis to mobile traditions and customs of the Community and interpreters were the real intellectual organizers of Hindu Law. In Western jurisprudence the primary rule of interpretation has been accepted as that of 'literal interpretation'. Among the ancients, Jaimini propounded the literal construction as the cordinal rule of interpretation. However, he recommended a departure from the laid text, in case of the text being not clear. In that case, intention may be gathered by recourse to the principles of synthetical or contextual construction. It is interesting thus to notice that some of these principles are not dissimilar to Western rules of interpretation. It is to be noted that the Indian mind was well alive to the need of interpretation and had developed a science of interpretation containing rules which have been discussed in Chapter 8 and which justifies the observation of Colebrooke that the logic of 'Mimansa' is the logic of law. It was through this logic that the Smritikars made a dynamic use of the texts that made Hindu Law alive and alert to time and place. The technique adopted by them was to bring law in harmony with life and its reality, all the time manifesting in social action, thought and behaviour the time-geist so that the content of law remains adequate to serve the social purpose and to give cohesion and strength to law. Law, thus was fixed but progressive.

It would thus be seen that 'Mimansa' is a comprehensive philosophy of law which performed the desired functions in the life of law. In conflict-situations, it performed social-engineering or balancing of interests. It may truly be called, at its unconscious organic level, as 'Volksgeist' of savigny, the collective consciousness of the people or the general will. To refine men, it was termed as 'Reason', to solve problems, it may be termed as 'justice' and for punishing people or to compel them to maintain rightful conduct, it was the 'Danda'.

It is an admitted fact that the object of law is to administer justice. According to Salmond law is a means to an end, the end being to achieve justice in a given situation. In recent years, voluminous legal literature has grown on the relation of law and justice, still we find ourselves in wilderness, as to the purpose of law and its administration when we come face to face with the problem of administration of 'unjust' laws. The ancients had the words 'Nyaya' and 'Dharma' as distinct linguistic expressions to use for justice and law respectively but this is a very late development seen in the wake of 'Nayaya Philosophy'. Be that as it may, the author's researches into this important facet of law has revealed that if, as the ancients did, we draw inspiration from the integrating concept of duty and responsibility in contradistinction to justice which is oriented on 'rights', we can advance towards our goal of constructive planning of society. 'Just' and 'unjust', like 'right' and 'wrong' had, in the ancient legal philosophy, its sole reference to 'Dharma' which was nothing, as has already been pointed out, but a total synthesis of Indian Culture. In this connection the author has examined in Chapter 9 the current meanings of 'justice' in the Western legal theory with a view to finding out how the concept of 'Nyaya' served a superior purpose of not only providing a happy life to the citizen but also the true freedom which can be enjoyed only by recognizing the fact of human worth side by side with the realization of social responsibility. Justice, in this sense, is the operation of 'Dharma' of the ancients which successfully handled the problems of law and life, without any rigid theorisation. The notion of Dharma including both 'right' (rightful conduct) and justice (giving everyman his own) fulfils our 'object'. How this could be done has been explained in Chapter 10.

The word 'Nayaya' to which the author has adverted previously was in the beginning, logic, used to arrive at a correct judgment which was later identified with justice administered impartially without any element of arbitrariness, and still reaching the correct conclusion in accordance with law. It has been shown in Chapter 10 that the essence of right or Dharma lies in what the ancients did by a synthesis of Indian Culture and the spiritualization of its thought. When thought is spiritualised and culture absorbed in a man's actions and activities, the ideal of justice is not for to achieve. The doctrine of justice, having in it the idea of 'Nayaya', has been examined in details by examining the relation of Rita, Truth, and the Law of Karma and their influence on 'Nayaya'. The doctrine of justice in the Gita, that immortal discourse by Lord Krishna, is the doctrine of functions, i.e., doing one's duty well. It has been shown in this connection that this aspect of justice comes closer to modern analytical approach where justice is looked upon as the functions allotted to courts, rather than an ideal. In ancient India it is an instrument, an agent, a means to achieve 'Dharma', which enjoins a duty to work in such a way that an individual's acts subserves common good and this obligation to work in this way is a duty and service. It is not a 'right' or a 'claim' on others. If is a fulfilment rather than a demand. It has been shown in the Chapter stated above (Chapter 10) that the theory of Karma is the theory of natural justice. It is an application of the law of conservation of energy in human action. 'Karma' is the rule of law, in the spiritual world if it may be so called. It is the expression of law and justice both. The ancient Indian mind was not claim-conscious. The law of Karma, then, as a theory of justice, tends more towards the idea of rule of law or law as an autonomous and self-regulating scheme of this world, which is at the same time independent of any ulterior power, not identifiable with it. The theory of punishment and penance, to which reference has been made while dealing with the doctrine of Justice, operates as exculpating sins and wrongs.

Justice has further been found to be what is ultimately right. It is in this conceptual framework of 'Right' that all creative human energy of thought and action can be utilized and directed. Rights is what is true, good and beautiful. Concept of right is first expressed as 'Rit' and later as 'Dharma' which is its mutation. In Plato's absolute justice and Aristotle's total justice we hear echoes of the ancient's Rit as right or righteousness. Its totality consists in 'Dharma'. An examination of these important aspects of justice takes us to 'Nayaya' or positive justice. Manu's famous observation that justice consists in the application of law to the cases arising between members of a State and *Sukra's* dual purpose of justice as a discrimination of good from what is bad and its utilitarian facet, have been investigated into to realize that justice should not only confirm to "right" and "good" and "beautiful" but should also be administered speedily, and this explains the wisdom of the saying: 'Justice delayed is justice denied' which the ancients realized in their own time in the heary past.

The review of the theory of Justice is undertaken to show that the main ideals of justice or its theories were present in Indian Legal Philosophy albeit they were submerged in the substratum of the culture which was religious, ethical and spiritual. In the West, materialism has reached its highest summit and it can be safely asserted that the Western Culture is materialistic. This being so, it is obvious that it (materialistic culture) should affect justice adversely which in its train must have a deleterious effect upon all those concepts, which are allied or ancillary to the doctrine of justice. Materialism has given rise to legal positivism and sociological pragmatism. The former, in its attempt to make law a science, isolates it from all the other related influences like historical, ethical and psychological etc. The latter makes law an empirical study based on facts but rejects ethical and ideological elements. Under these circumstances both of them have failed to provide a viable legal theory which may be capable of dealing with various legal problems that arise everywhere and which baffle solution. The Scandinavians, realizing the impossibility of finding a solution of these problems, have, in utter futility, sought an easy escape in rejecting the very notion of justice, together with authority of law and its binding force. They have, therefore, denied the very reality of law and have designated it as a mere 'label' and a psychological device. This tantamounts to a denial of the science of law. The ancient Indian legal theory, on the other hand, with its spiritual cult, has viewed law not in isolation but in relation to life in all its facets–as a part of the whole of 'Existence'. Law was thus never divorced from value without which law becomes an empty category. In this lay the dynamism of the ancient law.

In the ultimate Chapter of this book (Chap. 11), the author has endeavoured to examine some important concepts of law, without which, the author feels, a thorough and complete appraisal of the jurisprudence of the ancients would not be worthwhile. The Indian Legal Philosophy is robed in religion and mythology and therefore, a conceptual analysis of law cannot be expected. As has been pointed out, the Dharmasastras were more directive than analytical, and the Law of Karma was considered by people to be operating as a law of moral causation through birth and death. There are people who believe that Hindus did not have an efficient system of criminal law but this view has been controverted by S. Vardachariar who quotes Holdsworth as saying that even the English criminal law, in the beginning, was in rudimentary form and the boundary line between civil and criminal law was uncertain. Many offences, instead of being penal, were remedial. Our ancients maintained that it was the duty of the king to maintain the moral as well as the social order. The aim of King's justice was to reform and to correct the criminal and so greater emphasis was placed on civil liability so that the wronged could be compensated, though punishment was also awarded. Hindu criminal law was not based on English ideas of breach of "King's Peace", which according to this author, was only meant to increase the power of the King in a political society. In Ancient India, disputes relating to debts and gifts may be settled by settlement and the King would not interfere but in regard to criminal law, as Medhatithi points out, the offenders had to be punished irrespective of any settlement arrived at between the parties. A discussion relating to security of the State and the weeding out of anti-social elements, finds a place in this Chapter.

Penance, expiration, and post-mortuary punishments were an outcome of a system based on religious and philosophical theories. But this was so also in Europe in the Middle Ages.

A privileged position is found with regard to the Brahmins but that was justified because of a Brahmin's life of piety and his role in the Vedic Culture. Capital sentence was not awarded to a Brahmin for this very reason. The ancients were aware of the evil potentialities of human nature and so they emphasised the deterrent aspect of punishment. They believed that without a State and its power to punish will result in a State of "Matsya-Nyaya", i.e., where a bigger fish will devour the smaller ones and so the King had to be armed with the power of punishment. These were of various types, a reference to which would be found in this Chapter.

However, the aim of the law was also to reform the character of the offenders. The same sentiment is expressed in that great epic 'The Mahabharat'. Punishment was also meant to purify the wrong doer and if the offender is wrongly forgiven the sin falls on the King.

It is interesting to find that in Ancient India, we find tort as an action for civil liability. This is evidenced by a private action called "Vadicrat", (action by plaintiff), the plaintiff could demand compensation. How the King deals with various offences and does justice is seen in a distinction being made between wrongs known as "*Nrapasraya*" and "*Vadikrat*". The former are instituted at the instance of the King, and the latter by private individuals.

The Sastras did not make a clear distinction between private wrongs and public wrongs as elements of both tend to merge together. It is submitted that this was beneficial to the people because a poor litigant could get compensation for the injury to make good the personal loss. The aim of criminal law was "Kantak Sodhana" (weeding out thorns). It has a two-fold purpose--to allow the State to employ extra-ordinary means to avert a political disaster and to weed out thorns from the society. Thus the ancient Indian law was founded upon the concept of 'Dharma' where high regard is paid to duty.

A review of the law of contract carried out in this Chapter would show that the ancients guaranteed the security of property and person. To them contract is fulfilling of a promise, which in turn, becomes an expression of truthfulness. Contracts were of many kinds: of debts, pledges, mortgages, bailments, sales, partnerships, hire-purchases, etc. Who is competent to contract?,--all, except minors, extremely senile, those charged with grave sins, sanyasis, those addicted to vices like drinking and whoring. Their agreements are invalid. It is interesting to note here that the doctrine of 'social-contract' was built upon contract and the question has been discussed by this author at the proper place, by surveying the evolution of contract in the Western world and contrasting its evolution in Ancient India. Through the all-pervading concept of dharma, it has been indicated that the notion of dharma expressed the idea of a rule as well as a general notion of law, right, duty, political obligations, constitution and social contract etc. It has been shown that the modern concept of contract is a 'psuedo-dharma-concept', trying only to emphasise the importance of the freedom of the individual will without reference to social responsibility.

The next important concept that became necessary to consider is the concept of 'Property'. The law of property had reached maturity in the ancient times. A clear distinction was made between possession, ownership, and prescription. It has been revealed to this humble author that the whole concept of property, as it stood then, was in consonance with culture converging on spirit and so the matter of property was not allowed to acquire a super-imposing value. Having acquired harmony through a spiritual and moral scheme, property was considered as only providing security and was not allowed to acquire the status of political power. In this context, ideas concerning justification of property have been examined taking into account the evolution of this concept through the countries and a brief treatment has been given to the various kinds of property that exist today. This survey testifies to the fact that the whole legal theory of the West relating to property is, in truth, a justification for the accumulation and existence of property and for the need to regulate it. It is only now that the Westerners have become conscious of the danger of abnormal accumulation of property in a few hands. In contrast to this, the Indian mind, from the very beginning, allowed a proper place to 'property' in the social set-up, never permitting it to grow abnormally. Indian culture, with its planned social system through 'Varnas', struck a balance in such a way that no one would covet other people's wealth nor could one accumulate property out of greed beyond one's need.

Any abuse of property makes it liable to confiscation. It was clearly understood by the ancients that private property is nothing but an extension of man's ego and his love of 'self'. In a valuable books: 'Life and Thoughts of Mahatma Gandhi' it has been mentioned that the great Mahatma never considered capital to be an evil in itself but its wrong use makes capital an evil. Land must be distributed justly. The slogan: " सबै भूमि गोपाल की " had a social meaning and was meant as a movement for liquidation of ownership of land. The above is almost a reversal towards the ancient ideal relating to property.

The other part of the law, i.e. adjective law, which concerns itself with procedure, was chiefly concerned with 'Vyavahara' which has been considered in earlier Chapters as a law for litigation in Courts. The aim was to find out the truth in a dispute and to do justice. In order that the real significance, validity, and purpose of procedure in ancient Indian law may be judged and evaluated, tenets of procedure, in Western jurisprudence have been examined to show that the procedural safeguards were put upon a very high pedestal making it something like "Raj Dharma" of the ancient Indian Law and performed the most important function of not only ensuring justice but also of ensuring the more valuable rights–the Human Rights.

The rules of procedure will remain an empty dream if the 'rule of law' had not its proper place and in this, as elsewhere, the ancients did not lag behind. It has been shown that the Western jurists, in their jurisprudence, which is mainly materialistic laid emphasis on procedure to achieve the aim of law, i.e. justice which, in turn, could be secured only through rule of law. Much has been made of this doctrine and this discussion finds a place in this Chapter which results in the finding that procedural law can be exploited for concentrating political power, but no where do we find any factor like 'dharma' operating to exercise its spiritual influence to aid the society in a conflict between the individual and the 'State'. In 'Dharma' this conflict is reconciled not by rule of law or public order or due process or public policy, but by its own intrinsic vitality.

The ancients protected an individual's rights through law. This is evident by the fact that justice was evenly and equally done by the King by the law of 'Dharma'. However, one cannot fail to notice that whereas as has been shown earlier, greater emphasis was laid on rights in the Western legal thought, in ancient India, rights were considered as allowances, benefits, and obligations. This changed the whole tenor of rights. The Western jurists thought that no moral limitations could be placed on economic self-interest of the individuals. Rights were made the foundations of a social order. In England, these individual rights have been twisted, and twisted again and again, so much so, that it is impossible to recognize them. In America, they have been put in an iron-jacket. Naturally there has been a general reaction against the doctrine of natural rights which have become synonymous with an exaggerated individualism which is unconcerned with social purposes and indifferent to degradation and deprivation of a great mass of humanity. Duguit, rightly rejects the doctrine of individual rights for these reasons. A discussion on these matters became relevant and account has been taken of the various ideas connected therewith in its periphery. This has led this author to believe that the doctrine of rights thrives on distrust and dies in arrogance. It presupposes a conflict-ridden culture. The Western Culture aims at harmony and co-existence but not in integration and synthesis. The Indian culture being 'integral' no protection by way of a doctrine of rights was needed. State, individuals, and classes were integrated by the great concept of Dharma which alone was the right of the individual. Law was not an aspect of Government nor was it an indifferent spectator to the activities of the individual. 'Dharma' was the concern of man--a complete philosophy of life and action. Man was called upon to do his duty to self, to his family, his society and his State, and in doing so he was only performing his dharma and the resultant upshot was a spectrum on which one can witness, rights, individual and natural, in various colours.

The fundamental principle advocated by the doctrine of 'Dharma' was to convince man that by doing his duty as ordained by Dharma was the highest attainment and this strict adherence to the law of Dharma would not only give man happiness in this world and would make him a participator in righteous conduct, but would also make him a part and parcel of ultimate reality. Any deviation from the parth shown by dharma was an invitation to misery. He was made conscious that dharma is his right and dharma is his duty. It was thus clear to him that the only way to own right was to perform one's duty well. Duty was considered, as if it were, the only passport to right or title. In this context, the great aphorism of Mahatma Gandhi can be quoted with advantage:

> "If we all discharge our duties, rights will not be far to seek. If leaving duties unperformed, we run after rights, they will escape us like a will O' the wasp. The more we pursue them, the farther will they fly".

It would thus be manifest that in order to reach 'Brahman', the metaphysical reality one should perform true deed, i.e. duty. In the West the juristic 'Summum bonum' is reached by natural rights, common law, public policy, equity, justice etc., but due to their limitations the destination eludes us. The ancient concept of dharma had, within its ambit, all the legal ideologies of the West but shorn off of their antagonisms. The various amendments of our constitution only go to prove the imperfections of the legal theory and juridical postulates of today. If dharma is made the foundation stone of our legal frame-work most of the ills from which we suffer would vanish like thin air. This is not a Utopian idea as it had been operated upon in the ancient times, and a revival of it would usher in an era of peace and plenty and thus make man's life on this globe worthliving.

The vast literature of knowledge as found in the Vedas and other scriptures and sacred books can be fruitfully utilised by us for enriching our lives. The ancient wisdom can be correlated with modern thought and by their synthesis a new science of jurisprudence can be formulated. When such a science is born it would be our own–Indian jurisprudence. That jurisprudence will be capable of solving the problems with which we are confronted today in our country. Our experience of the legal system, that we have at present, is not very encouraging. It is not even satisfactory. As has been pleaded in this thesis, this is mainly due to the jurisprudential thought that we have borrowed from elsewhere which is alien to our culture and heritage. The Vedas and the related literature are there to unravel the mystery of life and with it of the whole existence. Law exists for a wholesome existence and it is clear that this law ought to be so moulded and reoriented to make this possible. Why go far, we have enough fund of knowledge which we can make use of. This knowledge is neither outdated nor inappropriate for meeting the challenges of the present-day-India. Even in the field of jurisprudence we should not be unmindful of the unity of existence or else we will be letting loose the forces of destruction which would be perilous to our very social existence. A study of ancient legal theory of India, with its emphasis on the spiritual side of law, can provide the needed impetus and encouragement in this direction.

The distinct quality of ancient Indian legal theory that has emerged from the studies of this humble author is, as has already been referred to above, the spiritual approach of the ancients to human problems with which law is intimately related. This spiritual approach is not concerned with the mystic experiences and their intricacies but is purely and mainly confined to that view of law which takes into consideration the whole 'Existence' and then goes to build the legal theories and concepts which naturally find a unity and cohesion with cosmic existence, consisting of its various facets–natural, social, cultural, economic, political, legal and moral. This author has endeavoured to designate this approach of law as "spiritual jurisprudence". The spiritual jurisprudence looks to the unity behind all the names and forms of law. The whole being and becoming of law is impregnated with oneness of Essence which is Existence as well as Value. As such by knowing a part we can know the whole, by knowing one we can know all. Its totality may be beyond conception and comprehension of logic and language but its reality is a matter of fact and part of feeling and experience. When seen in this light, Ancient Indian concepts of law like order (*Rit*), authority (*Vrata*), practice (*Achāra*), precept (*Sāstras*), litigation (*Vyavahār*), administration (*Sāsana*), justice (*Nyayā*) represent and reflect that one Reality which in all its totality and particularity is called Dharma. It pervades all of them and is a living reality for the people of Ancient India. This is what has been pleaded in the 'Epilogue'.

1

Philosophical Roots of Ancient Indian Jurisprudence

In order to understand and appreciate ancient Indian jurisprudence it is necessary to start from its foundations upon which the theoretical superstructure was built. Some of the theories were, afterwards, modified or conditioned and to some extent even forsaken or abandoned, due to the exigencies of social and political life of later ages. Invasions by other people and influence of foreign ideas have created great tensions and consequent re-adjustments which are reflected in the evolution of legal theory as we shall notice hereafter. To understand the philosophic base of law we must directly turn to the Rig-Vedic thought,[1] which is considered as the sheet anchor of Indian culture and civilisation wherein the Indian mind is seen embedded with all its potency, vitality and simplicity. This mind which is latent with us, can be still considered to be the substratum for a legal reconstruction of the present Indian life. To achieve our objective a review of theories about the creation of this universe, the nature of law, the theory of Karma, the nature of wrong, evil and suffering, and the theory of the ends of life become relevant. Such a review will also help find out the fibre of legal thought out of which its whole pattern emerged.

I

In theories of creation, we find certain considerations, objectives and preferences which continue to take precedence in Indian mind.

Our investigation brings forth three predominent views. The first is embodied in the Rig Veda (X Mandal, 90 Sukta)[2] wherein we find that creation starts with Yajna or sacrifice. In Yajna or sacrifice the Pursha (jivatma) is sacrificed. "When we speak of sacrifice in India, "Observes, Lionel D. Barnett in his book 'Hindu Gods and Heroes' (Page 51 to 52), "we must clear our minds of the ideas which we have formed from reading of the Bible. The Mosaic conception of sacrifice was that of a religious ceremony denoting a moral relation between a personal God and his worshippers: in the sin-offerings and trespass-offerings was symbolised a reconciliation between man and his God who was angered by man's conscious or unconscious breach of the laws which had been imposed upon him for his spiritual welfare, while meat-offering and peace-offerings typified the worshipper's sense of gratitude for the Divine Love and wisdom that guarded him. Of such relations there is found in the Brahmanas no trace." The above quotation has been used to indicate that the idea of sacrifice is not confined only to Indian thought but is to be found in the Bible also but with a significant difference as would be evident from what is being stated hereafter.

Yajna which does not always involve necessarily sacrifice of animal or humanbeing, arises from the common mode of Aryan life and its activities. It is also an institutionalisation of the cult of fire, and an ancient Aryan way of collective life and common activity of which killing and roasting of animals, offering them to gods with due ceremonials and then distributing the meat as food to members of common mess with prayers, music, songs, etc., was a regular feature, out of this, literature of Veda must have originated. Yajna is the symbol of Vedic culture through which knowledge of Vedas was propogated. With substitution of animal sacrifices, specialisation of knowledge of Vedas and complicacies of procedure, Yajna became the organising and governing principle of Vedic thought and life. After giving due discount to religion we see that Yajna implies an organisation of work which is done by assignment of it and by distributing the duties and performance of functions in such a way that in it we can see the formation of the concept of duty and obligation together with the concept of authority. Again, it expresses the highest form of sociability when the Yajnic willingly participates; and in this process changed with its atmosphere of ceremonies, chants, prayers and symbolism, he feels himself often merged in the very activity, and some times gets the flashes of spiritual light. The theory behind

Yajna is that by its process which is both material and mystic, the nature is preserved and the powers called '*devtas*' are activated to do welfare of the people. Thus Gods, themselves, have become immortal by performing this function–i.e., Yajna. Sacrifice or Yajna is then "life principle, the soul of all Gods and all beings' (S.B. VIII vi.I, 10, IX iii. 2, 7, XIV. iii. 2, 1); or, what amounts to the same thing, the Triple Science or the ceremonies of the Three Vedas (Rig Veda, Atharva Veda and Yujur Veda) is their essence (S.B. X.iv.2.21)". (Lionel D. Barnett in his book "Hindu Gods and Heroes", Page 52). Vedas are born in Yajna and is Yajna. Vedas and Yajna go together. Yajna expresses an aspiration for an ideal social life which is sought in the Vedic prayer thus:

Assemble (Sam), speak in harmony (Sam)
May your minds be of one accord (Sam)
Your prayer (Mantra) be common (Samana)
Your assembly be common (Samana),
Common (Samana) your mind, united your thoughts.
I counsel you to common (Samana) purpose and
I worship with your (Samana) oblation.

(Rig Veda X 191. 2-3)

Yajna contains in itself all the main elements of a system, organisation and must have been an original mode of Aryan life, even before emergence of political and other institutions like territorial state, private property, marriage, slavery, etc. It was based on common living and sharing the goods of existence with all its attendant dangers and advantages.

Law is reflected, at first, in the Yajnic way of common social life. It is a mixture of custom, legend, doctrine, myth, magic and religion. It is only at a later stage that state comes into being and law begins to be associated with it and then it is institutionalised and its knowledge is enriched and specialised and consolidated by a class of persons for the purpose of maintaining 'dharma' and ordaining life in a 'strait-jacket' of morals, religion and law.

The sacrifice which took the form of a norm of conduct is put on a high pedestal in Indian life from the very beginning and gets reflected in religio-legal philosophy of ancient India, so much so that every thinking about law is oriented by it. It is from this idea of sacrifice that jural law and obligation are seen to arise. Sacrifice, in itself, is a process and in order to be validly performed had to be according to procedure with some end in view. How fascinating to find a parallel in common law where also all law was "grounded" in procedure. So was the case with the ancient Roman law. Shastrakars speak of legal trial as a sacrifice and punishment awarded to the accused formed a part of sacrifice. As sacrifice contemplated some and in view, this end is posited as welfare of the people. It is true that Yajna later on becomes lifeless ritual and is forsaken to a larger extent due to Buddhistic criticism but in its true meaning it heightens the norm of sacrifice. The King, seeking the welfare of his *praja* (people) and discharging his duties, is considered as performing 'Yajna' or sacrifice. It is then reflected in later thought which develops or strengthens 'Dharma' as law. This 'Dharma' then expresses the idea of sacrifice as consisting in duty which is fixed to uphold the social order, i.e., to hold it together. The great Divine song, The Gita, of the epic period, pleads for the same by extending its meaning, when it says that he who enjoys the gifts without giving them in return is indeed a thief (3.12). Thus this world becomes a mighty corporation of mutual service to one another. The righteous who eat the residue after fulfilling their duties as enjoined by the law of Yajna are freed from all sins.[3]

The importance of Yajna is to be measured by the praise showered upon it. In Sathpath Brahman, which is a Vedic treatise, it is considered as the only best deed of world.[4] It is the navel of this world. In Dharmasastras, Yajna is also considered as the very form of God. In its literal meaning Yajna means worship of gods, association with good people and Dana (distribution). It is not a more ritual but declares that the deed which is done for the welfare of the world is in itself Yajna. In Kalika Puran, it is said, by Yajna, gods are satisfied, in Yajna, world gets reputation, earth is supported by Yajna: Yajna alone saves the public.[5] For the protection and security of this world Ved Bhagwan (God of Vedas) took the form of Yajna, i.e., Ved Bhagwan went into Yajna.[6] Mahatma Gandhi pays his homage to this concept of Yajna as mentioned in the Gita and speaks of it as the 'Dynamics of this world–a wheel in motion'. To him Yajna means an act directed for the welfare of others, done without desiring any return for it whether of a temporal or spiritual nature. The spinning wheel to him is an auspicious symbol of Yajna, i.e., labour. He who eats his food without offering this sacrifice steals it. By giving up this sacrifice we become traitors to the country. (*Young India,* Jan.

1925).[7] Yajna, as we have already seen, is the manifestation of 'Dharma' which later on was established as law. If Yajna seems burdensome than it ceases to be Yajna. This type of jural attitude we need in our people when they obey law. Without this law is bound to be frustrated. Modern positivistic theories of law cannot generate this type of attitude. They merely bank upon 'force' or 'coercion' as the sole guarantee for the obedience of law which is only an indirect and external control sanctioned by law. On the other hand, Yajna as law is voluntary and a willing act and, therefore, operates directly. In it the person participates himself and feels one with it. What an irony that modern thinkers have begun to realise the importance of reverting to the idea of "willingness" as an indispensable part of the nature of law. To a great extent it is an admission of failure on the part of the so-called scientific thinkers of law. In fact, law cannot yield its meaning to any reactionary or extremist thinker. It is essentially a synthetic product. Ancient religio-juristic philosophy of India is a reminder of this view. Modern thinkers like Ehrlich, have begun seeking law in society besides its official modes and formalistic expressions. This is not new to Indian thinkers.

The notion of Yajna has seen a revival in the hands of Vinobha Bhave. He has started two movements– (i) 'Bhoodan Yajna' and (ii) Sampatidan Yajna–which are juristically relevant. It seems to this author that his main object in launching these movements is to achieve, without the aid of parliament, the goal of social justice which has a great jural relevance. Such campaigns can be correctly designated as social legislation by the society itself for the upliftment (economic) of the community. The concept of Yajna has inspired him to deny individual's ownership of land and to assert the ultimate ownership in God. He is claiming land for the landless and wealth for the poor. To him Dan (giving away) is not just charity but the just distribution. These movements are a prelude to what the social legislators would like to do in future. Thus, in essence, these are jural postulates as they provide a theoretical basis for future Indian law.

In yet another description of 'creation' in Rig Veda we find the idea of will and intelligence without which human action and progress becomes impossible. Thus in Sukta 129 of the Rig Veda (X Mandal) there is a manifestation of the teleological view of creation of this universe which has become famous as *Nasādiya Hymn*.[8]

Whatever, to the mystery of creation, be it untold or unknown, it is atleast certain that desire 'the first seed of mind' is the attribute of the Absolute (Reality) which, at this cosmic level implies creative force and will behind this Universe. A will and mental process implies original intelligence which was the basic urge of creation. This intelligence is not something outside the world or something above it. It is the part of the world. This Vedic Cosmic 'teleos' gives sanction to construct theories and to have purposeful thinking about law and life. Law like any other subject becomes a system and science, i.e., Shastra. Law or dharma becomes known and fit to be realised and obeyed in life and so is formulated in texts. This being so, Nayaya (logic) and Mimansa (interpretation) are recognised as essentials for any systematised development of law and there is ample evidence of their use in the historical evolution of ancient law. As an extension of this systematic urge, *dharma, artha, kama* and *moksa* become the ends of life. Consideration for common goods gets its place in the theory of justice; the concept of duty, whether legal or moral, gets rationale and expresses the need to cope with the direction of this metaphysical intelligence. When duty or Dharma is forgotten by people it gave rise to litigation which was termed as Vyavahar. In order to redress the disputes a King was needed to wield 'Danda' (Sceptre) (Manu VII. 18 to 24) to uphold Dharma judicial administration starts with the purpose of maintaining public order and enforcement of dharma or law including sacred or religious duty. Interpretation of law which is nothing but an application of dynamic creative intelligence upon the static text of law becomes necessary to re-determine it for making it suitable to life and its purposes. Due weight is to be given to the circumstances of time, place and habits of people. All these considerations which find their place in the Indian legal philosophy can be seen as progeny of this creative intelligence which is metaphysical with this universe. The mythical support of the axiomatic truth that Danda is related to Brahmana (God) in the same way as Dharma, finds favour with Manu who says: "For the King's sake the Lord formerly created his own son. Punishment, the protector of all creatures, an incarnation of dharma or the law, is formed of Brahmana's glory".[9] This view is reinforced by Kautilya in the following lines:

> "That sceptre, on which the well-being and progress of the science of logic, Veda and commerce depend, is known as punishment. That which treats danda is the law of punishment or science of government".[10]

He further observes that in the happiness of the subjects lies his (King's) happiness; in their welfare his welfare. Whatever pleases his subjects he shall consider as good.[11] Intelligence had its operation in the dynamics of law. Indian jurists of the past have always recognised reason (Viveka) as the source of law. Though in poetical literature mythological form of explanation is given yet Nyaya or logic plays its own part in dispensing justice. Punishment or the force of law is not merely a coercion exercised at the command of the Austinian superior but is impregnated with intelligence which takes into account the purposes of life and law. It will not allow a purely materialistic or positivistic or spiritual approach to life but a synthetic approach bringing in its fold all these three, thus reaching the high watermark of human intelligence.

Another important theory of creation is embodied in the hymn No. 190 of X Mandals of Rig Veda,[12] which gives us the twin ends of living as 'Rita' and 'Satya'. It is the height of Indian genius that order (also law) and truth which are abstractions are considered as creations prime to all other concrete creation in this Universe. Rita, which seems to be the oldest juristic concept of human civilisation expresses itself in the mind of the Rig Vedic seers as an ordering concept. Law is the first envisaged as an order in cosmos and then in human life. It is eternal law. Rit or law as order in human socio-political life is an extention of cosmic order. Therefore, the juridical law has its rationale of existence in the general concept or 'Order'. This law as order is also expressed in the form of prescription as 'dharmani'–eternal statutes. If order is the nature and necessity of human society and a guarantee of its existence it also becomes a theory of obligation. Duty has to be imposed to do one's function well to maintain order. This order or law is later spoken as 'dharma' which holds this universe and society together. Hence, it becomes the duty of everyone to follow law or order called dharma which is the metaphysical 'Is' and social or juristic 'Ought'. The whole idea of social solidarity which is now posed in the West as juristic ideal is grounded in Rit or order as conceived by the ancients. If order is the value in itself, it conform to order is 'right' or 'good' and its violation a wrong or evil which invites suffering. This suffering, when inflicted by authority, becomes punishment (Danda). Danda as the enforcement of this order is nothing but an aspect of Rit and in its later transformation, Dharma. To saints and sages this order becomes spiritual peace (शान्ति) with the message of universal peace as visualised by the ancients in India.

Predominance and foremost consideration is given to truth when it is stated as one of the first born and one of the twin ancestors of our world. Metaphysically, this 'truth' is the truth of the Existence, i.e., 'Reality'. Truth is satt (real), i.e., existence. This aspect is explored to its furtherest limit in Indian legal philosophy. In social relations this 'truth' is the agreement or coherence with precepts or actual State of facts. The judicial trial, after the Rig Vedic period, is spoken by the Sastrakars as an enquiry into truth, i.e., what has actually happened. Justice is impossible in the absence of ascertainment of truth. Justice is a deliberate act establishing coherence with truth. In other words, it reduces disorder into order and thus truth becomes the concomitant of Rit, the Order as law, because one enforces the other. Truth is as great as order. It is identified in Vedas with God. Similar is the view of Mahatma Gandhi who formulated the natural law doctrine of 'Satyagrah', i.e., the theory of non-cooperation with unjust law, by applying this principles of 'Truth'.

Law is not only a prescribed behaviour from without but also a recognition from within. It tends towards harmony and order in society. In the theory of justice this ordering in done according to law whose purpose is to uphold truth, which inspires faith in law. Justice in India is not born of conflicts in society. It has not arisen as a judgment presupposing a fight between adversaries. In Indian history there were no conflicts of institutions and waging of constitutional battles, or revolutions like those we have had in the West, where law could be seen at one extreme as the will or command of the ruler and at the other extreme as an expression of the greatest amount of political and social freedom of the individual portrayed by the doctrine of 'rights of man'. It is beyond our nascent ancient Indian mind to think of law as the sole monopoly of the State. The ancient Indian could never think of supremacy of political order over social order in generating law. The law or 'Dharma'* is considered as ruler of rulers. To do one's duty according to it is called right. The Nineteenth Century notion of rights as subjective to man and at times subversive of legal order, boosted as securities or reservations against State were not needed; because the idea of security was already built in the concept of 'Dharma' itself. This Dharma, the 'Right', implies 'harmony' or 'Samanvya' and is conducive to welfare. It gives spiritual peace and later, in the hands of religious thinkers, tends towards the religion of non-violence.

* The later transformation of Rit.

Dharma, therefore, is considered as the summum bonum of civilized existence.

II

In order to understand and to construe the ancient Indian legal philosophy, it is also relevant to examine the theories regarding this universe, Karma, evil and ends of life. From these theories issue forth the supreme position of law with its autonomy, dynamism and idealism; the role of reason in administration of justice and interpretation of law and a positive approach to its problems.

THE NATURE OF THE UNIVERSE

The theory that there is one Supreme God who rules this world by his fiat or will has logical implications in legal philosophy. The world or the universe is considered by vedic thinkers as something which is not created by any one out of 'nothing'. It is (अनादि) and was not created by the fiat or will of the Supreme God from without as it was so in semitic and christian religions. "The great strength of the religion of the Vedas is that the Vedic thinkers did not permit one God' to dominate the world and man's affairs in the world".[13] Even if in later Upanisadic period God is spoken of, it has a different meaning. "The many gods representing the visible phenomena of nature and the personifications of functions and the ultimate Brahman, all are integral parts of unitary culture and lived together. What is very prominent is that there has never been an idea of 'one God' in India. It was always the 'One' alongwith the 'Gods', There is no supreme with personality; what is supreme is just a presence, a Reality.[14] The relation created out of the theory of 'one God' and his worshipper is that of a master and a slave. "He is a revengeful warlord. . . . . He interfered rather too much with the world. . . . Stern monotheism, moreover, resulted in a shifting of responsibility of God's shoulders. . . . . Sin is an offence against God, who alone has to be satisfied".[15] Philosophically, if at all one God is needed to serve the purpose of starting the world on its course of development, i.e., "Arambhak". Prajapati and Visvakarmas serve as ritualistic representations "even when the diversified world is described as a person, either as the Virãt or the Person originated out of that Virãt, or as Hiranayagarbha (Golden Womb) or as Visva Karma (All Maker), there is no question of creation of this world by a supreme God, and there is no creation of the law or giving out of the law to the world through a Teacher.''[16] We find again a unity between diversified world and its law and the operations in that world according to that law. The Supreme God known to the Avesta (the sacred book of Zorastrianism) is not only the creator of this world but also creator of the law in the world.[17]

In Puranic times the concept of one God was thought necessary because both Buddhism and Jainism denied the existence of God. Attention was then drawn to the idea of the divine, and in times when it was in danger of being lost or 'relegated to the background'. The propogation of one God became necessary. But still it was not the conventional God, as (इश्वर), known to the popular Hinduism of today. ''First, there was the impact of Islam. By a natural process, not difficult to understand, the virile God of the conqueror overshadowed the impersonal Paramatma; and the Isvara that emerged was very much an image of the God of the Hebrews, Christians and Muslims. The Bhakti-cult, which grew into a fertile soil, provided by the minds of the decadent and supressed Hindus of the day, added to its stature. He could now grant prayers and forgive sins and liberate from rebirth.....''.[18]

There seems to be some parallelism in the growth of the stature of the supreme political authority and its impact upon the nature of law, and the supreme divine personality which influences and moulds man's attitude towards law. At first, King was merely a military leader in war and held an elective post. Gods then, were powers and energies, and people invoked them by prayers. Law was social habit sanctioned by religion. When King's office became hereditary imperialistic wars began and Emperor-King came into existence. In religion also, grew a tendency to concentrate all power in one being. All Gods were then seen as aspects of one God. Law administered in King's court became 'Vyavahar' or litigation. Though it had the sanction of religious authority, the idea of king as the foundation of justice began to be realised. A new type of law as ordinance of kings began to play an important role.

With the political changes, wrought by Muslim invasions and conquest, political power was wrested from the Hindus and their states became vassal states. This brought a change in the attitude towards God in religion. God in religion now allowed the worshipper to go to Him to escape from the hard realities and oppressive conditions of the times and to submit before Him, in all humility, and in a state of complete surrender. As law become the rule of oppression administered by foreign invaders, Dharma, the law, destitute of political support became merely dharma, the personal religion or personal law.

The excellence of the Ancient juristic theory is that it did not allow law to become the agency of State. The 'one and all' powerful and personal God was only a solace and harbinger of hope in the days when foreigners ruled here and left Hinduism with the will to preserve and subsist. In ancient India, as there was harmony between religious interests and maintained its position as ruler of rulers successfully.

THE NATURE OF LAW

Law, in its generic sense, is the rule of action. 'Rit' which appears also as jural law starts with this meaning. It is the dynamics of action in the world whether cosmic human or divine. It is because of this conception of 'Rit' that the Aryan race has been called a juristic race par excellence. At its cosmic level, Rit expresses the idea of order and is spoken of as eternal law. It is identified with the Divine itself. Later, due to historical reasons, Dharma takes place of Rit.* Dharma is the mystic force as well as the social obligation and as such holds this world and society together in its fold. It is the ultimate good, revealed in the Vedas, which themselves are impersonal and for guidance, is codified in socio-legal codes called Dharmasastras. When justice is administered by King's Court it is spoken of as Vyavahar or positive law. Danda or punishment is a means of the enforcement of Dharma. Thus Danda or punishment is identical with Dharma. Punishment is not to repress the criminal but must work as Dharma or justice which has its justification in the welfare of the criminal and the society equally in which he lives. For this purpose there should not be a mechanical application of law only. Indian jurists of the past evolved a systematic theory of the interpretation of law. Again, Law is not to be seen as imprisoned in a code but has plural sources outside it, like custom, traditions of the learned, reason, etc. To keep alive the spirit of enquiry and revision of views, Dharma (i.e., law, ultimate knowledge of Dharma), at its highest level is said to be mysterious. Its meaning is not always knowable to one person. This keeps alive the urge for reform of law and its adaptation

* See next Chapter.

in the light of human welfare and in social milieu. This law, at all levels, remains impersonal and objective, and in the highest sense typifies the doctrine of the 'Rule of Law', which has become the touchstone of modern democracies. This law, or Dharma, integrates matter and life on cosmic scale, and regulates the function of man in society, and institutions, in the best interests of the whole which is again spoken of as Dharma.

THE THEORY OF KARMA

If this universe is dynamic having a logical progression it should generate actions, and reactions in the physical, social and moral world. 'Karma' as the law of action, expresses this law of causation. By doing right actions (Karmas), man keeps pace with the purposes of this universe and partakes in this world-process by progressively realising his own personality or self. This self is not only the individual self but a portion of the universal self, the former has to work in harmony with the latter. The law or the rule of law, then gets authority for its imposition and criterion of its validity in the theory of Karma. The law of Karma, which is eternal, ordains that a man has to bear the fruits of his 'Karma', be they good or bad. The theory of punishment is based upon this theory of causation, i.e., the theory of Karma of which it (punishment) is a voluntary and conscious participant.

The doctrine of Karma operates due to its own potency. It is independent of God which is only a factor in the scheme of the world and is not an overlord.[19] This autonomy of 'Karma' on the cosmic plane, is nothing but the counterpart of the rule of law in politically organised society. It also regulates the growth and evaluation of human personality and may be termed as the ancient law of evolution. It is not the blind operation of nature but is the product of the deeds of man according to the law of nature. It has its tendency towards progress and perfection. As such, it expresses the 'Universal Reason', unfolding itself in different stages to educate the self and bring about its moral regeneration and reclaiming 'Order' against deviation or disorder. It would thus be seen that it is only an aspect of Rit working through matter and life. The theory of miracles and 'avatars' (incarnations) has no place in the doctrine of 'Karma'. It is in the social systems of decadent ages only that such theories, foreign to Rig-Vedic Culture, could have their foothold.

The theory of Karma, though scientific in its approach, yet degenerated into what is called 'Karma Kand' in post-Vedic period.

The 'Karmavad' of Gita was a revival of the doctrine of Karma and teaches us to do our duty for its own sake without caring for results. In a different way it is re-enforcement of Dharma or law which is in itself the good. The concepts of heaven and hell are later illogical developments and are due to the weakening of human spirit in post-Vedic ages. The Indian of the Vedic period believes in the life on earth and scarcely prays for heaven. The persecuted Hindus of Bhakti Period is found to be indifferent to social responsibility and ultimately surrenders himself to the supreme personal God. Saint Tulsidas of the late-medieval periods says:

'निर्बल के बलराम' और
होई सोइ राम रचि राखा ।

But he remembers the law of Karma when he says:

'कर्म प्रधान विश्व करि राखा,
जो जस कीन्ह सो तस फल चाखा' ।

It is very difficult to reconcile these two views except by thinking that the law of Karma was only faintly remembered in periods of history when India had to face the effects of foreign rule.

The Punishment of the criminal as already pointed out, can only be justified on the basis of the doctrine of Karma. Punishment is an operation and enforcement of Karma. In order to be correct it becomes what is just. The theory of justice derives its force from the theory of Karma. It is directed by Shastras that punishment, in order to become just or right, ought to be proportionate to the wrong and meted out only with impartiality detachment and with a sense of duty and service. Then only it fulfils the requirements of 'Right Karma'. On the other hand, if it is not proportionate or is meted out to the criminal with partiality, the law of Karma is disturbed and the judge or the ruler, it is said, suffers the consequences of his unjust act. This law of Karma being rational and moral, helps to replace the mechanical trials by rational ones. As a theory of action it gives strength to law as a fact which is a social habit or a custom and reinforces law as one's own proper function and duty–'Swadharma'–the law proper to one's station in life which needs doing of one's 'Karmas'.

WRONG, EVIL, SUFFERING

Wrong in the early Vedic thought is disorder 'Arit' or deviation from the straight course of Rit. Mimansa which keeps alive this Vedic idea says that evil is also the deviation from the parth of the law. The deviation which is brought about by one's limitations can be restored and man can keep pace with the rhythm of this law. Good is only the conformity with law. Good actions result in happiness. Happiness, in other words, consists in so ordaining one's actions as to be in conformity with law. Sin or evil is then the state of deviation. Where there is evil, there is suffering or reverse movement of the law of progression. As evil is merely a negation of good, i.e., law, it cannot be called real or positive. Evil is only a non-conformity with law. It can be remedied. In Vedic thought and life evil plays only a minor part. But in Buddhism this evil assumes the form of 'World tragedy' which prompted Buddha to visualise world full of sorrow. But in truth, Buddha's emphasis upon suffering is philosophical. He wants to solve the problem of death, decay and disease. He becomes a rationalist and shows a positive approach to life at a time when Vedic rituals degenerated into wastage and violence, reduced themselves to stale forms, devoid of spirit and became unsuitable for rational enquiry. Puranas resound with the note of optimism and heighten the dignity of man even more than Gods. The assertion of the dignity of man is the confirmation of the theory of Karma.

ENDS OF LIFE

In the ancient Vedic thought only three ends or values of life were recognised. Dharma (Law), Arth (Man's life, also economic welfare), and Kama (enjoyment of life). Vedic people were full of vitality and strength and they seldom thought of release from life. The ideal of 'Moksa' as release from the cycle of birth and rebirth, as cessation of life was recognised only to accommodate Buddhistic ideal of 'Nirvan'. Even in the Upanisads positive realisation or knowledge of reality remains to be the end. Besides this, there are only two stages of life in Vedic thought–a full religious life and a full civil life. These were possible at the same time for a householder. The life of Sanyas and that of Vanaprastha was not sanctioned by the Vedas. They were incorporated due to the spreading influence of Buddhism. For this reason we also notice in later ages, a negative attitude towards life which was accentuated in times of invasion and domination by aliens.

In such circumstances, the Indian Culture had to turn to spiritual welfare at the cost of the material. Spiritualism helped in integrating the divisive forces of the times as is menifest in the legal philosophy of the period of the foreign rule, which henceforward began to reflect the precarious civic existence of the citizen. In pre-independence period, (before 1947 A.D.), the Indian mind grew conscious of the servile political condition and began to pine for freedom. The juristic thought of this period is mingled with the aspiration for Swaraj and formulates the theory of the non-cooperation with unjust laws. But its attitude is negative and passive. In post-independence era an active, positive and constructive approach is called for. The ancient legal theory is a remembrance of its glorious past and an incentive for designing, devising and framing, the law suitable to the temper of Indian mind and adequate to the needs of the body politic.

Notes and References

1. This Rig Vedic thought is in itself an evolute or rather amalgam of the Aryan and the Indus Valley Civilisations.
2. Verses:
    1. The perfect Being has thousands of hands, thousands of eyes and thousands of feet. Having pervaded the whole earth he remains ten fingers in surplus (i.e., he is endless).
    2. All present, past and future (objects of this universe) are the Perfect Being. And (He) is the Lord of immortality and all that grows and develop with food.
    3. Such is his greatness, and the Perfect Being is greater than this. All the Beings are his one-fourth; his three-fourth, which is immortal is in the heaven.
    4. With three-fourth the Perfect Being rose upwards; one-fourth of Him again remained here; thence he spread on all sides, over what eats and what eats not.
    5. From him Virat was born; from Virat the Purusa (in the form of Jivatma). As soon as he was born, (he) separated himself (from Virat in the form of gods, men, lower animals, etc.), then (he created) and earth the then the body.
    6. When gods performed a sacrifice with the Perfect Being as its oblation, the spring was its 'ghee', the summer its fuel and the autumn its oblation.
    7. They be sprinkled the first born Purusa, as to be sacrificed, on the sacred grass. Therewith the gods, the Sadhyas and the seers that are, all sacrificed.

8. From that Sarvahut sacrifice the butter mixed with curd was gathered up. He (or It) created these creatures of the air, of forest, and those of the Village.
9. From that Sarvahut sacrifice were born the RKs and the Samans; from that were born the meters; from that were born the ritualistic formula.
10. From that, horses were born, and all those have two rows of teeth; from that cows were born; from that, goats and sheep were born.
11. When they divided the Perfect Being into how many parts did they make? What was his Mouth? What the two arms? What the two things and what are said his two feet?
12. *Brahmana* was his mouth; Ksatriya was made of his two arms; then his two thighs became Vais'ya; from feet *Sudra* was born.
13. The moon was born from (his) mind; from (his) eye the Sun was born. From (his) mouth Indra and Agni (were born), from (his) breath mind wind was born.
14. From (his) navel was (produced) the middle region; from (his) head was evolved the sky; from his two feet the earth; the quarters from (his) ear. Thus they made the worlds.
15. Seven were his enclosing (sticks); twenty-one were made (his) fuel; when the gods, performing the sacrifice, bound the Perfect Being as a victim.
16. With the sacrifice gods sacrificed the victim. These were the first Ordinances. Those mighty ones attained the heaven where the ancients *Sadhyas* and gods are dwelling''.

    From--The New Vedic selection by Pt. N. Kanta Nath Shastry Telang and Dr. Braj Bihari Chaubcy--Prachya Bharti Prakashan, Varanasi, 1965 (pp: 400 to 416).

3. Fundamentals of Gita by Shri Bhusan Gupta, p. 13.
4. Quoted in Gayatri Yajna Vidhan (Hindi) by Sri Ram Sharma, p. 1 (Published by Akhand Jyoti Press, Mathura)
5. *Ibid.*, p. 63
6. *Ibid.*, p. 127.
7. Gita, the Mother--M.K. Gandhi edited by J.P. Chandra, p. 112.
8. Verses:
    1. There was neither the non-existent nor was the existent; there was neither the region nor the sky that is above. What did cover it? Where, in whose protection? Was there water, unfathomable, deep?
    2. There was neither death, nor immortality. There was not the distinct knowledge of night and day. That one breathed without wind by its will power. Other than that there was nothing beyond.
    3. The darkness was concealed with darkness in the beginning. All this (world) was indistinguishable water. That which existed, was covered with all pervading void; through the power of austerity that one was born.
    4. Desire, that was the first seed of the mind came upon that in the beginning. The sages having searched in their heart with wisdom, found out the bond

of existent in the non-existent.

5. Their (web of effects which) was extended like the ray of the Sun, was it across or was it below? Or was it above? There were impregnators; there were great forces; food was below, and consumers (were) above.
6. Who knows truly? Who shall have here proclaim whence it is born, whence it's vivid creation? Gods are later by the creation of this universe. Then who knows whence it has come into being?
7. Whence this vivid creation has come into being; either he held it or if he did not (then who held it?). He who is the Lord of this (creation) is in the highest heaven: certainly he knows it; or if he does not know (then who knows?).

(Translation by Pt. N. Kanta Nath Sastry Telang and Dr. Braj Bihari Chaubey in their book 'The New Vedic Selection', Published by Prachya Bharti Prakashan, Varanasi, 1965, pp. 446 to 459).

9. Manu, VII-14
10. Kautilya's Arthsastra, Chapter 4
11. *Ibid.,* Book II,: Chapter 19.
12. Verses:
    1. From fervour kindled to its height Eternal Law and Truth were born.
    2. From that same billowy flood of Sea the year was afterwords produced Ordainer of the days and nights (Sic), Lord over all the close the eye.
    3. Dhatar the greater, then formed in due order Sun and Moon.

    He formed in order heaven and earth, the regions of the air and light.

    (Translation by Griffith-included in a 'A Source Book in Indian Philosophy'. Edited by S. Radha Krishnan and Charles. A. Moore Pub., Princeton University Press, P.B. 1971, p. 25).
13. Fundamental Problems in Indian Philosophy by Khunhan Raja p. 151, Para 29.
14. *Ibid.,* p. 154, Para 35.
15. *Ibid.,* p. 149, Para 24.
16. *Ibid.,* p. 147, Para 19.
17. *Ibid.,* p. 146, Para 19.
18. Evolution of Hindi Pantheon by Dr. Sampurnanand, pp. 78-79.
19. Fundamental Problems in Indian Philosophy, by Kunhan Raja, p. 340, Para 6.

2

Law as Order–Rit

The first idea of law that arose in the Indian mind is that of 'Rit' as 'Order'. This order is inclusive of physical as well as legal, social, moral and ritualistic ones. More than that, it is also the order of ideas and signifies the very concept of idea or form by which alone comprehension or cognition can be possible of thoughts and actions. This is the 'form' or category of understanding and the aspect of the movement of the dynamic reality. The first cosmological creations were the twins of 'Rit' and 'Satya'. From ethico-legal point of view Rit is law and Satya is truth. But from the point of view of reality, Rit is order and Satya is existence (Satta).[1(a)] Both are the aspects of reality. Thus order and existence go together. They sanctify each other and are the warp and woof of Indian civilisation and culture. Gods and other beings were created afterwards in the list of creation.[1(b)] Rit as eternal order or eternal law is mentioned first, as without form no matter of reality can be manifested. Reality has been expressed as ordered whole and material essence which culminates in the Atman or Brahman of the Upanisadic philosophy. Because of the concept of Rit, as omnipresence and comprehension of complete cosmos, it has been called the 'Crude Precursor' of Vedantic Brahman–the epitome of Indian Philosophy.

I

IDEA OF RIT OR ORDER IN VEDIC THOUGHT

Indian thinking about law starts from this concept of Rit. It is said in Rig Veda that Divinity manifests itself through splendour and through law.[1(c)] The all pervading Being is born of eternal law and is eternal law itself.[2] In its literal meaning Rit is the course of things.[3] In its primary or physical sense Rit is the path of Zodiac with which apparent motions of 'Devas' (luminaries) are confined and which is dotted by *Nakshatras*. The devas are said to be born in Rit and are governed by it.[4] From this primary and physical sense, the meaning of Rit as an ordering principle of the universe extends to human life in society, in its normative and secondary sense it is understood as ethical, religious, legal and social order.

Rit also means 'proper' or 'right'. 'Right', a derivative of Rit, means literally straight and thus implies straight or right conduct as against 'crooked' or tortuous path of life. In old English it is 'riht' in German 'recht' and in Latin 'rectus'.[5] It is surprising that even French 'droit' and Italian 'diritto' we find an echo of the sound of 'Rit'. Rit becomes the expression of order, organisation and system of every type of social life. In religion, Rit is the order created by sacrifice that enables the performer of ritual to live in harmony with Gods; in order to achieve social harmony, it is submitted, the division of society into classes called as 'Varna' system was also in a large measure a reflection of this 'rit'; and in aesthetics it is the expression of that beauty which expresses through order and symmetry. In ethics, Rit is right ordering of conduct; and as law 'Rit' is the preservation of order and awarding of punishment to wrong doer when there is a violation of the 'seven laws'* by 'an-ritti' (अनृति) acts. Rit is order and coherence; its negation 'An-rit' is chaos, disorder and death. In human dealing it is complementary to Satya or Sattva the standard of truthfulness in conduct which squares with the whole 'Existence of Society'.

Rit as Legal Order

In ancient Indian legal theory there is no law-maker. Law in its essence is not the command of the King or the sovereign. Ontologically, Rit is not even the creation of gods, as gods are said to be created afterwards. Gods are only the keepers or guardians of law. Agni, declares law; Brahspati is the son of law; Usa (dawn) obeys law. Indian thought, from its earliest stages, expresses the idea of the "supermacy of law". On a cosmic scale this law works by

*The Seven Laws are mentioned in the Vedas but no one has yet been able to specify them and resolve this controversy as details are lost to us.

itself but on the social scene we hear of the seven laws, as stated above which constituted Rit or law. These seven laws, referred to, in Rig Veda were, it seems, the predecessors of the later formulation of law in Sutras and Smrities धर्म सूत्र, स्मृति In the Vedas Rit is associated with all gods but special mention is made of Varun who is the Keeper of Rit. Association of Rit with Varun has also juristic significance. There are many reasons for it. Firstly, he maintains the rigour of law and inspires awe. Varuna is the purest of Gods and is the highest ethically. He is so pure and holy that a mere performance of sacrifice will not ensure his favour for the abhors sin, or any thing which does not conform to Rit.[6] Secondly, he commands awe and respect. Thirdly, Varun is always aware of the deeds of men and is omnipresent in the theistic as opposed to pantheistic sense. Two men, even in the most secret of places, or at the end of the earth, cannot make plans or enter into contract,– a third person, Varuna is always there to witness the transaction.[7] This may not sound as strange because in secular law as in ancient Roman Law we find the presence, on such occasions of an anamolous personage, the libripens. The whole idea in both the cases was to provide evidence of the transaction. Fourthly, his ubiquity ensures that there is no escape for the sinner. He catches and binds the evil doers in his snare, so that they become diseased, especially with dropsy, and when they die they descend to the 'House of Clay' apparently a sort of gloomy subterranean region.[8] Fifthly, in Atharvaveda, Varun is seen as mighty emperor sitting in a great palace in heaven, often associated with gods around him. Most important of these was Mitra, मित्र , a god mainly connected with 'Vows and Compacts'. The contracts were enforced by Mitra, Varun sat with his scouts or spies who flew all over the world and brought back reports on the conduct of mortals.[9] This points out the fact that in later Vedic age, law began to be associated with King and State. Law of contract and crime must have been the early expressions of Rit. The association of Rit with Varun, after giving proper discount to the theological description indicates that Rit expressed the jural law. It was considered quite efficient in controlling society and some sort of organisation or legal system must have been in existence for the purpose of the enforcement of this law.

Rit preserved the physical as well as the social order. Acts opposed to Rit (Anrit acts) are then deviations from ordered living in society. Evil in early Rig Vedic thought is not a positive entity but happens to be a mere negation of orderliness. The wrongful acts as 'an-rit-acts' were considered primarily as violations of orderliness. They were viz. injuring the essence of food, kine, steads or bodies; adultery, witchcraft, drinking, senselessness, self-deception; stealing, robbery, false swearing, deceiving husbands; wrongs against inmates, against a friend or companion, a brother, a neighbour or stranger; cheating (chiefly at gambling, cattle lifting, incest Marriage of brother and sister) etc.,–are the wrongs which have been recorded. These were the violations of moral life as they were of social life and were considered as violations of Rit and were punished by Varuna. Rit, like a wheel, not only circumscribes the physical universe but enters into our social life and regulates it. Rit has been called the highest flight of Rig Vedic thought; by virtue of which 'order' as the primary fulfilment of law has become the main concern of the Indian mind. The Indian mind even today seems to have a frightened sense of alarm of lawlessness, disorder and chaos, so much so that it cannot but eschew the philosophy of anarchism. Further, as India is suffering from lack of resources, inertia, explosion of population and antipathy of its neighbours, she can hardly afford to lose sight of stability and order. In ancient India all the later constructions of juristic theory were oriented on this idea of order, which has been equated by Vedic philosophers with existence itself.

Atleast five concepts of law were prevalent in Vedic age. First, we have the idea of a divinely ordained rule or set of rules for human action as in the conception of व्रतं Vratam and secondly in Purvi पूर्वी and Dirga Srata दीर्घ श्रुत्र where we have an idea of law as tradition of old customs which perhaps proved acceptable to the gods and hence point the way in which man may walk with safety. A third and closely related idea is contained in Vedic Maryada, मर्यादा an idea conceiving law as the recorded wisdom of old who learnt the safe course of human conduct. (Rig. Veda X. 5.6). Herein we find also the idea of law as a system of principles discovered philosophically, and perhaps, expressing the nature of things, to which, therefore, man ought to conform his conduct. In the fifth place, law seems to have been thought of as a reflection of the divine reason. For such of the creatures who are amenable to reason, it (law of divine reason) can only appeal and for those who are not endowed with reason it leaves them to be governed by this law. The former because of their free will may violate the law, the latter, however, cannot do anything else than to obey it.[10] How interesting, that a parallel idea is found later, much later in the Western jurisprudence by the Schoolmen as reflected in the writings of St. Acquinas.

These ideas of law, of course according to Radha Binod Pal, are not presented to us as distinct from each other, but every one of them is grafted on the others and on the idea of law as the order, the harmony, the *status quo* of the universe, i.e., Rit.[11] The idea of व्रतं Vratam, to which a reference has been made a little earlier, is the embodiment of Rit. It expresses the idea of authority in law and makes it violable and its non-observance is met with punishment at the hands of gods whose Vratam is violated. Vratam is the Ordinance of gods. Vedic Rishis considered it a guidance to mortals. It has been maintained that Vedic स्वधा Swadha is also derived from Rit. This Swadha is conceived as quality or disposition of nature, the essence of a person or thing as derived from its growth, i.e., its nature and potency, developing from within from spontaneous energy inherent in material objects without the intervention of any external agency. Here it seems to lie the authority of custom or usage पूर्वा and दीर्घ श्रुत्र . What is found in past and what has long tradition demands our respect because its observance and repetition makes it consistent with nature. What is not contrary to Swadha स्वधा is liable to be repeated frequently.[12] This is similar to Aristotelian 'nature of the thing'. Dharma in its meaning reflects स्वधा when it has the meaning of 'nature of the thing' or its characteristic function.

In later Vedic age we see a major change. The word 'Rit' falls into disuse. In Atharvaveda it becomes one of the expressions of 'Dharma'. It is also identified with truth. There were many reasons for this transformation. Firstly, the prestige of Varun, the Keeper of Rit began to wane and he was consigned to the position of an Indian Neptune. Secondly, Aryans had to fight wars constantly for a couple of centuries before they could establish themselves in India. They needed more of the blessings of the war god 'Indra' who was at first merely a tribal god but later shot into prominence at the cost of 'Varun'. Thirdly, to fight wars for a long time it became necessary to plan the functions of organisation by a division of labour for all time, to gear up the war machinery. The society was divided by the principle of division of labour to bring in the highest degree of efficiency. The concept of Rit was not so appropriate to govern the relations of these classes interse. Some new orientation was needed which was affected by the concept of Dharma. Fourthly, Rit being rigid and inflexible was suitable only to govern a simple collective life where procedure was rudimentary and trial must have been mechanical having its mode in ordeals. The Rit-era was that state of social existence where there was not much of private property and no division of classes. King was only a leader in war, State was not territorial and observance of law was more a matter of habit or custom. Later a distinction between Rit and Vratam arose. It was thought that Rit could not be violated wilfully whereas Vratam as commands of gods could be so violated. Wilful wrongs were then associated with 'Vratam'. Lastly, Rit was replaced by 'Dharma' to compete Bhuddhistic influence of 'Dharma'. Dharman, an old Vedic word, meaning law as eternal statute suffered a change of gender from neuter to masculine and Dharman became Dharma to offset Dharmma of Bhuddhism which was gaining popularity.

Idea of Order in Post-Vedic Juristic Thought

(a) The theory of the creation of Dharmas Social Order: As has been adverted before at the end of Rig Vedic age the society was divided in four classes and the concept of Rit was found ill-suited to govern the relations of these classes interse. It was, therefore, necessary to so construct the social order as would avert the mutual clashes and conflicts which might lead to disorder and chaos. Since 'Rit' was found inadequate, a concept like Dharma became indispensable and consequently the juristic mind of ancient India found in latter an appropriate remedy to deal with the ills of the time. How this was rationalised becomes evident from the following description in Brahadara-nyaka Upanishad which is told in the form of a myth.

"The Creator, Prajapati first created, the god Brahma. He represented Intelligence. But the Creator was not satisfied only with that. He felt that he should create other gods also if creation were to be a complete manifestation of the various powers in him. He created the Kaatriya gods, Indra, Varuna, Soma, Rudra, Prajanya, Yama and others. They were the embodiments of power, valour, brilliance, fearlessness, the tendency to govern and such other qualities.

But the Creator was not satisfied even with these gods. He saw that there was still something wanting in creation. So he created the Vaisya gods, the eight Vasus, Aditya, the Maruts and so on.

But then he saw that the society of gods he wanted to evolve was not yet complete so he added Pusan to the creation. He represents the 'Sudra principle, namely, manual labour and service.

Even this did not satisfy the Creator. He, therefore, created Dharma or the law which binds all, which keeps all in their own places and which strengthens all who act according to it. Those who do not follow law, they fall away, however, strong they might be. Those who follow the law are stronger than the strongest because they adhere to the law. He who speaks the law, speaks the truth. He who speaks the truth, speaks the law. Truth and the law are one.

Corresponding to this creation of his in the heavens, Prajapati created human society also on the same pattern and laid down the law for all the four *Varnas*. The law lays down the functions of the four pillars of the social system. Those who follow the law and perform their functions accordingly have nothing to fear. They are stronger than the strongest and they are bound to be happier than the happiest.

Intelligence, sacrifice, disinterested service are the characteristics of the Brahmins. Valour, Chivalry, forgiveness, ability to rule are the characteristics of the Ksatriyas. Trade, co-operation, agriculture and distribution of material wealth are the characteristics of the Vaisyas. Ungrudging manual labour, and service are the characteristics of the Sudras.

To choose our functions according to our powers and to attune our powers to the functions that we take up, is the only way to follow the law and maintain social harmony.[13]

In Plato's 'Republic' which is later in chronological order, we find echo of this ordering scheme where society was divided into classes. He also expresses such division in the form of a myth: God used gold for the composition of rulers, silver for soldiers, and iron and brass for that of the class of farmers and craftsmen. The proposed classification was meant for the purpose of attaining excellence through specialisation. Plato's principle of justice like Dharma is conditioning of the proper functioning of society. It is like Dharma 'the citizen's sense of duty of his station'. It is that righteousness which is the result of performance of duties. Justice is the conception of social morality and a definition of the code of social ethics which no less than law, and perhaps even more than law, underlies the play of social relations.[14] In his theory of justice Plato gave a theory of right. The Greeks "had no word corresponding to the Latin *Jus*. Jus implies not only Right but also, and still more, Remedy: it is something concrete, 'which is recognised, and can be enforced, by a human authority'. It is the sum of the actual rules, whether created by usage or by judicial decision or by Statute (lex), on which courts proceed. While, the Romans thus thought and spoke of a single concrete *jus* and of *lex* as a part thereof, the Greeks thought and spoke of an abstract and absolute Right (...), by the side of which they set, as the one expression of concrete law, the old and traditional Use (...) whether written or unwritten, of the community.[15] While the scheme of social order remained a dream in Greece it has already become a living reality and a principle of integration in India. In Greece a mere theoretical formulation of the ordering principle of society as the principle of Justice or Right proved 'fatal to any concrete law, and ideal Justice resident in the pure reason of the philosopher-King, was made to abolish all law and all legislation'.[16] Due to the political orientation of Greek culture it initiated a struggle between Right and Law or usage, which has culminated into a controversy between natural law and positivism. Plato, himself was conscious of it. He thought that Ideal Justice was opposed to traditional usage of the Greek State.[17]

Dharma, then owes its creation to the need of order. But it is not merely a social obligation and a characteristic function but also the ultimate social value. As a mystic force it is the ruling spirit of this world. According to Indian thinking this world is sentient and intelligent and as such it is realised that in order to achieve victory of good over evil and to progress in the right direction, some all-pervading and all inclusive concept ought to be accepted. The ancients find 'Dharma' as a fulfilment of this urge.

(b) *Danda as Preservation of Order in Civil Society:* The function of law as order is not merely the preservation of order in physical, social and moral spheres but is also to ensure administration of justice by the instrument of the coercive mechanism in a civil society with its political institution like the state and thus to maintain order. Rit orders life by nature, dharma by imposing duty to perform proper function and Danda by exerting force. The primary meaning of Danda is a stick. Its secondary meaning may be easily inferred from it. Danda may be translated as 'military force', 'coercion', 'punishment', 'a fine', or according to its function as 'justice'. Ancients had not always a good opinion about human nature and they thought Danda was needed. In the benighted ages in which most ancient writers on law and morals believed themselves to be living, mankind could only be disciplined to observe the sacred law by fear of punishment.[18] According to Manu, 'Danda' (punishment) alone governs all created beings, Danda (punishment) alone protects them, Danda watches over them while they sleep, the wise declare Danda to be identical with Law (Manu-VII-18). The whole world is kept in order by punishment for a guiltless man is hard to find; through fear of punishment the world provides enjoyment. The root from which the word 'Danda' comes is 'Dama' which means to restrain. According to Sukraniti 'Dama' is weaning away from wrong conduct, this is achieved by punishment. The means by which a person is restrained (from misconduct) is Danda.[19] Danda is not a mere chastisement. In describing the King's duty, Yajna Valkya and Narad use the expression स्थापयेत्पथि as meaning 'put him back on the right path', which Mitakshara interprets as "having punished (a person) according to the nature of the wrong, the King must re-establish the person in the performance of Swadharma".[20] In ethico-religious legal theory of ancient India, justification is sought in the theory of creation of Danda. Manu says: "The Lord created his own son and made him law incarnate for the protection of the entire living world; it was endowed with Brahma's own vigour as Law's administration as danda". (Manu-VII-17). Manu believed that before the administration of justice by king arose there was the state of self-help. It was the age of Matsya Nyaya in which bigger fish devoured the smaller one. This view is supported by Kautilya when he says "when the law of punishment is kept in abeyance a great fish swallows a small one; for in absence of a magistrate, the strong will swallow the small and the weak; but under his protection the weak resist the strong. The object of keeping men to their paths is accomplished by punishment.[21] Here law of punishment is equated with science of government and it is said that progress of the science of logic, the three Vedas, and Commerce depend upon Danda which alone can procure safety and security to life and these in turn are dependent upon discipline.[22] With this end in view the procedural and administrative rules multiply and police regulations and safety measures are formulated with varied needs of well-organised state like that of Moryan State in times of Kautilya. The end of law administered by State is expressed as 'Kantak, Sodhana' i.e., removing the thorns; maintaining peace and order in society. "Kantak Sodhana" sets forth different measures such as police regulations and administration of criminal law with a view to get rid of such thorns or obnoxious people who are a danger to the country.[23] This process starts from Manu and culminates in Kautilya and becomes the justification for the development of a 'special law' as ordinance of king called *Raj Shasana* or administrative law.[24]

II

Order is the first and the ultimate justification of law. This has been partially proved by having a review of ancient Indian thinking about law. It is our business now to test the validity of this proposition in the light of Western theories of law. We should know that though the idea of Rit or order is complete as it reveals the nature, function and ideal of law, it can be better understood when viewed together with its doublet 'Satya' which is not only the metaphysical reality (Existence) but also the social reality imbued with all the value considerations involved in the existence of man–in society. In fact, in later Vedic age Rit was identified with Truth. Rit then inheres all the juridical idealism which is a necessary aspect of the existence of law and is vital to its understanding and knowledge.

The Idea of Order in Western Legal Theory

Law a craving of human mind which at first is reflected in order. This craving when applied to human organisation, evolves into set patters of behaviour and ultimately emerges as law which is a minimum standard for co-existence in a civilized society. In Aryan society this order is generalised in the concept of 'Rit', order in society becomes 'Dharma' and order in State takes the form of 'Danda'. All the three are intertwined. In the western legal philosophy the idea of 'order' as law expresses at first, in the natural law doctrine of the Greeks. The conception of Natural Law according to Friedmann, is the sign of man's consciousness of his position in this universe. *Heraclitus* found the essence of existence or 'being' in the rhythm of events. This he called destiny, order and reason of this world. *Nature, to him, was not merely substance but a relation or order of things governed by its own law*. In the Fifth Century B.C. the high state of political, social and spiritual development of the Greek city States and the resulting problems of political and social life, forced upon thinking people, a reflection on law and order. Laws changed frequently, in the democratic republic and the human and changing elements behind the laws became visible. Philosophers began to think about the reason for the validity of laws. At such a time the conception of nature as an order of things was bound to be utilised. With a generation, sceptical of itself, weary of arbitration of human government, conscious of oppression and injustice, nature came to be opposed to be 'tyranny of men. In Sophocles' Antigone "natural law as divine law is opposed to written law. The former is wise, the latter arbitrary. From this arise demands for justice which anticipate the principal demands for social justice, raised and disregarded again and again in modern history."[25] With the pre-occupation of Greek mind with 'Polis' (City State) which they loved and cherished, natural law took a political turn. In its later course of history in Europe it began to evaluate the interests which were competing in society, from time to time. Sometimes it made the state a means of good life of the individual and at other the individual a means for the benefit of State. And all the variations of this theme, only caused confusion. The theory of political justice in West is replete with contradictions. Thus the interests of both the individual and the State with varied intensity, gave rise to different kinds of socio-political and juridical doctrines in the West where we find a swing from conservation of order for its own sake to fomentation of revolutions; from freedom of the individual, to the glorification of the State; and from natural law to positive law. To the Indian mind the idea of order did not enter into its critical phase and remained the creative impulse of organisation of thought and life. It helped in ordering the society by allotting functions and dividing labour in order to obtain efficiency, skill and specialisation. These functions as duties were codified by the sages in 'dharmasastras'. To them, justice is not greater than Dharma–an ordered function in society is an obligation in law, a precept of religion, and an end of life which was objectively determined and fixed. Varna order in those times, was the only just order in society, the Ashram the just way of life and Dharma the only just mode of living in society. Justice in law becomes a search for truthfulness of facts, a means of upholding the law as Dharma. Further, positive law was the law which was laid down in the Dharmasastras. The King or monarch was only a guardian of Dharma and had no supreme juristic existence of his own. Natural law in the West could never embrace positive law. It could not keep to the path of order and exhibited explosive and subversive elements in it. As a result it was discredited in 19th Century by Bentham, Austin and their followers. Kelsen's positivism in 20th Century has even strongly reacted against natural law. He eliminated the idea of justice from the study of law. Natural law, considers law as ordering of life but with all its faith in 'order' it could not construct it. Analytical positivism is also a theory of law as order. But it limits itself to a logical order called conceptualism which is only one type of order. Sociological positivism also treats law as a means of ordering man's relations in society by adjusting or balancing interests as far as possible without friction or waste. But inspite of all its assertions it provides no guidance. It only emphasises the need for new methodology and technology of law. It is in fact not a theory but an assertion of a working attitude towards law. Mere study of facts called empiricism is also a reaction against metaphysics and ethics of natural law. By study of disjunctive facts one cannot construct a theory of law. Legal theory in the West had an adventurous course because political, social and economic ideologies and interests of different classes have left their imprint upon the theory in the course of civilisation. Legal philosophy in India could not take a similar course. Here neither political power was transferred from class to class nor was the political authority dissociated from religious authority. The rise of middle class due to industrialisation or the increase of the power of lower classes due to popular democracy did not take place. In India, juridical theory did not lose equilibrium and never swung from one extreme to another. The political power of classes was once for all harmonised with the functional distribution of duties. As such aspiration of classes (Varnas) were for ever fixed, and were socialised in the broad framework of Dharma which became a complete constitution of the society. Indian thought turned more towards synthesis and refinement of culture and progress of personality reaching higher and higher culminating in a culture alongwith material progress which ever attracted invaders. The above discussion which has been briefly undertaken into consideration the currents and counter-currents and cross-currents of various influences that worked on legal theory, in the West, is intended to show that, though we have adopted the British system of jurisprudence, yet we have not been able to achieve justice, political, social and economic through law. Instead of creating peace and harmony, we have only created disorder and conflicts which still remain to be resolved. Our future legal theory has still to evolve and give expression to our need of a just order. An organised, response from all the sections of people is the only sanction for our schemes of social reconstruction and creation of a new theoretical framework which suits the Indian genius and social conditions and is an imperative need to enforce and accomplish our projects of social reconstruction.

We have yet to interpret comprehensively Order, not merely as preservation of peace and security, but in its 'brahat' (wider) from Rit is 'universal order' in society which has yet to be realised as envisaged by ancient *Rishis* of India. In England the ideal of peace and order has been given top-priority by Hobbes, Bentham and Austin. In the light of these theories the state is reduced to a police institution and law is seen as a necessary evil by Bentham. In the pursuit of certainty the Westerners have tried to divorce morality from the science of law and in pursuit of logic they have rejected experience. Formalism in law has become the creed of legal scientists. In the hands of Kelsen even State is reduced to an order which is meant only to give unity to the legal system and is thus only a legal order. Law becomes a norm backed by the sanction of coercion and hence only a coercive order in the community. His law, or normative science, is divested of all considerations of ends and objectives. On the one hand the ordering impulse has prompted juristic mind of the West to go for the quest of certainty and unity by conceiving from bereft of content, and on the other, by breeding skepticism it has shown only the spectacle of disjointed contents bereft of form with the result that the very existence and essence of law has been deprived of its reality by Scandinavian realists. According to whom law is a mere label or a psychological device. The so-called jurisprudence of interests has culminated in Roscoe Pound. He puts the aim of law as ordering of human relations and adjustment of interests with the object of social engineering which is nothing else than *ad hoc* balancing of interests with minimum of friction and waste; without any manifest end in view. This theory of Pound owes its popularity because it helps in minimising the inherent danger of Marxism to order and existence of the democratic and free world. To avert this danger, allowance of concessions to explosive sections of society, i.e., workers are given. Historical school presents a variation on the theme of order. It views law as order existing by virtue, of the passage of time. This order is crystallised into custom by habit, is upheld by tradition and is said to have a mysterious residence in the 'common conscious of the people'. Historical movement, in England, was nurtured in the dread of the French Revolution. In Germany, it appeared as a reaction against a proposed codification of law on the basis of natural law and rationalistic theories which had a close affinity at that time, to the French Revolution–the arch-enemy of the existing order in the Europe of the 19th Century. Historical school restates the need of order and considers law as an aspect of general order and existence of life in the community which is governed by its own laws of growth and decay. The 'order-and-existence' is considered as good in itself.

In England, the analytical positivism of Austin is a by-product of 19th Century stability and order which necessarily gives a sense of complacency but when this sense disappears, disillusionment is bound to follow. Neo-Austinians began to modify and liberalise the doctrine by introducing elements and considerations which were already thought of as unworthy of it. This they did consciously in order to rationalise and justify the prevailing order which was shaking under the constant threats of Fascism and communism. Incorporation of ethical element here and there in the doctrine is the direct result of this awareness of the dangerous situation. The idea of order, in India from the very beginning, was saturated with the ethical element. Positivism courts order by disowning ethics. Nevertheless positivism of all forms and genre, in one way or the other, makes secret. If not open resorts to ethics which is nothing but an attempt to secure a wholesome existence of man-in-society. The latest dominant note in legal positivism is that of Professor Hart who expressly admits natural law into positivism, through its 'Minimum Content' which is a modernised and an attenuated version of order and peace as necessary to human survival and self-preservation as contemplated by Hobbes and Hume.[26] This again is a partial reinforcement of order, together with the existence of society with its values of life which is the net result of Western juristic theories shorn-off of their extravagances of over emphasis and extremities of reactions. All these excursions of legal theory in the West, have been an exercise in futility because they have failed to harmonise as order, with law as existence of man in society. So the Western thinkers, even to this day, have not succeeded in correlating order with existence properly. Indian sages understood the axiomatic truth that order is existence and existence is order. The norm of law is also a value of life. Inspite of all the different approaches to law one can hardly deny this plain truth. From cosmic law to positive law; from orient to occident; and from ancient Indian culture to Modern European civilisation; the truth is borne out, whatever be its mode, disguised or undisguised. Order is existence and existence is order. Order and existence go together.

Notes and References

1. (a) The Call of the Vedas–By Abinash Chandra Bose, p. 41 (Second Edition, 1960)
   (b) Rig. X. 190

(c) Rig Veda VII-190(3-4)

2. Rig Veda-4-40-5.
3. Source Book of Indian Philosophy--By Radha Krishna, p. 27.
4. *Ibid.*
5. Chamber's Twentieth Dictionary.
6. The wonder that was India by A.L. Basham. Published by Rupa and Co., P.B. 1967, pp. 238-39.
7. *Ibid.*, 239; Atharva Veda, IV, 16.2.
8. *Ibid.*, p. 239.
9. *Ibid.*, p. 238.
10. History of Hindu Law by Radha Binod Pal, pp. 173-74 (Tagore Law Lectures).
11. *Ibid.*, p. 174.
12. *Ibid.*, pp. 164, 404 to 406.
13. 'Upanishads in Story and Dialogue--By R.R. Diwakar. Bhartiya Vidhya Bhawan, pp. 94 to 95.
14. Greek Political Theory--Plato and His Predecessors, p. 179, by Sir Ernest Barker, Published by Methuen, London, 4th Edition, 1951.
15. *Ibid.*, p. 180
16. *Ibid.*
17. *Ibid.*, p. 180 (Foot Note 2.)
18. The Wonder That was India by A.L. Basham p. 115, P.B. Edition 1967.
19. The Hindu Judicial System, Lectures by S. Vardachariar, p. 82.
20. *Ibid.*, p. 83.
21. Kautilya's Arthsastra (Chapter 4, The End of Sciences).
22. *Ibid.*, Chapts. IV, V.
23. Dr. Bhandarkar--Some Aspects of Ancient Hindu Polity, p. 14. The Mahindra Chandra Nandy Lectures, 1925, Published by Banaras Hindu University, 1929.
24. This is dealt in Chapter VIII.
25. Friedmann--Legal Theory, p. 198 (5th Edition 1967).
26. Natural Law by d' Entreves; p. 191. Published by Hutchinson University Library, London.

3

Law as Culture–Dharma

Jurisprudence, broken up in so-called schools today ill-provides a whole view of law. An understanding of the nature and function of law then becomes difficult. The jurists of these schools behave like the leaders of political parties who thrive by criticising their opponents. The student is at a loss to understand and has to read between the lines to make his way through them. This fragmentation and regimentation in the field of jurisprudence is the by-product of scientific and materialistic approach to law in Europe initiated by renaissance and nationalism which gave a spur to separatist and conflicting tendencies in Western culture and civilisation. The need of a complete synthesis is now felt by western jurists and they are in search of a constructive juridique. The developing countries can scarcely afford to suffer the sins of these movements because they need a better understanding of law in order to solve their problems of law and society. Legal theory is a theory of human and social existence and is a method of securing the well-being of human beings upon whom a legal system is imposed. The province of law is nothing but "the establishment of rules for regulation of human conduct amidst diversity of inclinations and desires, so as to reconcile and harmonise the wishes of the individual with the interests of community in which ultimately the interest of the individual is also involved: it curtails the fictitious freedom of unregulated desire by subordinating the particular nature of individual man to the discipline of the community acting upon universal rational principles and thereby gradually tends to bring about the higher freedom which consists in the dependence of the individual on the dictates of reason while governing the community is also his''.[1] Thus jurisprudence is an understanding of the science of law but this study depends for its depth and insight into the knowledge of human nature with all its aspirations and failings, the bonds of social obligation and responsibility, the inbuilt values and the process of evolution directing itself towards progressive realisation of the ends of life with all the counter moves, limitations, physical and institutional, which put hurdles for conscious planning through law which is all the more urgent and is to be done all the same with the greatest consideration, caution and foresight.

Ancient Indian legal philosophy arises from the very scheme of life and is the very aspect of it. It has no prejudices against religion, ethics and politics but is interwined with them. It unfolds a complete universe of law. The dharmic philosophy is encyclopaedic--in its approach to law and provides a source of inspiration--a juristic heaven to a fatigued Western jurist and a founding rock for any scheme of social reconstruction.

In the West itself, at first legal theory did not view law in a narrow technical sense as something laid down by the sovereign political authority and backed by force. It represents the aspects of individual and social life with all the considerations of its religion and ethics. It was spoken of as an embodiment of eternal justice, a gift of gods, a discovery of sages, the rule of God or reason or nature seated in the hearts of men, etc. It was not considered subordinate to King but was considered to be the King of all kings. Law was not considered as something 'made' but an existence which was a part of local, tribal and national life. The modern imperative theory of law is only a sequel of the doctrine of sovereignty formulated by Bodin and Hobbes in the Sixteenth and Seventeenth Centuries. This view of law is the negation of the very spirit of common law which has its myth that it cannot be made and is to be obeyed even by Kings.[2]

Natural law thinking is not absent in the Indian legal philosophy. Juristic thinking ensures from the concept of Rit as eternal order. In Brhadarnyaka Upanisad (1.4.14), this law or eternal order is equated with truth. Law is viewed by Apastamba of Sutra period as that which is approved by Aryan society. To Manu, Yajnavalkya, Vasistha and Baudhayana, it is embodied in the virtuous conduct of 'Sistas' (virtuous learned men) and practice of good men,--Sadachara. Law has been declared as self-existent and King of Kings in Vyavahara Darpana.[3]

Positive thinking about law is not absent in the ancient legal theory. In Kautilya's language it is a command enforced by sanctions i.e., *rājnam ājnā*. In Narada Smriti the reason of the existence of positive law is contemplated in the context of Dharma. We are informed that when "performance of duty having fallen into disuse positive law (Vyavahara) has been introduced and the King as superintending the law is known as '*Danda-dhara*' or wielder of danda, the power to punish". Sukra Nitisara specifically states punishment as the sanction of law but it is to be used to maintain the people, each in his proper sphere. Jaimini States that 'Dharma' is the desired object, 'Arth' is characterised by command. It means that Dharma is to be enforced through force. The reason is that it then becomes more efficacious. Dharma or law is upheld by different classes in a different way. Brahmins keep to Dharma by knowledge and education, Ksatriyas protect it by might, Vaisyas observe it through truthful and fair dealing and Sudras serve it by service and duty. Dharma has then the sanction of knowledge, force, truth and duty. It was due to this all pervading concept of Dharma that the ancients made it a foundation of their juridical thought in the conviction that in it lies the complete mystery of law. It is, therefore, necessary to unravel its meaning in all its aspects.[4]

I

DIFFERENT MEANINGS OF DHARMA

Metaphysically, Dharma is the mystic force which pervades and regulates this universe and is the law of its being. Religiously, it is the sacrificial act or ritual. In its moral meaning, it is the end of life higher than Arth and Kama and expresses the belief in conservation of moral values and in the eternal moral order which is based on 'cosmic archetypal ideation which persists immutably and which is utterly independent and indifferent to merely human preferences".[5] Socially, Dharma is the complete 'Constitution of Hindu Society' and signifies those principles which are said to uphold society, expressing its culture which makes life worth-living. As such "Dharma is an instrument of cohesion and integration which imparts flavour to the whole corpus of values which go by the name of Indian Culture".[6] It represented, the "privileges, duties and obligations of man, his standard of conduct as a member of the Aryan community, as a member of the one of the castes (Varna) and as a member in particular stage of life (Asrama)[7]. Dharma-rules were "agreed upon in assemblies'' in a great measure[8] and represented social habits. Dharma is not so absolute but is relative according to one's own status. In its normal meaning Dharma gives coherence and direction to all life, the harmony of the whole man who finds the right way for just law of living.[9] It is then the totality of duties which bears upon the individual and totality of rules to which he must conform if he does not want to fall. So the whole legal theory of ancient India has its axis in Dharma.[10] In its juridical meaning Dharma is custom, law and righteous conduct sanctioned by dharmasastras, reason, authority, conscience, etc. It is Dharma which gives authority to king to rule. Dharma, then, is the ruler of rulers and is a mystic force which destroys the wicked ruler bent upon violating its Ordinances. Dharma when preserved, preserves and when violated destroys.[11] As a concept of power, Dharma, derives its potency from the idea of '*Vrata*' a Rig Vedic concept which has the connotation of law. Accordingly, if the content of sovereignty is force (Danda) it must solely be used for enforcing the Ordinances of Dharma.[12] As early as Vedic times, the concept of '*Raja-dharma*' or Dharma of the state was considered to be the main function of the Vedic King.[13] In the Buddhist literature there is the same insistence on the primacy of Dharma over Danda. ***In politics, Dharma acted as a check upon royal absolutism***. The King could be dethroned if he acted against the distates of Dharma. This is sanctioned by Manu.

Dharma has in it elasticity and comprehension. In Sanskrit, no term relating to human life and conduct is dissociated from its ethical sense. Terms like jus, recht, droit, diritto signify more than one meaning and express the idea of right as well as law. For the juridical purposes Dharma expresses the notion of law, justice and duty. To our mind, bred and nurtured in professional notion of law, ancient Indian concept of law as Dharma may seem vague, indistinct and confusing as an amalgam of law, religion and ethics, but the truth is that law is in fact of such nature. No exact definition of law can be possible nor is necessary. The dissociation of law from society, and morals have been effected only due to the prolonged struggle and reactions against theocratic and feudalistic conception of law, i.e., the ties of human fidelity and divine guidance, the exaggerated emphasis upon individual free will. In this way individualistic jurisprudence came into being. ''If individualistic civilisation were now to give away before the one based on a socialistic conception of the social tie, all the positions of our jurisprudence will have to be reconsidered.''[14]

TWO PROBLEMS OF LAW

Law is knowledge, participation and regulation. It is a concept of recognition and control; without having a clear knowledge of its nature and the secret of its binding force, all our approaches to it are partial, and we can neither be able to make it a workable instrument of social change nor can get popular support and co-operation for the success of our planning through law.

Therefore, two problems of philosophy of law are: (1) The difficulty of identification of nature and content of law, and (2) the difficulty of ensuring its obedience by the people, i.e., its effectiveness. The first is epistemological dealing with the theory of knowledge of law and the second is ethical, searching for justification of duty to obey law. These are, also, the two tests to be applied in determining a complete theory of law. It is, therefore, necessary to ascertain whether the concept of Dharma, as a theory of law in ancient India qualifies itself to be so. Examination of legal theories will reveal to us the extent they suffer from over-emphasis and exaggeration by undermining the essential elements of law, and by affecting elimination or delimitation of its relevant sphere or scope. A complete concept of law includes the meaning of law, i.e., its true nature and function, its correlation with a community, its acceptance as standard or value, its potency to deal with fundamental issues of social and individual life, and proper developed machinery to accomplish its ends and methods to mirror changing concepts of justice, transference of power and shifting interests, etc.

What is to be identified as law: Law is a synthetic concept. In Western Jurisprudence, it has ceased to be so, because of the birth of different political ideologies and social theories which have their impact upon legal theory, with the effect that a limited aspect of law is identified as law. The result is that a part is identified as a whole. Every legal theory wants to appropriate the juristic field to itself exclusively. Consequently, law is treated as a property or monopolised sphere or a hand maid of a particular class of society, at a particular time, when it holds political power and wields social influence. Jurisprudence then, becomes, directly or indirectly the justification or propoganda of the class in power. Law, from ancient times to present day in the West is the story or a spectacle of changing phases of the panorama of legal theory of different interests called jurisprudence. Karl Marx tried to seek remedy of this state of affairs by preaching the end of class-war and recognising the interest of only one class, i.e., workers. Jurisprudence of interests culminating in sociological pragmatism of Roscoe Pound has given recognition to all types of interests and has preached business of law to be balancing of interests without friction and waste. His jurisprudence has become an accounting or auditing and maintaining or balance of interests, and law-making a business management, i.e., recognition and satisfying of different demands representing different interests. This business has to be entrusted to the jurist who does not work on the basis of any ideology but with all the consciousness, responsibility and skill of a social Engineer. Dharma, as law, demands more than such social engineering. Dharma, while reconciling various interests of society also attempts to keep in tact the value and ideology which would make a man perfect in every sense as a member of a social group. It emphasises that its principal function is the welfare of the people and this welfare cannot be secured mechanically by the agency of law, and so, social engineering bereft of values, will not be worthwhile. Ideologies like individualism, socialism, capitalism, anarchism etc. are partial approaches to the solution of the problems of law and life. Dharma, the ancient Indian legal theory of law does not suffer from any danger of becoming a doctrine creating imbalances in society nor is it regressive. Of course, it may suffer deterioration by enslavement and by imposition of a foreign legal system. On such occasions, Dharma is likely to receive a setback. Dharma, as law, as has been already stated, is a complete aspect of law and more than that it is law of law itself. Law in the West is fragmented. In India, it is a complete symbol of juristic matter, form, function, programme and objectives. Today when we are striving to have social justice by adhering to socialism, we are incurring the displeasure of classes. Social justice, which is our goal, today, can easily be achieved, not by accepting any 'isms' but by adhering to the concept of dharma which not only takes into account the welfare of society at large but also of each individual, prescribing for his righteous conduct. If everyman does his duty well and rightly, society is bound to flourish in every way and social justice will not be far to seek. It is tragic that so great a country like India, with so great a cultural heritage cannot bring all its legal acts and ideals to one alter or one whole when there is a concept like Dharma which fulfilled this want of ours in ancient India. In those days our legal theory was an amalgam of matter and spirit of life in contradistinction to the present day theories which are only inclined towards materialism.

We have discussed the nature of Dharma which identifies the sum and substance of ancient Indian Life, culture and law. In order to bring into focus the excellence of Dharma as law, it will be worthwhile to examine critically the Western legal thought. Idealism, in Western legal philosophy is expressed by natural law theory. Natural law thinking started in ancient Greek civilisation with observation of order, regularity, uniformity, harmony, etc., in physical nature which appealed to the thinkers and they wanted to incorporate the same qualities in legal systems. These thinkers wanted to order life according to reason. On the political and legal planes, they made natural justice the end as they made virtue the end of the moral life of the individual. Natural law offered the doctrine of natural justice as ideal justice. In ancient India the controlling power of reason to bring order in life and thereby creating just conditions for living a virtuous life, was reflected truly in Rit and later in Dharma. Dharma is the very law of the universe, its characteristic function and the direction of its movement which is nothing else than the good of the humanity. Dharma is the total frame-work of all human thought and action. It is not a static concept but a dynamic one. By its very nature it is flexible and variable according to time and place (Yugas). Dharma is a standard measurement of all thought and action or required resultant of all rules and procedures of law or a conversion table of all individual and social action. This Dharma has equation with right, law and justice and covers not only the filed of moral 'ought' but also governs the entire universe of the discourse of law. Dharma has multiple sources e.g., the Vedas, the Smritis, reason, testimony and custom, etc. It completely answers 'the question what is law as it comprehends the complete theory of law. The Greek natural law theory at its inception was comprehensive like our Rit and Dharma but soon sowed the seed of discord. It created a dualism in legal theory by separating the law of the state and law of Nature which proved ruinous to the future of legal theory. This dualism resulted, in failure to recognise positive law as law proper because it could not express the ideal of justice. Natural law, in early medieval socholastic thought ran counter to the State. But later, it lent its support to it when religious authority donned a political mantle also. It then considered positive law as an earthly expression of the will of God, and the margin between ideal law and actual law began to blur. The 18th Century recognised that law as law which ensured freedom of the individual and his right to property. Modern natural law recognises as law that which is just and provides a minimum standard of living. Modern natural law recognises positive law which has in it the element of 'value'. This value may not be absolute but be relative to time and place, nevertheless they (thinkers) consider it as necessary. In sum, it can be said that Natural Law under-rates positive law and thrives upon vague feelings of frustration and appeals to ideal law.

Historical jurisprudence of Savigny answers the question, what is law, by pointing to what resides invisibly in the general consciousness of a people, which is called 'Volksrecht' by Savigny and 'Volksgeist' by Puchta. It is a mystic and romantic concept like that of Dharma which is also a mystic force which holds the Varna society together. To this extent Savigny's doctrine is similar to Dharma. But it is not a complete theory because it is reactionary and favours only a certain mode of law e.g. custom. His doctrine reacts against the movement of codification started in France under the influence of natural law. He forges fetters for the legislator and the codifier of law and thereby betrays 'juristic pessimism' as regards the rational development of law. Again, his deification of 'Volk' has lent a theoretical support to fascist tendencies. The doctrine of Henry Maine is an anthropological approach to the evolution of law; it is application of the evolutionary theory of Darwin with its faith in progress but is swayed by Hegelian idea of 'freedom' as a value in itself culminating in his dictum 'Status to contract'. In a way he represents the progressive view of the dharmic doctrine but he falls short of it because firstly, he unduly favour legislation as a source of law and secondly, he has implicit faith in the freedom of the individual as the sole end of law.

Utilitarianism both individual and social, makes happiness the end of law. In this it approaches a characteristic of Dharma which is conducive to the welfare of the people. But in utilitarianism this concern for happiness is vitiated by improper emphasis given either to the individual or the society. Benthamite utilitarianism holds happiness as the end of legislation but its view of happiness is one sided. Bentham bases his doctrine upon the individual's ego or his self-interest. To him happiness is that which makes an individual happy. His theory undermines the interest of society because society to him is a misnomer and a fiction, i.e., not more than the aggregate of the individuals. With its hedonistic calculus and its slogan of 'the greatest good of the greatest number', this theory fails to lead him convincingly from psychological egoism to ethical altruism, as the bridge between self-interest and interest of all, is unbridgeable. Again, he considers law as a necessary evil and inspite of his zeal for reform pleads for minimum of law and subscribes to the notion of law merely as a command of the sovereign. Social utilitarianism of hering postulates society as real, considers, law as a partnership between the individual and the society and the end of law as balancing of interests. Though he recognizes subjective elements like love, honour, friendship, etc. Yet his doctrine can fall an easy prey to any political ideology, which purports to undermine individual in the name of society. Inspite of the fact that he has a greater juristic canvas, he still adheres to the definition of law as a command of the state.

Pound's sociological positivism also known as pragmatism with all its overemphasis upon method, is more of a reaction against formalistic and metaphysical approaches because it asserts and propogates an 'ideological void', and an aversion to precept or formula. When he considers law as a means of civilisation, displays juristic optimism and desires the maximum satisfaction of human wants by balancing of interests without friction or waste or with least friction and waste, called social engineering, he expresses pseudo-dharmic view. Dharma–is condusive to human welfare; and aims at progress of society and perfection of individual personality. It prefers good to pleasurable and has equation with the Good or the Right or the Duty; rises above the mere satisfaction of human desires and physical wants and by sublimating these leads to the spiritual engineering of life. The mere consciousness of the responsibility that the jurist is a social Engineer without any ideology is a false parallelism to 'doing ones duty for its own sake'. Without any grounding in values; it is nothing but to reduce 'elan vital' or life force into the mechanical energy of an automation. The moral insensibility of a social engineer makes the whole task of engineering a craft. This half-hearted approach with delusive statistics, extensive programme without predetermined values of life is a return of technicalism and formalism in jurisprudence. The assertion of the highest degree of juristic freedom in absence of self-guidance with the highest degree of duty or responsibility to the juristic task may be possible in logic or theory but not a practice. The aversion to theory, ethics and metaphysics is reactionary, in kind and obviously prepostrous. A true religion cannot afford to have prejudices towards any other religion. So is the case of any jurisprudential theory which must necessarily be broad minded.

"Scientism" is the belief "that with the same techniques, that have worked in physical sciences we can eventually create an exact science of man.[15] But this is a false hope, for, human conduct cannot be interpreted well by this 'Scientism'. It is forgotten that "human relationships do not belong to engineering, mathematics, chess which other problems which can be perfectly solved". [16(a)] But this happens in a mechanistic society and "when they have turned away in dispair from these 'problems', they begin asking for more and better 'machinery' where in fact there cannot be any machinery at all".[16(b)] Felix S. Cohen observes that it is fallacious to infer that "settling of such disputes is the sole norm of law. It is the right settling of conflicts, the right delimitation of interests, which the law ought to secure. And since the problems raised by litigation are always parts of larger wholes in which individual values and values beyond the spheres of the opposed parties are involved, this rightness will depend upon factors beyond the immediate conflicting interests which the law adjusts. Thus although law is limited in its direct application to outward conduct, it must take into account the spiritual values it calls into being".[17] There is the need of more human legal philosophy which must look for the goods of human existence and goals of life beyond the pale of social controversy. Law cannot exist without balancing of interests in some way or other but this preliminary is not the end of law. The dharmic theory of law does also the balancing of the interests of society. This balancing of interests is put on permanent footing in Varna system. But in the Indian Legal Theory this incidental function is the beginning of law as Dharma, whereas in the Western American sociological theory it has become the end of law.

There is another jurist[18] who comes forward as a sociological positivist but idealism creeps in his theory. In him we find an explicit denial and an implicit assertion of ethics like that of Dharma. In his theory of 'social solidarity' which is almost identical to the 'Varna' system of ancient India we witness a cohesive principle and a division of labour and consequent specialisation of functions. To this extent he seems to affirm the concept of Dharma. However, as a sociological positivist he denies the ethical value in law. To him, a juridical obligation is an obligation to do what is a social value, that is, not to do what is anti-social. The criterion of social principle is the social reaction which is capable of being socially organised. This amoral social obligation is liable to political exploitation by irresponsible individualism as well as fascist totalitarianism. Again, this type of so-called positive interpretation is at bottom Hegelian. "The idea of freedom is replaced by an idea of 'the social'. The inexorable law is not progressive unfolding of freedom as an idea; it is progressive unfolding of 'the social' by organisation of the social reaction against the anti-social".[19] Leon Duguit then, considers law as a social fact and a resultant of social interdependence which is also a fact and which, in its turn, is the requirement of social solidarity. It emerges as an ideal and value in itself. If it is not, as he asserts, then in the opinion of this humble author Duguit seems to have conceived human society as an extention of organisation of ants who in their co-operative instinct must be expressing perfectly his idea of social interdependence. In the society of ants there are not privileges except perhaps that of the queen Ant. There are no rights, no sovereignty but only a spectacle of doing work ceaselessly based on the working ants who do their duty on the basis of instinct. This is true, especially in the light of the view that his 'sense of justice is an after-thought and a later development worked out in self-defence. Unlike, Duguit's social solidarity which has been examined and shown as lacking, in a vital aspect of law "Dharma" does not enter into antagonisms, and refutation of theories but merges them (theories) into one another in such a way that it becomes "unity in diversity". In its form it is as terrible as the vision like that of the divine in cosmic form (Virat) and as soothing like the vision of the divine in Gentle Human Form–described in the Gita (Chapter IX). This concept of Dharma as law is the richest legacy of the Indian legal philosophy bequeathed to the world of jurisprudence.

Analytical positivism looks to the form as the identification of law. To Austin, law is a command of the sovereign, to Kelsen it is a norm. Both of them make law destitute of morality. H.L.A. Hart modifies the position of Austin when he says that laws or rules of law also have their internal aspect, i.e., provide a criterion of criticism. Scandinavian realists resemble modern schools in their positivistic outlook and in their desire to eliminate metaphysics. To them law can be explained in terms of observable facts and study of such facts, is the province of the science of law. To Olivercrona, rules of law are not subjective states of mind expressed by the notion of command but are 'independent imperatives'. To Ross, Valid law means "the abstract set of normative ideas which serve as a scheme of interpretation for the phenomena of law in action.[20] To Lundstedt, law is simply the fact of social existence in organised groups and the conditions which make possible the co-existence of masses of people. His slogan is: "That nothing is valid which can be proved as a fact."[21] Notwithstanding these differences among them, the Scandinavians agree in denying the possibility of a science of justice or values. To them, these are purely subjective states or reflections of class or political ideologies. It is not possible to construct a science on such a basis.[22] American realism identifies the nature of law in judicial process which took a start from what Holmes said as "the prophesies of what the country will do in fact, and nothing more pretentious are what I mean by law."[23] It tends to indeterminism and lacks constructive approach to jurisprudence or legal theory because it implies the study of indeterminate and inarticulate extra legal factors. Analytical positivists or 'realists' confuse law either with form or circumstances or process. The partial studies of analytical positivists and realists make their so- called studies of real law, –unrealistic. It is the bane of the Western jurisprudence to suffer from particularity, partiality, limitedness and fragmentation in their views about law. The western jurisprudence exhibits the wear and tear of the materialistic civilisation with all its clashes of ideologies. They appear to make jurisprudence the hand maid to wash their dirty ideological linen. The West cannot view law as a whole which like the Vedantic Brahman is more than the aggregate of rules and theories about law and transcends their meaning and scope in which it is immanent. To the ancients, law symbolised the representative mode of Indian thinking and is a reflection of the totality of Indian Culture.

The author has endeavoured to discuss in the foregoing pages the leaders of Western jurisprudential thought with a view to ascertain the nature of law. The discussion leads this humble author to believe that each and every Western thinkers, while expounding the nature of law, has taken into consideration only a partial view of law. The Western jurists have approached the problem of identification of law either from the point of view of form, or its function, or its purpose or its methodology or its growth and evolution. It is here that we perceive the lacuna. Law cannot be understood in this way. Law is an integrated, synthetic and complete concept and any attempt to explore its true nature has to be equally integrated and syntheticised bringing in its wake the totality and pervasiveness of life itself for which law exists. By comparison, at appropriate places, it has been shown now the ancients tackled the problem of the nature of law by relating it to the nature of life and to the whole existence.

II

WHEREIN LIES THE BINDING NATURE OF LAW?

The impact of Dharma as law was so powerful on the Indian mind of past ages that they could not think of disowning it and endeavoured to preserve it assiduously by willingly and conscientiously letting it guide their lives according to its imperative. They thought that they were bound to obey law which they inherited by birth and there never arose a question in their minds as to why law was binding because they knew that it contains its authority and sanction from within, themselves. P.N. Sen, the learned author of "Hindu Jurisprudence" further explains the reason for the binding nature of Dharma. According to the sacred law the kind has its own function to perform which is partly general and partly special in its character; it is general insofar as it is his duty to obey the law himself like other individuals, and it is special insofar as unlike other individuals, it is his duty to enforce its obedience in others to a certain extent. The law is supreme; the will of the king is not the originator, and its sanction is not derived from any extrinsic or accidental agency, for it contains its sanction from within itself in the certainty that obedience to law will lead to welfare and its violation to misery. It may, however, be asked whence this certainty arises. Is it to be supposed that law represents commands issuing from God whose will holds them by attaching due reward or punishment to actions in conformity with or in violation of these commands? No doubt this may seem to be the most natural stand point, but, in fact Mimansakas who may be said to have dealt with the Philosophy of the law did not introduce divine intervention in order to explain the fruition of human action; they maintained that every action had an invisible force which subsisted even after the cessation of the action, and brought about the due consequence either in this life, or, at any rate in the life to come. This invisible force was designated by them as Apurva–. In this way, it is to be noted that they recognised the impersonal force of law without admitting Deus ex machina.[24(a)] The ancient Indians were also certain that its obedience will lead to selfare. The same question perturbs the modern jurists who have thought of abolishing or disowning state, and society to seek freedom. Indian mind too has sought complete freedom from society and state but it has sought it in the spiritual realm, i.e., Kevaliya (Salvation) usually after spending life of duty and dedication to Dharma. To them, problem of the binding nature of law lies resolved from the very beginning in various ways:

1. Metaphysically, Dharma as law is the mystic force which is governing this world. It is the law of its very being, as such the rules of Dharma are felt binding because Dharma is an obligation or a bond due to the very nature of man himself who must have some Dharma.
2. Sociologically Dharma is to be enforced because of its literal and etymological meaning. "The most general sense provided by its root 'Dhri' which signifies the action of maintaining, sustaining or supporting and which has produced *fre* in Latin (*fretus*, depending upon daring to) and *fir* (*firmus* strong in physical and moral senses whence solid, hard and durable). *Dharma* is what is firm and durable, what sustains and maintains, what hinders fainting and falling".[24(b)] According to K. Balasubrahmania Iyer in its abstract conception it means "underlying fundamental law of ones being, that which holds a thing together, makes it what it is prevents it from breaking up and changing it into something else. In other words, the characteristic function, peculiar property, fundamental attribute or essential nature of a thing is its Dharma, the law of its being. Further enlarged and idealised, it has come to mean that which makes the world what it is and holds all its parts together as one whole. It has the same significance as the English phrase 'world order'.[25]
3. "In external terms *dharma* is the action which, provided it is conformable to the order of things, permits man to realise his destiny to the full, sustains him in this life, and assures his well-being after death".[26]
4. In internal sense "*dharma* signifies the obligation, binding upon man who desires that his actions should bear fruit, to submit himself to the laws which govern the universe, and to direct his life in consequence. That obligation constitutes his duty–"[27] This duty of the individual is to his family, to his society to his God, to his higher self–all are called Dharma.
5. In yet another sense Dharma is binding because it is the distinguishing feature of man that he is conscious of his obligation to do his duty, and can deliberately impose upon

himself the obligation to do his duty. Obligation of following Dharma was also rationalised by the theory of the origin or Dharma. Ancient Indian society, which was from the very beginning organised on the principle of division of labour–called *Varna*, system, postulated functional separation. It was feared that the principle of division of labour which was meant for increased efficiency and specialisation might tend towards schism and disintegration. Hence Dharma was forged as an integrating and co-ordinating force. Brahadaranyka Upanisad says: God created one as Brahman, as an embodiment of intelligence, then Ksatriya as of power, then Vaisya of trade and then Sudra as of service and felt not satisfied at each act of his creation, because weak would not be able to exist against strong in such a scheme of creation. He created Dharma above all these classes to impose duty on all and to be obeyed by all. By Dharma they will 'hold together' and by it the weak will be able to assert against the strong when he had a rightful claim. The rationale of this Upanisadic story is that Dharma is an integrating force and mechanism of all the four sections of society. That is how Dharma has acquired the meaning of 'holding together' all the parts of society. It unites individual to himself, as well as to society in the same way as it unites different classes to one another and the society as a whole. The individual, class and society are integrated for all time. To make it a more permanent hold the Indian thinkers have been wise enough to conceive it also as somewhat relative, flexible, and modifiable, according to 'desh, kala and yugh (place, time and age) according to which its contents could be varied. By this method its collapse is avoided. It is also asserted at times of extreme emergency Dharma need not to be followed. This is succintly contained in the popular maxim आपत काले मर्यादा नास्ति which in the Western juristic literature is–necessity needs no law. For such emergent times, it is rationalised by holding that Dharma, ultimately cannot be known, its aspect is shrouded in mystery, as no one can know, Dharma completely for all time. But the test is whether the particular act is conducive to the welfare and stability of society. It is also said that Dharma is known by one who knows social welfare.

In the sum, the question why Dharma is binding is not very difficult to answer. Firstly, it is binding from within because it is the mystic force of this universe as a whole, a characteristic quality of everything, and distinctive feature of man's rationality to abide by Dharma or law. Secondly, it is binding because it is an integrating agency brought into being for smooth functioning of the ancient society which had divided itself into different classes and allotted different functions to each of these classes. In order to hold them together, they found in 'Dharma' the cohesive and co-ordinating instrument. Thirdly, in order that man may lead a virtuous life, he has of his own free will, to impose upon himself such duties and obligation which may subserve this purpose. Fourthly, Dharma is considered as the highest end of life.[28] Fifthly, Dharma leads essentially to the welfare of the people. As a dynamic concept Dharma permits man to depart from it in times of crisis when such departure may be thought of to be conducive to general welfare, with variations according to time and place. Dharma is also binding as injunctions of the Vedas and Dharmasastras. And lastly, as a symbol of what is great and good in the Indian Culture and civilisation, Dharma strikes the chord of feeling in the heart of an enlightened ancient Indian citizen, which is a foretaste of spirituality. If at all Ancient Indian jurisprudence is to be called by any name it is to be called by the name of "spiritual jurisprudence" of which Dharma is the cult and culture itself. Dharma is then binding in every way by its etymology and ontology; by right and ritual by judgment and conscience, by the Vedic injunction and virtuous conduct, in one word for self-realisation, social unity and human welfare. Dharma permeates and transcends every branch of Indian life and thought and is the emblem of its spirituality which is the natural phase of evolution an eternal aspiration and the everlasting source of strength and vitality. How else, India after invasions, persecutions, subjugation, mutilation, with all the foreign imitations and borrowings of language, dress and ways of thinking could survive through centuries; how else, surrounded by antagonistic states, jingoistic psychosis, make-believe propoganda and hostile culture it could still exist; how also would she (India) survive with its over-population, deficient recourses, inefficient controls, and disorganising forces. For the future and in the present if the great task of ensuring to every citizen justice, social, political and economic, is to be fulfilled it is 'Dharma' alone or a concept based on Dharma which can help achieve these objects. Dharma, by its juristic light would enlighten all the parts of Indian thought and action.

Materialistic Western jurisprudence, which is a by-product of exploration of matter, commercialisation of life and its values, promotions of the prospects of material comforts, turning towards territorial aggrandisements, germinating warring ideologies, nurturing or nurtured by disharmonies of social and individual existence, cannot think of such a concept of law as Dharma.

In the West early legal philosophy was born out of dissatisfaction from life in urban Greece. In Rome it developed as a protest against particularity and inequalities of life together with rigidities of the legal system which was faced with diverse problems of heterogeneous population. In early medieval times the legal philosophy out of disgust with the State, and in the later out of its allignment with the same, made itself a means of propogation of the christian doctrine. With the renaissance and the consequent decline of the authority of Church it secularised the field of jurisprudence and boosted the political authority of the king and state against its rivals–Feudalism and Church. In Seventeenth and Eighteenth Centuries with the diminution of the kingly power it expresses the supremacy of the parliament and gave a slogan of the 'Right of man'. In 19th Century, it tried to secure freedom to the individual, and the right to his property. At present it is trying to impose restrictions on both property and freedom. By discarding the cardinal principles of unity of law with life, and the purpose for which law exists, i.e., value, the legal theory of today has miserably failed to become viable and is groping in the dark to fall upon some mystique as an alternative. Present confusion in the legal theory can hardly appeal to Indian mind which sees oneness in multiplicity; which is nourished by the idea of service and sacrifice; and which is neither inimical to 'State' nor averse to religion or ethics. To Indians who have been traditionally cherishing Dharma and whose genius and culture have imbibed its tenets, Dharma contains in itself jus positivism as well as jus naturale and is a principle of division as well as unity, and a coherent scheme of life as well as the ideal of perfection. In one word it is the epitome of Indian civilisation and culture.

As against this, we cannot get so complete an answer in Western jurisprudence to the question why law is binding. Natural law thinkers feel obliged to be bound by law if law is just. The historical jurists will consider law as binding if it is the expression or recognition of habit, usage, or custom. To sociological jurists, law is the condition of social life and is binding because it is an expression of pubic opinion and is a means of social control and has organised force of community at its back. The American realism will accept that law as binding which agrees with the judge's hunch.

This brief survey of the different schools of jurisprudence shows that not even one school agrees with the other on the question why law is binding. Let us now turn our attention to legal positivism which has given special importance to enforcement of law. This enforcement, the positivists point out is secured by the element of force behind the rule of law. It is submitted that this does not solve completely the problem why law is binding because even despite this element of force behind law innumerable violations take place, which in their turn, call for further needs to enact more laws. Even then the situation does not improve. This is a further pointer to the fact that force alone is not sufficient a reason or an exhausting reason to make law binding. For the analytical jurists coercion is the sole explanation for the obedience of law. This is a feeble argument, as obligation to obey law can neither be determined by logic nor can this obligation be forsaken by it. In their endeavour to explain the binding nature of law, the analytical jurists have either failed or have tried to give such explanations which are similar to moral explanations, though the positivists, in their very thesis, have discarded the moral aspect of law. The problem thus continues to remain insoluble. Austin brings in the notion of political community which has the character of habitual obedience as its trait and which is conditioned by fear of punishment. Obligation of law does not depend upon its being a coercive force alone, but its being a good thing. The doctrine of Dharma explains the nature of law better because it manifestly includes the value of good in law and for this very reason the natural law doctrine which has been consigned to the grave due to its destructive and revolutionary role throughout the history has revived again and again for it adds the element of value to the proposition of law without which legal obligation cannot be explained. Hans Kelsen, the author of 'the pure theory of law' could not completely explain the phenomena of law when he held that law is a norm expressing its normal activity by 'legal ought' as distinguished from 'moral ought'. Again he could not logically answer the question 'why law is binding'. He postulated that the reason for the validity of law is to be traced only formally and ultimately to the basic norm but the condition for its validity lies in the 'minimum effectiveness' of a legal order. Instead of 'habitual obedience' of Austin he has used minimum effectiveness as a guarantee for the obedience of law. He has not clarified the nature of effectiveness further because he must have felt the logical difficulty of unavoidable involvement with morality. The Neo-Austinian Holland, includes in the study of jurisprudence which he calls the formal science of positive law "considerations of moral phenomena, and scheme of purposes" when he gives guidance to a jurist who has accumulated material to formulate the formal science.[29] Salmond expressly admits that justice is the end of law and law is an instrument of justice. His concept of justice is utilitarian one which he expresses as 'human welfare'. H.L.A. Hart criticises Austin for not explaining the idea of obligation towards law properly. Hart admits that law has an internal aspect, and is binding because "there should be a critical reflective attitude to certain patterns of behaviour as a common standard, and that this should display itself in criticism.....all of which find their characteristic expression in normative terminology of 'ought', 'must', and 'should', 'right' and 'wrong'.[30] If positivism admits this much and yet distinguishes law from morality, in whatever manner, the position of positivism is certainly shaken. American realism (of LLeweLLyn) is only a ferment and the separation between law and justice or between 'is' and ought is only provisional. In the Scandinavian realism the idea of obligation is brought to its logical conclusion. Hagerstorm discards value and the whole science of ought together with the notion of duty and other moral concepts as emotional responses brought into being by 'word magic' like that of primitive law. He considers that word-magic is still effective in its modernised form in the present legal systems. This seems to be the natural consequence of rejecting morality, whereby it becomes quite manifest that binding effect of law can neither be proved nor be considered in law, as it is seen operating upon human minds only by magic alone and nothing else. It is as much as dethroning jurisprudence and enthroning magic. K. Oliver Cronna, his disciple, expressly says that there is no such thing as 'binding force of law'; he calls it illusory or 'meaningless' and 'nonsensical' which exists only as an idea in the minds of individuals. It has no juristic explanation and is only a mirage of language. Yet according to him the 'feeling of being bound is positive and needs to be explained. To him it stems from the psychological associations, connected with this mode of expression by certain agencies.[31] In our minds, he says, the imperative expression is connected with the idea of force, and it is on account of this purely psychological effect of the imperative form of law that we feel ourselves to be under a legal obligation, i.e., we feel bound. Law to him is a regulated force and the binding force of law is to bound in the physical force behind it which is manifested and exercised whenever there is a need for doing so. This position is the same as that taken by Austin with the difference that the word "habitual obedience" has not been used. However, the theory which treats 'binding force' purely as a psychological matter cannot be trustworthy because law cannot be enforced relying only on psychology of fear. If law is force, or force is the sole explanation of law jurisprudence will be transformed into a science of penology, or some dismal art of exciting fear in the minds of people. A. Ross, another Scandinavian realist seems to realise that law cannot be explained validly in terms of force. He comes very near to our notion of Dharma as binding from within, but in a different way when he says that valid law "means the abstract set of normative ideas which serve as a scheme of interpretation for the phenomena of law in action, which again means that these norms are effectively followed because they are experienced and felt to be socially binding."[32] They are felt so by the judge and other legal authorities who apply the law. According to A.V. Lundstedt law is something which is purely subjective. He denies the existence of legal rules as abstract propositions binding individuals. "Behind 'law' the only 'reality' he can find is a highly complex congeries of psychological factors, influencing the conduct of officials and private individuals and in turn being influenced by this conduct. Obligation in Lundstedt's view, depends upon the subjective feeling of moral duty; therefore, he cannot admit the possibility of objective law or rules of law."[33] Here we find that 'binding force of law' is purely the moral aspect which the positivists do not admit. Though Lundstedt for sakes metaphysics and ethics yet he conceives legal activities to be indispensable for the existence of society which is the only *raisond' etre* for these activities. Further, his constructive juridique looks to the benefit of society or social welfare as motive for all activities of law. In truth the positivist has realised that 'obedience is a fact which cannot be proved by logic, which is the only method available to him. Finding himself in this quandary he rejects the whole problem by saying that the problem is factual and so needs no theorisation.

The fallacy becomes quite apparent to him. To avoid it, either the positivist takes the fact of obedience for granted or leaves the theory incomplete. Some of the positivists, as has been stated earlier, consider the fact of obedience a moral problem only and not at legal one as they do not find any logical link between law and its obedience. With due difference, it is submitted that this exposes their helplessness. This is the most vulnerable point in positivistic jurisprudence. Some of the Neo-Austinians like Salmond have taken recourse 'value' or some other considerations. If it is so, then rejection of value, normativity and ideology is not worthwhile. Law in order to be a study must have extraneous reference beyond itself in the society and human nature and its purposes; and in one way or the other legal theory has to tilt towards some greater concept than that of law. Positive law, then need not feel shy of morality. Because of the unique experience of natural law doctrine which had subversive and revolutionary character, the Western jurists are scared of morality. This is somewhat justified in their own context because a burnt child dreads the fire.

What then, is the net result of the Western materialistic tradition culminating in positivism in jurisprudential though? Briefly stated it begins with a rejection of morality (Austin), then a rejection of concepts like sovereignty, command, personality, rights, justice, separation of powers (Kelsen) than again the rejection of concepts together with 'the binding force' or validity of law, the objectivity of legal rules take place (Scandinavian realists). After the departure of ethics, metaphysics, normativity, all conceptual thinking and the main doctrines, law seems to be that which has laid down or some probability of pressure of 'meaningless scraps of paper' or labels or nonesense or 'mere fantasies of mind'. How can a jurisprudence with such theories succeed in Indian when it has failed in the West? In such circumstances we are left without any cogent, coherent, and viable legal theory which may meet the needs of the times. In the West where they (legal theories) originated, they have proved insufficient, incomplete, inappropriate and what not. The fact of revival of natural law theories is enough to prove this. It is high time that we learn the lessons of history. The ancient concept of Dharma has not been molested by political ideologies, class conflicts and all the harrowing propoganda and hatred of institutions. Why should then we not reclaim our own legal theory of 'Dharma' which will be the juristic fulfilment of the self-evident truth of the maxim 'know thy self'? why should not we plough our own land and raise our own crop? Why should we not transfuse our own legal philosophy in the body of our own law so that it may be in accord with our character and genius? Why should we be shy of 'Dharma' which displays the whole spectrum of legal theory? Dharma is our characteristic quality, our function, duty, good, order, truth, existence, world process, welfare, true interpretation (Mimansa), law in action (Vyavahar), custom (Achar) prescription, right, justice, and the ultimate victory of good over evil. In one word, it is the complete constitution for our social, moral, legal and religious existence. Nay, revival of Dharma may again lead to the concept of one world (वसुधैव कुटुम्बकम्) and universal brotherhood; and with its spiritual aura and mystique may contribute towards universal peace.

Notes and References

1. Hindu Jurisprudence by Priya Nath Sen, Tagore Law Lectures, 1909, Published by University of Calcutta, 1918, p. 1-2.
2. Cultural Heritage of India, Vol. II, p. 575, Published by Ram Krishna Mission, Institute of Culture.
3. *Ibid.*, pp. 516-18.
4. Dharma in later Vedic literature replaced Rit, as the eternal order, for the reasons pointed out in the last Chapter, wherein a reference was made to the fact that Buddhists adopted Dharma and popularised it and began to win over masses by 'propogation of their main doctrine by the name of Dharma which was a Pali version of Dharman. Buddha seems to have chosen this word, because it was possible to follow 'Dharma' without attaching oneself to divine idea' which was advocated by him. (Ref. Call of Vedas by A.C. Bose; 1960, p. 192). The concept of 'Dharma' which is nothing but a version of 'Dharman' of the Vedas, in Pali was accommodated by Hindu theorists as 'Dharma' with a subtle change in gender. This, considerably minimised the influence of Buddhism, the main rival of the Vedic religion. It was associated by Vedic adherents with 'Yama', the God of Justice.
5. Quoted in Indian Thought through the ages by B.G. Gokhale, Asia Publishing House, p. 27.
6. *Ibid.*, p. 46.
7. Kane–quoted by S. Vardhachariar in his book "Hindu Judicial System" by S. Vardhachariar, p. 36.
8. Hindu Judicial System by S. Vardhachariar, p. 36.
9. Hindu Ideals–quoted by K. Bala Subramania, p. 51, Published by Vidhya Bhawan.
10. The Classical Law of India by Robert Lingat, p. 5.
11. Manu (VII-15).

12. Indian Thought Through the Ages–By Gokhale, p. 43.
13. *Ibid.*, p. 43, View of Sinha Stated.
14. Vinogradoff, Historical Jurisprudence, quoted by S. Vardhachariar in his Book Hindu Judicial System at p. 30.
15. W.H. White, quoted by Dennis Lloyd in his book–Introduction to Jurisprudence, Ist Edition– p. 179 F.T. 22.
16. (a) and (b) Dennis Lloyd–Introduction to Jurisprudence, Ist Edition– p. 199, Foot Note 41. J.B. Priestley quoted.
17. Ethical Systems and Legal Ideals–Felix S. Cohen, 1959, p. 89.
18. Leon Duguit.
19. Interpretations of Legal History–By R. Pound, 3rd Edition, 1946, pp. 86-87, Harvard University Press.
20. Ross quoted by Dias in his 'Jurisprudence', 3rd Edition, p. 541.
21. Dias, Jurisprudence, 3rd Edition, p. 541.
22. *Ibid.*, p. 542.
23. O.W. Holmes, The Path of Law (1897), Extract in Introduction to Jurisprudence (1st Edition) by Dennis Lloyd, p. 211.
24. (a) The General Principles of Hindu Jurisprudence–By Priya Nath Sen, Tagore L.L.Pub., 1918, pp. 26-27.
24. (b) The Classical Law of India by Robert Lingat, p. 3.
25. Hindu Ideals, pp. 21 to 23, Pub.–B.V.B., 1969, Bombay.
26. Classical Law of India by R. Lingat, pp. 3-4.
27. *Ibid.*, pp. 3-4.
28. Except Moksa (Liberation) which one can attain only after cessation of earthly life. Moksa was included in the list of ends due to Buddhistic influence of 'Nirvan' as adverted to in the first Chapter. Again Moksa is possible through a life of Dharma.
29. The Elements of Jurispurdence by T.E. Holland, 7th Edition, p. 7.
30. The Concept of Law by H.L.A. Hart (1972), p. 56 (ELBS).
31. R.W.M. Dias, Jurisprudence (3rd Edition, 1970, p. 540)
32. John D. Finch, Introduction to Legal Theory, 1970, p. 123 (quoted by Rose).
33. J. Walter Jones, Historical Introduction to the Theory of Law (Footnote) at pp. 201 to 202.

4

Law as Authority–Its Evolution from Vrata to Danda

I

If law is a directive for human action, it must be an authorised one. The concept of authority has so great a philosophic significance that it takes within its fold all the basic inquiries about law. It is "a high level abstraction and any thorough inquiry into its roles, types, conditions and functions is no less than a quest for an inclusive philosophy and science of law and politics."[1] It is a concept of "Legitimate power" and while expressing formal legal validity of a rule of law it has to take into account the justification, the reasonableness and rightfulness of the rule. In order to do so it (law) takes for granted the corresponding belief in the corpus of values, which creates the psychological attitude in man who is a free willing agent to follow law and this provides to the law, the sole guarantee, of its existence and effectiveness. For this new values also find entrance to make it representative and viable. The formal linguistic expression of law as command or order or directive to the members of a legal community without reference to the 'agreed norm' or notion of reasonableness or the value of overall well-being leads one in logical difficulties and problems which are hard to be circumvented and solved (as has been amply demonstrated in the previous Chapter). Any formulation of the notion of law devoid of a comprehensive discussion of its authority, is bound to be inadequate and would need new orientation and a rethinking so that it may not be completely rejected by legal theorists as illogical and unconvincing. In ancient Indian legal philosophy, mythology, metaphysics, and teleology–all participated in supplying law its logic, its justification, and thus generated the psychology of obedience, reverence, fear of and faith in law. Authority as a concept of legal philosophy is seen here to arise from the very nature of the universe, which is sentient, with purpose of well being of all. Not only does it give a choice to men to participate in the progressive realisation of this purpose but persuades them to do so by the agency of myths, legends and doctrine to explain the direction and course of universal teleos. The notion of Rit (discussed in Chapter 2), the physical and spiritual dynamics of this world which expresses law as right and order in human life; the concept of Dharma–the characteristic quality and function of things and beings in this world which fastens obligation to follow law; the notion of व्रत (Ordinance) a formal linguistic expression of law as command; the notion of right, reasonableness and welfare; the genesis of state and creation and application of 'Danda' originally by God and later by the learned; all have contributed to the concept of law as endowed with authority. Be they mythological or man-made makes little difference as long as they have legal consequences which are relevant to the notion of authority. This authority held royal absolutism in check under the rule of law and enjoined on the individual to do his duty.

THE NOTION OF AUTHORITY IN POSITIVIST JURISPRUDENCE OF THE WEST

A sociological jurist, like Max Weber, understands the notion of authority in terms of legitimacy but describes it purely as a psychosis. As C.J. Friedrich points out: "The legitimacy of an order according to Weber may be guaranteed (1) purely internally (i.e., subjectively) in three ways: (a) purely emotionally; by emotional devotion; by faith in the order's absolute validity as an expression of ultimate values (moral, aesthetic and others); and (b) religious; by the faith that salvation depends upon it (the orders) maintenance; or (2) also (or only) by expectation of specific external consequences, that is by interests; but these expectations are of a particular kind".[2] As Friedrich points out this approach stressed the psychological aspect of legitimacy, to him, devotion, faith and expectations as psychological factors are more transitional phases which cannot explain the concept of legitimacy. He observes "an order is provided by its having a basis in positive law. Legitimacy is related to right and justice; without clarification of what is to be understood by the rightness and justice of law, legitimacy cannot be comprehended either. Hitler's rule was legal but it was not legitimate. It had a basis in law, but none in right and justice. This rule possessed unheard of power but it lacked authority to a large extent''.[3] Legitimacy, even if considered in the authority of the will of the majority, must be related to the higher reason of a system of values which point to reasoned elaboration or rationality. Hence not 'devotion' or 'faith' or similar psychic phenomena provide genuine authority; not legitimacy either but 'augmentation', i.e., the reinforcement by reason, expresses itself in the judgment of the old, the learned and the wise; only by such a relationship to reason, that is to say, only by reasoned elaboration in terms of the community's ideas, values, and beliefs, is authority added to the exercise of power, whether autocratic or democratic.[4] In the final analysis, the authority of law accordingly, ''rests upon its reasonableness–that is to say its justice–that the legitimacy of a constitution, a statute, or a decision rests upon its rightfulness and that its legality rests upon its accord with positive laws''.[5]

EXTERNAL AND POLITICAL ASPECT OF AUTHORITY

Political considerations had led Austin to conceive the sovereign as the sole authority of law. As this sovereign is a human being, or a group of human beings, which he terms as determinate human authority, calls for a complete rejection of natural law theory and the common law doctrine of the 'rule of law'. The common law postulated that the king is bound by the common law and the law of God, as we know that doctrine of the rule of law is derived from this supremacy of common law. The result is that authority has to be identified with political authority and power in the State. In reply to the question why the sovereign has got authority to lay down law, it is pointed out that sovereign is a political superior and citizens are political inferiors, and so they are subject to the authority of the sovereign. By this logic law is viewed as the command of the sovereign. The subjection of political inferiors creates the mechanical habit of obedience in the bulk of the community or people at large. The law-breakers are coerced into obedience just as the gun man coerces the bank manager to hand over the bag. This is the total explanation of the question why one is obliged to obey law. People, in such a case obey law partly because of political condition of being subjects and partly because of the threat of punishment; the guarantee of obedience lies in the formation of the habit of obedience.

The consequence of such a theory of authority is that only modern legal systems, where political power is concentrated to in persons or bodies, can alone be called legal systems embodying in themselves the principle of authority. Further, law is the law only to the extent it is the expression of the sovereign will or is dependent for its recognition upon, the sovereign which is the biggest political gun that gets the mark of legal validity. This arid characterisation of authority makes jurisprudence as something which is concerned with mere description and distribution of political power and reduces the essential element of authority of law to a formal and external criterion. This has virtually been the office of Analytical positivism. Accordingly, the problems of legal systems become problems of logical analysis and processing of material to facilitate, to ascertain, or to determine the will of the sovereign power which alone is considered to give unity and certainty to the legal system as a whole. The legal authority, in this way, is traced to the fact of political power. This seems to render all conceptualisation of authority as nonsense. This virtually is the position reached by Scandinavian realists who call for the rejection of the concept of authority. Thus, jurisprudence becomes only a systematic description and exposition of the legal propositions and rules without the need of any rational criticism or of a theory of justification. Law becomes merely an arsenal of rules, a skilful and a professional game devoid of any purpose and social significance, a class-book-jurisprudence or theoretical branch of study without reference to interests, cultural values, and ideals of human life. Frightened by this consequence, the neo-Austinians, like Salmond, have reverted back to the end of law as justice. Hart has included minimum of natural law and recognised the internal aspect of rules; sociological jurists also reacted against this view. They have emphasized the instrumentality of law for social purposes and ends. Natural law thinkers, of all grades and degrees, have brought in the considerations of value in relation to time and place. Yet all these piecemeal approaches have not converged into a comprehensive approach as they maintain their own grooves of thoughts or preferences and fail to give a synthetic view of law and its authority which ought to include all the aspects of human life and culture. Such a comprehensive and synthetic view we have in the legal theory of ancient India.

EVOLUTION OF THE CONCEPT OF AUTHORITY IN ANCIENT INDIAN LAW

This universe has been conceived of by the Rig Vedic Indians as sentient with purpose, menifesting all the aspects of life and action. The first sign or germ of the notion of authority lies in the very scheme and being of this Universe–the eternal teleos. This gives rationale to any direction or authorised guidance to human beings which proceeds from law. Law becomes then a functional participation in the purpose of this world and is expressed as Rit. Thus we see the concept of 'Authority' arising out of the purposeful universe.[6] This purpose of the universe, in relation to human beings is the welfare, perfection and happiness, all rolled into one. From this ensues the regulation of life and activity by means of reason which not only imposes restrictions on individuals to act in a particular manner but also, in doing so, contributes to, the theory of law, by influencing human conduct in various ways viz.; volition, interpretation and administration. The idea of reasonableness and justice are clearly seen in such comprehension of the concept of law. According to the ancients a law devoid of reasonableness and justice is not law but "Adharma", the negation of 'Dharma', and hence devoid of any authority. Reason or Reasonableness, to which we have alluded, is inherently, seated in Dharma and men's conduct has to be in accord with this 'Dharma'. In this sense the authority of law is contained in the concept of Dharma which has reference to what is right, just and reasonable. Dharma is then internally what is right and externally what we may call law. 'Authority', in this sense only, is capable of persuading men to desist from evil. As early as the Rig Vedic times, Indian mind put forward the doctrine of free will. According to Rishi Vasistha God gave to man and man alone a conscience so that he may decide for himself what is right and what is wrong. Rishi Vamdev conceived 'self-interest' or 'egoism' to be the starting point of his theory of law. "If law is to be respected it is perhaps because that will ensure one's own benefit... But it must be said to the credit of these early Vedic philosophers that they do not at the same time fail to lay stress on the ethical foundation of law".[7] Man, according to "Rishi Mahidas of Brahmana period, is endowed with "capacity to reason, and it is necessary for the ordering of his sensations and experiences, to reason from particular to general.....Reason postulates the subordination of conscious ego to its environment and consequently requires a certain concordance between egoistic and altrustic impulses. This gives rise to the legal sense and the legal impulse, and these manifest themselves in an inclination towards external order.[8] Yajnavalkya of Sutra period expresses the philosophy of self-love आत्म काम but for proper function of this doctrine of self-love one has to keep in mind the Kathoupanishadic distinction between what is pleasurable (प्रेय) and what is good (श्रेय). According to him, authority of law enforces 'Dharma' or the good and relates it to the ideal living which is a better form of self-love. Thus man has a conscience to judge and the reason to regulate his life for the attainment of higher ends of life which in his own interest are to be pursued and practised. The notion of authority then gets formal expression as 'ought' or command in the concept of (व्रतं) which is an embodiment of 'Rit' ऋत. This Vratam (व्रतं) consists of a body of rules ordained or dictated divinely. "It is indeed looked upon as the command of this or that deity and its non-observance is met by punishment at the hands of the deity whose व्रतं is violated".[9] Radha Binod Pal has distinguished व्रतं from ऋतं Both Vratam and Ritam are conceived as invoilable; they are so in as much as any violation of them will at once be followed by penalties. But while there scarcely seems to be any possibility of wilful violation of Rit, with Vrata, human beings are conceived as having great deal of freedom.[10] Vratas are also expressed as injunctions of religio-legal philosophy and are further classified into negative and positive (शिष्ट and प्रतिषिद्ध). The authority of law in order to be worthy, be such as would direct human behaviour not because of any political power but because of its own in-built potency. Law thus retains its authority, preserves its sanctity, and sustains itself as an emblem of Justice and Reason and guarantees human welfare. A number of Vratas have been enjoined by gods according to which social habit or habitual obedience has been inculcated. Religious Vratas of today are social counterparts of the legal rules and have served the purpose of a jural consciousness of the civilised society. They are a sort of jural postulates which have been conceived by Kohler and adopted by Pound in his sociological theory of law.

One of the socio-religious Vrata which is prescribed of Jainism and Buddhism, and adopted also by Hinduism is Ahimsa or non-violence. "Ahimsa is not only a moral or religious Vrat or vow but has deep jural significance; it is supplementary to the dictates of law which receive a social recognition. Formal law forbids violence under the threat of punishment, whereas Ahimsa enjoins the practice of non-violence by forgiveness, pardon and expiation. It is not only a reaction against Vedic ritualism but is the voice of reason which speaks of non-interference with and non-injury to persons and beings. Without the propogation of non-violence, law would have failed to convince us and would have appeared as a brute force destitute of the legitimate authority. In the inculcation of 'Karuna' and 'Maitri', i.e., active compassion and service and a great tolerance of other beliefs we get the greatest success of law. Like Ahimsa, the other Vrata of "truth" is also a legal ideal. The whole purpose of legal procedure in legal philosophy of India is a search for truth. The law of contracts is based upon good faith and truthfulness, i.e., it demands that one should be true to ones word. It is said in Rig Veda that Law and Truth were born together as twins. Truth is knowledge of existence as well as existence itself and is acclaimed as the God himself. Similarly, the Vrat of अस्तेय (Asteya) enjoins not to commit theft, and अपरिग्रह (Aparigrah) enjoins not to commit adultery. In fact, most of the offences are committed as a result of lust and greed; law and punishment are only needed for keeping this part of human nature in control. Similarly, other Vows or Vratas work for the enforcement of law. In fact, these types of Vratas are true specimen of social legislation or living law because they are legislated by society and not by the State. The social counterpart of the force of laws or 'dand' lies in the doctrine of Karma or causation which can uphold the authority of Dharma without the instrument of force. It becomes the moral retribution and possesses such a convincing force of its potency and efficacy that in ancient times it had so much controlling and regulating force that the doctrine of danda must have appeared as its offshoot or a by-product or supplementary to it. Modern jurisprudence which was deviated from its path has been torn to pieces and now is making defensive attempts to justify itself by acknowledging secretly the semi-religious and ethical base in 'willingness', 'recognition', social welfare, utility, freedom, etc. Inspite of the touch of modernity and sophistication given to them, the legal theory has failed to sustain itself and is bound to revert to the ancient base of law consisting of morality and religion which commanded authority with reverence.

Authority has two kinds. The first commands obedience, the second confers power to legislate. Authority to command obedience, as we have seen, is derived from the concept of Vrata which is the form of Rit. Authority to legislate is derived from the conception of this universe which is permeated with conscious designing, i.e., Legislation in a wider sense. This authority to legislate was rationalised by the Indian thinkers in the form of a myth. In the Mahabharat, the great epic we notice how Dharma had deteriorated and fallen. Though the concept of धर्मन् , as eternal statute (its plural धर्माणी , eternal statutes) was in existence yet it had to be reinforced. Bhisma points out that at first there was "neither sovereignty nor sovereign, neither punishment nor punisher (..............). At that time the people used to govern themselves by means of justice or righteousness (dharma). In later times, however, they began to degenerate and were assailed successively by the vices of intoxication, greed, wrath and self-indulgence. The world was disturbed, and the Vedas as well as justice perished; the gods were frightened; and they sought the protection of Brahma. The great God created for their sake and for the good of the world a gigantic treatise consisting of one thousand Chapters which treated the four-fold ends of life–Dharma, Artha, Kama and Moksha. This was called Dandniti (The law of punishment) and became the arche type out of which successive summaries were prepared by gods Siva and Indra, and the sages Brihaspati and Sukra".[11] This is the genesis of all Dharma Sutras and Smritis and Commentaries which lay down rules which declare, or discover or interpret the rules of law which have been codified in Dharma Sastra which is the most important source of law. Bhisma does not consider human nature as intrinsically bad. It is only due to external influences and change of times and 'Yuga' that dharma loses its hold on human beings. As such, codifications of dharma becomes an authoritative source, not from within but from without, having divine sanction to *ad hoc* considerations of social situations. Authority was then seated in the reason or intelligence of that Supreme God and in nothing else. To Manu reason is also one of the sources of law. Even the authority of Dharma was not so absolute as to be autocratic. Dharma could be violated in exceptional circumstances (Refer to Chapter 3). All this shows that the authority of law in its ultimate analysis, is a manifestation of reasonableness.

It would thus seem that law exists on the basis of this authority and whenever it is violated, the violation; depending upon its nature is dealt with by 'Danda', i.e., punishment. This is not all. The ancient sages have interestingly, given an explanation for the need of punishment. The origin of punishment or coercive force as Danda lies in a myth. According to Manu the lord created the instrument of punishment, in the form of his own son so that the king may protect 'Dharma'. Punishment, he says is the protector of all creatures. It is the incarnation of law, i.e., Dharma (Manu VII-14). But this punishment must be right. It is specifically said that if the punishment is not inflicted properly and after due consideration, it destroys every thing (Manu VII-19). In this way punishment is identified with Dharma, i.e., what is just and reasonable. In other words, the authority of Punishment lies in Dharma which is an embodiment of Reason. The King possessed summa potestas (Aisvarya) and this protestas had to be exercised rightfully and justly. Though punishment is considered as the foundation of civil life and the keeper of virtues, yet all the benefits of such life in the state will not be available without its judicious use. In the conception of danda lie merged the political interests of state, the social interests of the group and the moral interests of the individual. This merger takes place through the agency of Dharma.

II

The development of the concept of authority in Western jurisprudence is not only interesting but also strange. At first, the authority of law appears as 'divine authority' and law becomes divinely ordained or divinely dictated body of rules, as the code of Hammurabi which is believed to have been handed down by the sun-God, ready made, or as the Masaic law of the Ten commandents of the Lord. When in later ages, conflicts were created between the State and Church, then the religious authority of God as the authority of law, lost its ground. Another source of authority of law was seen in nature. This thought found its origin in Greek philosophy and resulted in the doctrine of natural rights, with exaggerated emphasis upon freedom of the individual and sanctity of property. Consequently, a great distrust has been created in the minds of men towards the State, as they fear their property may be expropriated at any time. Reaction has set against natural law land the authority of nature as a result of which nature as the authority of law has lost its appeal to the modern man. Yet, in another way, authority of law was located in the political power of the state. Law began to be conceived of as the will of the Roman emperor. It was then conceptualised in the principle of sovereignty. This found favour later with the lawyers of the Sixteenth and the Seventeenth Centuries who supported royal authority. With the popularity of democracies, parliament became powerful and sovereignty or authority of law was located in the parliament. Again with republics, having concerned for the welfare of the people, this sovereignty was sought in the general will of the people as the single, ultimate, unchallengeable power and source of all law. This general will is more of a fiction than a fact. It seems that by such a concept the principle of authority has lost all its worth and significance. It may boost every law as the will of the people and instead of God or Nature or Religion it has posited a political God in the form of people.

Be it a fradulent or hypocritical humage paid to this political god, the essential truth which is borne out is that both law and state are meant ultimately for the people. It is for the welfare of people or the good of the community wherein lies the reason of the existence of State and law. In this sense, the authority is grounded in reasonableness is not absolute power but only a legitimate exercise of power and the principle of sovereignty in its last analysis is only the principle of knowing the source of legitimate power or authority. But this basic truth is seldom realised by those who run the machinery of law and State. Inspite of the fact that the doctrine of sovereignty, as supreme and absolute power has lost its ground in political and legal theory, it has still in the psychology of the functionaries of State and law. When we know that all the governmental functions are to be performed and administration of justice by courts is to be done with the aim of the welfare of the people, it is disconcerting to note that parliament, at times, becomes hypersensitive of its power and authority begins to view judiciary with irrational prejudice as such becomes jealous of its power of judicial review. Judiciary is not far behind in retaliating by exhibiting its own professional prejudices. One claims to represent the will of the people and the other, the conscience of the nation. Both are working manifestly and consciously for the welfare of the people. But unknowingly they are looking to the sphere of their authority as their own exclusive property and are apprehensive of its encroachment or tresspass. The whole orientation of the theory of authority is not so much on the theory of rights and powers as it is on the theory of duties and service. Most of our problems of law and politics can be solved by setting a right this authority-complex of ours.

The ancient legal philosophy of India can perform the therapeutic function in this direction to cure the ailing body of jurisprudence. In the foregoing paragraphs an attempt has been made by comparison of the Western jurisprudential thought, regarding authority of law, and the ancient Indian legal philosophical basis of authority and it has been logically proved that the concept of authority in Western thought is not clear and has no ethical base which may be strong and solid enough to embrace all the facts of 'authority' of law. On the other hand, as has been shown, the ancient concept of authority is built upon solid foundations of 'Dharma' which not only has the element of coercion, which is not borne out of mere fear, but has also the promptings of inner responses towards law and its authority. 'Dharma' is all righteousness, morality and such conduct by individuals which subserves, social interests and contributes to social and individual welfare. It is that master-concept which harmonises and integrates all the aspects of human life with which law is closely and intimately related and concerned. If this harmonisation and integration is not achieved, law becomes inspid, empty, and insular. It is in this respect that the authority of law as 'Dharma' becomes relevant in its many manifestations viz. order, culture, precept, practice, and administration of justice. The whole world of law in all its unity and diversity lends moral tone and viability to the theory and practice of law. In this lies its enduring source of authority.

Notes and References

1. Quoted in "Studies in Jurisprudence and Criminal Theory–By Jerome Hall-Ed. 1958, p. 95.
2. Philosophy of Law in Historical Perspective by Carl Joachim Friedrich, p. 203 (Second Edition). Weber Quoted pp. 202-03.
3. *Ibid.*, p. 203.
4. *Ibid.*
5. *Ibid.*, pp. 203-04.
6. Ref. Chapt. I, 'Theories of Creation; Visvamitra's Concept of God, in 'History of Hindu Law by Radha Binod Pal, Tagore Law Lectures, pp. 118-46.
7. *Ibid.*, p. 144.
8. *Ibid.*, pp. 192-93.
9. *Ibid.*, p. 163.
10. *Ibid.*, p. 165.
11. The Ideas of Sovereignty and State in Indian Political Thought-By K.M. Panikkar, Published by Bhartiya Vidya Bhawan, 1963, pp. 17-18.

5

Law as Practice (Custom) and Precept (Text)–Achara (Acara) and Sastra

I

Many important concepts of Indian Legal Philosophy are derived from the primalnotion of Rita. The Chief among them is Rig-Vedic 'Swadha' (स्वधा) the inherent potency or nature of things or beings and actions or ideas. As an aspect of Rita it has special relevance to law in the form of custom (Achara). According to Professor Berolzheimer the sanction of Achara or Custom as law arises from this Swadha. To Radha Binod Pal the concept has a deeper philosophic significance. Swadha "is indeed conceivei of as the quality or disposition of nature, the essence of a person or thing, as derived from its genesis and growth. It is the order or construction of nature as a generative and creative force, developing from the spontaneous energy inherent in material objects without the intervention of any external agency".[1] Herein seems to lie the authority of custom or usage. Whatever is पूर्वा is (that has gone before in the past) whatever is दीर्घश्रुत्, (long and continuous) demands our respect because the very fact of its being done or observed by so many and so often, makes it probably consistent and habitual with our nature. What is contrary to स्वधा could not have been repeated so often. Moreover, such customs have proved acceptable to the gods to human society and sanctioned by Rit or law–as safe conduct in social life in not being punished point the way in which man may walk with safety.[2] The concept of Swadha is closely related to the Vedic मर्यादा which, to the ancients, meant the conceiving of law as recorded wisdom of the wise men of yore who had learned the safe course of human conduct–by treading the same path.

Custom, in its organic function and creation, is crystalisation in settled mode or pattern of behaviour, a psychological force called habit. This habit, the so-called second nature of man gives the first expression of law in form of custom. Custom is then the first visible seed of human legal system and manifests the first idea of wrong which is nothing but a conceptual product of man's non-participation in settled and accepted mode of social life, with the feeling of uneasiness and apprehension of public sensure, as an evil consequence invoking the displeasure of the social group and gods.[3] The doctrine of "living law" of Ehrlich is the modern expression of the old Indian concept of "Swadha" which has the efficacy of bringing a mass of man under its fold by inner organic force without, coercion and does not call for any indirect and incidental means for enforcement of law. Law, then, becomes an organic function of society, and realises itself into pattern-following habit of man. This pattern-forming habit is also the unavoidable and main presupposition or axiom of Austinian theory of law, and is expressed as "habitual obedience". Who pays disguised tribute to the efficacy of custom. The nature of man-in-group, in relation to automatic and spontaneous creation of law, without the need of conscious willing at the initial stage, has been idolised by Savigny as Volksgeist, i.e., the spirit of the people, the fountain source of law. 'Swadha', then may be taken to reside as common consciousness and a mystic force whose external form is custom. According to Salmond custom embodies those principles which have commanded themselves to national conscience as principles of justice and public utility.[4] Its existence as established usages is the basis of a rational expectation of its continuance in future.[5] In this way, custom gave predictability and stability to ancient legal orders which were oriented on custom and usage. According to modern sociological analysis "Custom in fact is not merely a pervailing habit, but also a rule or norm of action. The rule is supported on the emotional side by two sets of forces. There is firstly a sentiment or group of emotional dispositions attaching to custom as such, and condemning its breach. In this sentiment there is a rational element, the recognition, however, vague, of the importance of order, and the necessity of knowing what to expect in given situation. Around these, cluster the social feelings; and the obedience of customary rules is one of the most elementary ways in which the individual responds to the call of social life and realizes his dependence upon the group."[6] There is an assumption of goodness in custom. This assumption imparts it an '*emotional ethical value.*' Violation of the rule of custom is taken as an insult and offence against the group life and outlook. Hopes and ideals of the group are reflected in its customs, and acquire sanctity through legend and myth.

There are four main sources of Ancient Indian law. They are: (1) Sruti or Veda, (2) Smriti or Tradition, (3) Custom, (4) Digest and Commentaries (The last named belong to the medieval period mainly, but were worked out later also).

Law, in Ancient Indian Legal theory, is said to have divine origin in the Vedas which are revealed texts. Divinity is an early mode of thinking, religion a means of social control and theology the general frame of knowledge. But this belief, of the divine origin of law is not confined to Indian law alone. It is a universal feature which is found in all legal systems of the world. We have already mentioned earlier that Hammurabi received the code from the Sun-God. This is supported also by S. Vardhachariar who observes: "Hammurabi was believed to have received his Code from the Sun-God. Moses received the Commandments from Jehovah. Similar beliefs were entertained as to the laws of Lycurgus in Greece and Numa in Rome".[7] The theory of common law that the fundamental rules of law had been derived from a divine source also reinforces this belief. Keble J. said as late as 1653 that there was no law in England which was not the laws of God. For there are very many consequences reasoned out of the scriptures. Even Blackstone held the view that all human law rested on the twin foundations of law of Nature and the Law of Revelation. Vinogradaff also observes: "Looking back on the historical evolution of Jurisprudence, we may discern three stages, the first stage of thought is dominated by the idea of Providence. In this respect, there is no fundamental difference between the Heathen world and the Christian world. All societies place in the centre of their conception of the human world, the idea of the guidance of Providence".[8]

Muslims also claimed their law to be of divine origin, but they made a distinction between that part of the Koran which was in

God's own words and the other parts, i.e., the Prophet's precepts which were inspired by God but were expressed in the words of the Prophet. Similar distinction is made in case of Hindu Law. As regards the Vedas, orthodox Hindu theory would not even accept that they are 'God's words because even God must be regarded as Being, while the Vedas are claimed to be A pourusheya (not uttered by any being, human or divine) and hence Eternal''.[9] The Vedas are not useful for getting direct statement of rules of law. They refer to the different parts of *dharma* from which inference can only be drawn about some aspects of law. The formal treatment of 'dharma' is given in Smritis (remembered texts from the Vedas: known or unknown). Here we get a systematic exposition of the ancient Indian law. In theory, Smritis were repositories of secret revelations, but in fact, they arose as reinterpretations of the Vedas and included the already prevailing law agreed by assemblies. Smritis imply human agency in the declaration of law as their authors were human beings. At first, they were not considered sacred due to their human authorship, but were treated as subsidiary to the Vedas. It is only later that they acquired a prestige similar to that of Revelations. In the next stage they (Smritis) exercise even more authority than the Vedas. Commentators like "Vignaneswara and Mitramisra were prepared to assert that anything in the Srutis (Revelation) bearing on Vyavahara was only in the nature of *Anuvada* (statement of what is found prevailing in the world) and where a practice so referred to had ceased to be followed or to command general approval, it might be treated as no longer authoritative or binding.[10] (According to Jayaswal one of the earliest *Smritis* makes an explicit statement that the rules of Dharma originated in 'Samya' or as communal rules which were agreed upon in assemblies and the Vedas were only of secondary authority in regard to them. The learned author refers to the Sutra of Apasthamba (आपस्तम्ब) which states that the conventions of people conversant with Dharma are authority and also the Vedas. (धर्मज्ञ समय; प्रमाण; वेदाश्च) [11] From the point of view of historical truth the Sutra of Apasthamba reveals that at the beginning all law was convention or custom. It had unconscious growth and was of non-litiguous nature. Later law-texts uphold the authority of customs which were prevailing at that time and transform them into written law or declared law. The jurists, legislators, and judges of the later stage only rationalise this customary law, i.e., modify, reform and supplement it and reduce it into a system. In India, this process must have had its course when Smritis replaced the authority of unrecorded custom. In this manner the legal formula as a direction and pattern of social life coincided with that body of law which was considered to be of divine origin. It seems the theory of divine sources of law was an expedient to uphold the authority of law in the absence of centralised authority of courts and kings. After Smriti period, there ushered in the period of Digests and commentators which flourished from 700 A.D. to 1700 A.D. Prof. Paras Diwan holds the view that after legal development had been carried out by the Digest and Commentaries, custom was incorporated by Digest writers and commentators.[12]

THEORIES ABOUT CUSTOMARY LAW

There are two theories about the importance of custom as source of law in ancient Indian law. According to one view custom is a formative and primary source of law. The other view holds that it is only a material and secondary source of law. They resemble the historical and analytical schools of customary law in Western jurisprudence.

(1) Sadachara or Good Custom as the Source of Law

Altekar traces the evolution of ancient Indian law through the agency of Sadachar, the Good custom. In his view,[13] when Sadachar also spelt as Sadacara or good custom or the practices of the virtuous Veda-knowing people, were recognised as source of Dharma or law, the first great concession was given to custom. The category of Sadachar was not at first extensive but later it became so, as a result of which various types of customs were included in it by Smriticars and Commentators. "Sadacara has been defined in several works as the conduct of ideally selfless Veda-knowing persons who are above temptations, jealousy and passions."[14] The behaviour of such persons at first appeared rather as guidance in spiritual matters than in secular ones like social customs and in positive law. Sadachar signified the customs and traditions approved by society and the need to define it precisely was not realised at first. Accordingly, as pointed out by the Mahabharat, it is indefinable and is, what is inferred from the conduct of cultured persons. It appears that Sadachar began to acquire a wider meaning as it was not confined only to the virtuous and the Veda-knowing people became widespread among others as well. Taittiryaranyaka also points that 'dharma' need not only be inferred from the persons who are of too rigid and narrow a nature. It implies that some customs can be accepted as 'dharma', even if they were not followed by the cultured few, if practised and followed by the uncultured many. This was actually done lateron. Practically, it was thus not necessary in course of time to respect the fiction that Sadachar as custom must not be in opposition to Srutis and Smritis. This happened when Sruti and Smriti law became inoperative and new custom arose. Further, in case of doubt, it was conveniently assumed that they were based upon a lost text or Sruti. Again "the condition of conformity with sacred text was to be insisted only in the case of religious and spiritual practices; it could be dispensed with in the case of social and legal usages. Established legal usages based upon equity and reason will always prevail over the dicta of Dharmasastra, Commentators and digest writers, while expounding the Vyavahara or positive law, pointed out how it is almost entirely based upon usages and practices established in society; they have hardly anything to do with Sruti and Smriti texts. Nilkantha observes that relation between usages and Vyavahar law is as closed as that between usages and grammer".[15] The practices of Sadachar were recognised in some cases by Smritikars even when they were opposed to the sacred texts. To justify the exclusion of certain practices sanctioned by sacred text a theory was developed according to which dharma changed epochwise; what was practicable in Krta or Treta or Dvapara age may be impracticable for Kali age.[16] As time want on, the customs, of social or religious nature developed new diverse forms with the changes in social structures. This was noticed by Bhaudhayana of early times. As a result of which Brahaspati of 7th Century and Kautilya included in (Caritra, चरित्र Charitra which meant secular custom) a recognised source of law, such practices and customs which were in consonance with dharma as well as those which were opposed to it. It was also pleaded that 'dharma' was so subtle that it was very difficult to be scrutinised. For making an allowance for such anti-shastric customs Brahaspati points out a practical reason. He observes that there would be a country-wide commotion, army may revolt and texes will be withheld if an established custom were sought to be stamped out merely because it was opposed to the sacred tests. According to Mitramisra the custom opposed to Sruti and Smriti but universally accepted by the people in province cannot be stamped out. It is confessed that recognition of such anti-sastric custom may incur sin and cost a visit to hell but it will certainly avoid social boycott. Madhava, the commentator of Parasara also points out that if anti-vedic customs like prostitution or drinking are tolerated by society, they cannot be stopped even by Government. Many medieval writers have also realised the force of custom in opposition to the Vedic injunctions and sacred texts. Therefore, it is only in early writers that we find the assertion that customs are recognised only if they do not go counter to the sacred texts. Medieval commentators and digest writers do not subscribe to this dictum. Even early writers like Manu and Vishnu sought support from the theory of Kalivarjya according to which certain practices were not considered suitable for Kali-Yuga (an age of the decline of dharma). This they did in order to permit the supression of Sastric provisions which did not accord with the prevalent usages of society. They also withheld recognition of some practices which became unpopular according to prevalent moral tone of the times e.g., the practice of Niyoga and intercaste marriages were condemned by them though they were permitted by earlier sacred texts.

The scope of Sadachar in time to come, became more extensive when it included :(1) *Kuldharma*, (2) *Jatidharma*, and (3) *Deshdharma*. These consisted generally of custom and unwritten laws. Draupdi's marriage to five brothers, though against proper conduct was sanctioned by Kuldharma. Jatidharma consisted of customs and practices of castes and sub-castes. It included their customs, conventions and usages of trade, profession and guilds, and determined the rights, liabilities and responsibilities of their members and of the guilds. People, according to their Jatidharma have their own customs of marriage, divorce, re-marriage and adoption, even when they had no sanction in Sastras. Sadachar as 'Desh Dharma' denoted the customs and practices which were peculiar to the provinces, and differed according to the prevailing usages of the people of the respective provinces. So much so that in the matter of adoption the different schools interpreted the injunction of Vasistha differently according to their 'desh dharma'. "The differences in the order of succession; in the powers of the father over the ancestral property; in the scope and devolution of Stridhan and the powers to dispose it, which we see today in the Mitaksara and Dayabhag law, is primarily due to the divergent Deshdharma....... The admission of Sakulyas (cognates) as heirs in Bengal, the recognition of the Krtrima son in Mithila, special proprietary rights of women recognised in Bombay State, are all primarily due to the different Des'adharmas of the localities concerned. These instances will show

—

how great a part Sadacara has played in moulding and developing Hindu law, when Smritis had ceased to be composed''.[17] These divergencies have now, to a great extent, been removed by recent legislative enactments.

Further the doctrine of Sadachar as conceived by the ancients had also an abrogative character. So we find that the earlier rules permitting Niyoga and inter-caste marriages, were changed. This was, perhaps, due to orthodox beliefs of the Sutrakars.

Altekar has traced the whole course of development of customary law only through the encompassing doctrine of Sadachar. However, we are also informed by Sen Gupta that customs of secular character specially usages of people of lowly occupations who were beyond the pale of sacred law and those of agriculturists, traders, usurers, etc. were tolerated simply because there was no sinfulness in following them. There were also certain customs and usages which were tolerated and recognised on the ground of political considerations or royal policy without scrutinising their character, whether sacred or profane. Such was the case of the laws and customs of conquered territories after subjugation.[18] As time passed, it is said, the attitude towards laws of conquered territories probably was extended to all customs so that more and more customs came to be recognised as law, more than what Gautma or Apastamba (Sutrakars) ever conceived of and perhaps a very substantial part of the lives of population came to be regulated by customary law without a critical study of their authority.[19]

(2) Impact of Sastric Law Upon Custom: Lingat's Theory

Robert Lingat, in his book ''The Classical Law of India'' states that in Roman Jurisprudence the doctrine of consensus occupies a significant place. This doctrine of consensus, which amounts to saying that all law is the result of consensus, is foreign to Indian Juristic thinking, and plays only a minor role except in the case of 'conventions' which are considered as one of the sources of dharma. Custom is purely a human development in the sense that it develops at the level of human groups involved in social interaction. However, Hindus did not consider its origin in the manner like that of Roman jurisconsults of the classical period, who thought of its origin in convention. Law is born of a more or less conscious agreement of wills of those called upon to obey it. The Indian law cannot be explained on this basis. Its origin eludes human memory, confers upon itself a force which it neither had nor has it in Eastern civilisations.[20] Custom in its pure aspect, is indifferent to religious consequences and may be in accordance with the precepts of Sastras but may also be in conflict with them. It has been defined by Katyana as all that man practices, whether or not it conforms to dharma, simply because it is the constant usage of the country. It has its authority because of its inveterate character. The rule of custom has reference to factual circumstance and is a phenomenon governed by time and place.

In contrast to this, law promulgated by Sastras differ from custom both in its object and origin. "As its intention is to teach dharma, it prescribes duties and obligations of a religious character. It shows men the conduct they should follow in order to acquire spiritual benefits. To act in conformity with it is to secure merits, which according to law of Karma will produce fruits in course of life or after it".[21] Law, which is communicated by Sastras does not arise from the will of men. It rules the moral world, just as physical law rules the phenomena of nature. The rules of conduct and the duties which they enunciate are pre-condition of the realisation of social order as it was intended by the Creator. These rules existed before they were transcribed. They were not conceived by the authors of the dharmasastras but were discovered in the texts in which divine will is expressed. They are also found in traditions. These rules govern the activities of men, they are not influenced by them.[22]

A study of Lingat's theory reveals further that Dharma is not the result of consent or agreement (explicit or implicit) of the people and is not changeable according to time and place. According to him the theory of Yugas or Kalivarjivas does not disprove this view of dharma. In the theory of Yugas which we discussed to show the relativity of dharma, Lingat, however, attaches little importance when he says "that although the rules of conduct prescribed by the Sastras retain eternally their redemptive quality, they are not always good to follow. Laid down by Sages for the perfect man of the Golden Age, they cannot be enjoined upon men of our days without discretion. The latter find, as Manu says (IX. 2-4), that the pursuit of interest or pleasure tends to take precedence over the acquisition of spiritual merit. Human nature is such that one cannot force it without destroying the effect desired. Hence, it would be better to dissuade men from, or even to prohibit certain percepts of the Sastras than to try to impose them without regard for whether they will work".[23] Manu addressing the "Snatak" (Student) points out that he should abstain from observing that dharma which has inauspicious consequences or which is rejected by the world. (Ch. IX, 176). Vijnanesvara, the commentator of

Yajnavalkya (II. 117) "prohibits the eldest son being given a larger share at partition of ancestral property than any of his younger brother even though such a preferential share is permitted by Manu and Yajnavalkya". This he disapproves because such preference is rejected by the world at large. However, the theory of Yugas is not to be equated with instability or changeability of dharma. He quotes the remarks of Medhatithi, the commentator of Manu, regarding certain rites thus: "that no one in our days has the means to perform them or desires the results which performance to them procures, or even that faith in their efficacy has vanished. But they do not any the less retain their validity, and they are always capable of being performed. A rule of dharma cannot be abrogated by dissuetude".[24] So is the opinion of *Devanna-bhatta the author of Smritichandrika (Circa 1150 A.D.)*, who allows that a practice may not be followed due to popular aversion but asserts that a contrary custom cannot abrogate the Sastric rule. As a matter of fact according to such an interpretation of the learned author the theory of Yugas affects human capability to follow dharma but it does not diminish or change the character of dharma. It is urged by texts that men should always uphold dharma. The king is especially enjoined to follow dharma and by his proper performance of his task the king can do away with the effect of Kali age. The theory of Yugas has no reference to dharma in general but to dharmas, i.e., particular meritorious acts whose effect would change according to the Ages and, therefore, allows some to be performed in preference to others. The doctrine (Yugas) recommends those acts which require less effort on the part of men and this may be interpreted as due to decreasing influence of dharma. The bull of Dharma, according to Medhatithi losesone foot with every succeeding Yuga due to the diminution of the moral sense of men from Krta to Kali Age. Manu says that in the Krta-Age what is essential is austerity (tapas) in treta knowledge (Jnana) in dvapara sacrifice (Yajna), Kali-Age, simply gift (dana) (I-86). Whatever the use which was made by jurists and authors of dharmasastras to be of a relative character. According to them, moral imperatives did not vary with ages but what varied was only the man's capacity to observe-them. Authors of dharmasastras, inspite of their assertions of being the spokesmen of dharma of Yugas, do not legislate or lay down new dharma for their own ages. To them, law had its source ultimately in the Vedas, and that law was eternal. Had it been otherwise, there would have been no problem of interpretation as presumption of change saves the labour of the interpreter. According to Lingat[25] custom is no doubt an important source of law but the great importance given to it has created a sort of misunderstanding in the minds of certain writers like Nelson (he visited India in the 19th Century) whose decided opinion is that India was not governed by written laws but was governed solely by customs of different types prevailing at different places. Even the Privy Council in Collector of Madhura V/s Mootooramalinga Sathupathy 12 Moore's Indian Appeals 397 held that "under the Hindu system of law clear proof of usages will outweigh the written text of law. The judicial view of the Privy Council is a reflection of the attitude of the colonisers to minimise the importance of written law whereby they could see the immediate necessity to have the appointment of law commission to codify Indian law on the basis of juristic notions very disagreeable and alien to Indian Culture. It is submitted that this view held by the Privy Council and others writers is only partially true. Sastras might have recognised custom but that does not mean that the role of Sastric law as minimal and negligible. It is by the acumen of commentators and digest writers that the rule of custom was organised into a juridical framework. Even when dharmic rule was not followed, the same commended respect, had veneration, and wielded influence to such a degree that it was considered by people a model for their lives, and was viewed as a legal category of a higher kind. Therefore, such customs and usages which were repellant to the dharmic view of life or in other words which were contrary to accepted patterns of good conduct were rejected or modified to an extent necessary. The rule of customary law, being oral, and having organic life and growth, was modified in the light of Sastric Culture. When usage or custom, in conflict to Sastric law, was tolerated it had no capacity for further extension beyond its locality and remained a local custom merely. On the other hand, the rule of dharma had unlimited power of radiation and was a general model for all. This would indicate that dharma had a quality to influence custom and to mould it according to its ideal requirements. Thus, influence of dharma can be compared with the influence of Roman law on the continental customary law. Roman law had great prestige in the countries of Europe and was considered as the very revelation of law, "the ratio scripts or written reason", and an ideal for legislation. Dharmasastra held the similar prestige in India, and the gaps in customary rules were filled in by written law of the Sastras, and the raw material of custom thereby got in ideal framework. In Europe, the customary law, repugnant to Roman law was confined to its actual territory whereas the influence of Roman law was felt throughout the length and breadth of the continent. In England also, the customary law felt the curb from common law judges who evolved harsh tests for its recognition, thereby customary law could be rationalised and systematised. Similar function, it appears, was performed in India in the classical period and thereafter.

In view of this humble author there is a difference of approach about law between the West and in the East. Whereas in the West, it has always been believed that the life of a community is determined by political power, in India, it has never been so, not only in the ancient times but also in the modern age. This may appear to be a very old assertion but as it is true, it has to be accepted. In order to prove it, one has only to look at the various attempts made by political theorists to amend and modify the basic fabric of Indian law and the resultant failures. This is so because in their zeal to make India a secular State, the politicians have, failed to comprehend correctly the significance and vitality of Indian Culture, its genius, its Volksgeist which is rooted in a legal philosophy of its own which is a happy blending of materialistic as well as spiritual values. It would thus be clear that in ancient India what influenced and determined the life of the community was 'Dharma', an amalgam of law, order, good conduct and religion. The last-mentioned, not in the narrow, orthodox sense but in a very broad and liberal sense meaning the universal religion bringing into its fold all the diverse beliefs and faiths and thus exhibiting examplary tolerance towards them and so fulfilling the main task of secularism.

The humble author has attempted to discuss the two prevailing viess in the field of customary law with a view to arrive at his own conclusions. He has been led to believe that Altekar is conscious that Hindu law of today needs to be reformed. By tracing the evolution of the ancient Indian law he tries to show that it was not a sealed booked but has always been admitting changes. In his eagerness to advocate reform he has treated the 'Vedas' and the Smritis just like the fictions of Roman law whose legal form remained rigid but spirit or legal reality was allowed a change according to the call of the times. This interpretation is too rationalistic to give a correct picture of the evolution of ancient Indian law. Law by its very nature in ancient times is amenable to changes in society but such changes are organic and the juristic or law-makers are not conscious that they are in fact changing the law deliberately. On the other hand,

Rebert Lingat has worked out his theory having in mind the concept of dharma as the great director of legal development. To him, custom become law only when it is admitted to the realm of dharma. In the long-run there would not be conflict between dharma and custom. Dharma may made room for custom but custom in order to be good law will automatically embrace dharma as the law laid down in Sastras. The whole treatment of the evolution of law proves to him that Indian law would have functioned as a developed system without having the need of the reception of English law.

Both views have been propounded by writers having preconceived ideas about ancient Indian law. Neither Indian law was dogmatic and averse to change, nor did it suffer from reformative zeal. Indian legal system was complete and was responsive both to change and stability. It was so dynamic as to re-vitalise and reorient its concepts and doctrines and needed no resolute efforts, conscious planning or wholesale adaptation of foreign law. Every step of its development was both natural and purposive quite in accord with its requirements. Both the thinkers agree as regards the completeness and viability of our ancient legal system which had the capacity to preserve and to renew as well. It seems that views oriented on Benthamite ultitarianism and civilian reverence are quite-in-appropriate for over-rating certain sources of Ancient Indian law because it is a denial of its essential spirituality.

Spirituality enables the thinkers of ancient India to see the whole in the part; to them every part is miniature universe, law with all its unity and diversity bears the stamp of this spirituality. When seen in this light it becomes an expression of harmony rather than that of discord and with this all our exaggerations and variation of emphasis appear incongruous and unjust.

II

Polarisation in juristic theory has been due to antagonisms of schools which exaggerate the importance of one source which of law at the cost of another. Historical and analytical schools vie with each other in grading the sources of law. Analytical school of Austin is inclined more towards legislation and puts emphasis upon sovereign authority as the hall-mark of law. Historical School considers statehood and sovereignty as only incidental factors in the evolution of law. Law, it is asserted in the commulative product of the spirit of the people 'Volksgeist! Law to them is not what is imposed as extra but something organic and living, evolving from within the society. It is law, that is living actually, and not hypothesized by sovereign authority in the form of enactment or declaration, without reference to the volume of beliefs and values of those upon whom it is imposed. It is submitted that if one puts too much importance upon legislation or written text, one ignores the real source of law. It is as good as to equate law to pure subjection and enslavement. Without rational justification, legislation or book law cannot hope to direct human beings towards progressive realisation of patterns of life and conduct.

We have seen that legislation or Sastric law has a limited capacity. As such too much of legislation governing human conduct is not beneficial, for beyond a certain limit the hard core of human personality cannot be put under the Yoke of law and regulated for refinement. The force of law cannot surpass the limits of docile human nature without being an airy nothing; it has to seek its sanction beyond its form into the real content of life itself. On the other hand, too much reliance on autonomous and self-generative capacity of society to create law in the form of custom will be half-baked law. To leave the so-called legal instinct of people unguided, propelled by its own irrational forces, without being aware of needs and exigencies of times is an exhibition of an attitude of indifference towards the real problems of life and law. It is due to this wanton indifference that the historical school is guilty of the charge of juristic pessimism. It is submitted that once a society acquires normal health, it may be capable of generating law due to its intrinsic vigour and vitality but what about those societies which are debilitated on account of decadence? In such circumstance resort has to be had to deliberate planning through legislation, to remedy the ills of irrational habits and customs.

Western society, inspite of its scientific progress and material achievements has failed to take a full and complete view of life and has satisfied itself by delivering harangues on only the periphery of the problem. Most of the theories of Western jurisprudence inspite of scholarly expositions (are caricatures and propoganda stunts and) foster inconclusive and endless debates. The serious thinkers in the West have begun to realise the futility of all their legal concepts and are now in decision rejecting them for complete nonsense (the Scandinavians).

It appears to this humble author that the so-called debate between custom and legislation or text as the sources of law is in reality, nothing but a contest between people's participation and rational will in formulation of law. To the Indian mind both are important participants in law-making. Indian society was, from the very beginning, bred on the basis of participation and co-ordination, and distribution of functions by (Varna-system) though it got diseased later on, but it certainly exhibited talent of a high order, in social planning and in this it (Varna system) proved an ideal-hood to ward off ideological dangers. The inordinate aspirations of all classes were culled for all time and people's participation was made obligatory by the master concept of 'dharma'. All the concepts and sources of law merge in this great Sangam, i.e., Synthesis which is a miracle of Indian juristic genius. Roscoe Pound does not appear to give a new note but reinforces Indian view point when he says: Jurisprudence, Ethics, Economics, Politics and Sociology are distinct enough at the core, but shade out into each other; when we look at the core or chiefly at the core, the analytical distinctions are sound enough. But we shall not understand even that core and much less the debatable ground beyond, unless we are prepared to make continual deep incursions from each into each of the other. All the social sciences must be co-workers and emphatically all must be co-workers with jurisprudence''.[26]

As regards custom or texts as determinants of law, the Indian mind could not take a partial view. The fact of existence of custom was accepted, and its incorporation in the body of book-law, i.e., texts has not been denied by Indian jurists. Custom was recognised and was engrafted on Dharma or sacred law. But it was also modified and–assimilated by it. Both had their dual existence and their sharp contours and edges were blunted and softened by the rigorous interpretation done by Mimansakas. Their dualism need not be seen as antagonism but it is like the dualism of 'Purusha' and 'Prakriti' of Sankhya system which has been explained by the allegory of the perfect union or partnership of the robust blind and the keen-sighted crippled to the mutual advantage. The blind carrying the crippled on his shoulders gets the benefit of eyes and the crippled by this partnership get the advantage of other's feet. In this lies the fulfilment of each other. So is the case of the precept and the practice. Custom without precept or written law is bound to lack the vision and foresight to channelise and direct legal growth to marked ends and values. The book law, or precept or text or legislation without custom or law in practice becomes inert having no vitality and loses proximity or affinity with the individual and social life.

Pre-eminence given to custom in India, by Western writers evinces only the influence of historical school on the one hand and on the other it is a pretext for codification without need of mature understanding and deep insight in the cultural setting of Indian law and without realising the 'elan vital' of Indian society. Deep and sympathetic understanding of its forms, contents, and objectives should be a good prelude to its able legislation and better codification, which will furnish all the insight into its culture and genius of its people. Consequently, a grounding in the Ancient Indian legal philosophy is a prime to all undertakings of law.

The very fact that the Hindu Law has been codified hesitantly and that too partially, and the fact that Muslim law has remained untouched till this day speaks volumes of the inability of the rulers who toe the Western juristic paths without looking back to determine whether laws based upon allien and undigested concepts would usher in harmony and happiness in social relations. Nor is it justified to view Indian sources of law on the lines of Western theories as, instead of creating a law-abiding and peaceful society, it will only sow seeds of discord and internicine strifes.

Notes and References

1. History of Hindu Law (T.LL. By Radhabinod Paul, p. 165).
2. *Ibid.*, p. 165.
3. Notion of Custom enforced by ruling minority or Sovereign authority is something foreign to Indian thinking.
4. Jurisprudence by Salmond Tenth Edition, pp. 201-03.
5. *Ibid.*
6. M. Ginsberg, Sociology, p. 153; quoted in Fundametals of Sociology by Pascual Gisbert, p. 160.
7. S. Vardachariar, The Hindu Judicial System, Edn. 1946, pp. 32-33.
8. *Ibid.*, p. 34.
9. *Ibid.*, p. 35.
10. *Ibid.*, p. 36.
11. *Ibid.*
12. Modern Hindu Law by Paras Diwan, 1972, p. 45.
13. The Sources of Dharma-by Altekar, pp. 37-38.
14. *Ibid.*
15. *Ibid.*, pp. 39-40.
16. *Ibid.*, p. 40.

17. *Ibid.*, pp. 45-47.
18. Evolution of Ancient Indian Law, Tagore Law Lectures, 1950, by Dr. N.C. Sen-Gupta, p. 329, Published London Arthur Probsthain, Calcutta, Eastern Law House.
19. *Ibid.*, pp. 329-30.
20. The Classical Law of India by Robert Lingat, p. 177.
21. *Ibid.*, 176.
22. *Ibid.*
23. *Ibid.*, p. 189.
24. *Ibid.*, 191.
25. *Ibid.*, p. 203.
26. Roscoe Pound, 'Law and Morals', pp. 123-24.

6

Law as an Action in Courts–Vyavahar

In the Chapters that have gone before an attempt was made to critically examine the basis of ancient Indian law and its philosophy. Progressively, we arrived at finding the true nature of law by, analysing the abstract principles of 'Rit', Dharma, Vrata, Swadha, etc. all of which had immensely contributed to the formulation of Indian legal theory. Thus, so far, the investigation has been confined to more general, and abstract notions concerning law, in terms of order, culture, authority, custom and texts. The last two deserved a separate treatment because of the conflicting theories as to the superiority of one over the other. In a sense, this was a sort of transformation of law from abstract to concrete. So far so good. Nevertheless, still greater concentration on the abstract notions becomes necessary and unavoidable, to make our search for viable and meaningful legal theory and it is hopefully realised that this task must necessarily involve us into the functional aspect of law. In other words, it remains for us to consider how law actually functioned in courts. This would reveal the most concrete or positive aspect of law in the form of Vyavahar.

In ancient India, the action of law in courts is termed as Vyavahar. Vyavahar comprises all the basic elements of Indian legal philosophy. Katayayan, the famous Smriti-writer who according to Kane lived some where between 4th and 6th Centuries A.D. defines it in two ways. The first definition is based upon etymology where he refers mainly to procedure, and the second embracing the conventional sense of the word, meaning a dispute.

Etymologically Vyavahar meant a method or procedure resolving or removing doubt or doubts. Conventionally, it meant the 'dispute' between the parties.

The purpose of legal procedure according to Katyayana is to find out the truth when there is a dispute.[1] The purpose of trial has also been frequently mentioned by ancient Indian jurists as an enquiry into truth, i.e., तत्व बुभुत्सा.[2] Justice then becomes synonymous with truth. Katyayana gives another definition of Vyavahar thus: "when the ramifications of right conduct, that are together called dharma, and that can be established with efforts (of various kinds such as truthful speech... have been violated, the dispute (in a court between parties) which spirings from what is sought to be proved (such as debt) is said to be Vyavahar".[3] Taking them together we notice that Indian legal philosophy out of which ancient jurisprudence was born is concerned firstly with truth and secondly with the establishment of dharma which in its older form is Rit. Satya and Rit again emerge as the two aspects of Vyavahar, the law in action. They have been intuited by the Rig Vedic seer as the two phases of the Being (Rig Ved X, 190). Here the truth is not merely subjective and intellectural but is objective and factual. The order which is established is not a natural order but the Rit or Right of legal system. Rit and Satya, when become concrete they can be more clearly seen as the foundation of a legal system. Two deep seated principles in administration of justice according to Kane are found. They are: (1) fulfil your promises, (2) cause injury (himsa) to no one.[4] Keeping your promises is only an aspect of truth, as the truthfulness in word and deed; and causing injury means violating law or rightfulness, i.e., Rit. Need for Vyavahara arises only after deviation from right path or from a violation of duty. When both parties adhere strictly to truth in their statements, there is virtue or justice clearly enough, judicial procedure, written proof and a royal edict being quite unnecessary, in that case. When either of the two parties is suspected to have made a false statement, judicial procedure has to be resorted to, which depends on the evidence given by witnesses and documentary evidence".[5] It means Vyavahara or law in action does not contemplate or give rise to mechanical trial devoid of its moral task, to ascertain truth in doing justice. "Two views have been taken in different ages and by different systems of law as to the function of a judge. According to one, he is to use all the appropriate methods for the discovery of truth; according to the other he merely stands as an umpire between the parties to see that all the rules of the game are observed. Medieval English procedure was strongly inclined towards the second view. Vinogradoff makes his general assertion that ancient trial was not much more than a formulated struggle between the parties in which judges had to act more as umpires and wardens of order and fair play than as Investigators of truth (Vin. Hist. Jur., I.P. 348). This theory can have no place in a system like that propounded by the Dharmasastras, which regarded administration of justice not merely maintenance of public order, but a sacred and religious duty. This is made clear by the numerous texts''.[6(a)]

Two verses, –one of Manu, and the other of Narada–are very significant. The first compares the task of the king or Pradvivaka (Judicial officer) in arriving at the truth to that of a hunter who tracks his wounded game by the traces of blood. The second compares him to a surgeon who skilfully draws out foreign matter from the body in which it has got embedded. The Mahabharata compares the task of finding out of the truth to that of discovering the feet of a snake and warns the king against being misled by appearances.[6(b)]

The Smritis and commentaries give many meanings to the term 'Vyavahara' viz. civil law, positive law, legal procedure, litigation or dispute etc.[7] Thus, it may mean transaction or dealing, dispute or suit, legal capacity or means or deciding a matter. Kane has accepted the sense of law-suit or dispute in a court and legal procedure and thinks that this sense is very ancient.[8] In one word, it deals with justice done in courts and signifies 'legal transaction' and the rules of procedure or something like the *lex fori*. To make it a more serious and grave task, Vyavahara has been compared to a ritual to be performed in the sense of a 'Sacrifice'. The king in ancient Indian law is entrusted with the task of doing justice. He is bound to act according to the precepts of the Smriti. Brahaspati does not hesitate to identify a law case (Vyavahara) as a sacrificial act or Yajna. In the sacrifice (Yajna) Vishnu is the object of worship; in the case (Vyavahar) it is the king. The plaintiff who wins his suit is equal to the sacrificer (Yajnamana) and he who loses is like the victim ('Pasu', sacrificial animal). The plaint and defence are like, clarified butter, and the grounds of the plaint (Pratijna) like a vegetable offering (havis). The Vedas are here the Sastras, the judges the priests who officiate and the fine imposed resembles the ritual fee.[9] This exemplifies the pure religious feeling with which adjudication is viewed by ancient Indian mind to whom religion was not only a ritual but a theory of reality and a moving force to shape human behaviour in this world. It was said that the king should observe, very scruplously, the rules laid down in the text as if he is performing a sacrifice. He is bound by the terms of the Sastras, as a sacrificer is by the ritualistic manual.[10]

ANCIENT INDIAN SPECULATION ABOUT THE ORIGIN OF 'VYAVAHARA'

The origin of 'Vyavahara' as depicted by the ancients, and the speculations thereon in Indian jurisprudence, are interesting excursions into the realm of law. Narada declares that in ancient times people were truth-speaking and devoted to Dharma and there was no litigation because there was no hatred or envy. According to him litigation (Vyavahara) resulted when Dharma was no longer followed; and the king was created to attend to Vyavahara and wield Danda. Brahaspati repeats the same idea substituting covetousness (Lobha) for envy. Many states bluntly that a man, honest by nature, is very rare and hence the need for law.[11] This reason, may not seem true but it has great relevance. The sense of righteousness or dharma is at the base of the theory of Vyavahara. Vardachariar says that hatred and envy or hatred or covetousness is at the root of the trouble, the king's duty will not be discharged merely by compensating the victim; he must see to the observance of Dharma. Danda which is extolled and almost deified in the Dharmasastra literature is derived from 'Dama' meaning 'restraint'. The Sukraniti says that 'Damana' is restraining from wrong conduct. The means by which a person is thus restrained (from mischief) is 'Danda'. Gautaṃa pleads that Danda and teaching by the Acharya or preceptor deserve to be put on an equal footing with reforming or correcting the wrong doer.[12] While describing the king's duty Yajnavalkya and Narad use the expression 'स्थापयेत्पथि' i.e. to put him on the right path' and the Mitakshara interprets it as saying that having punished (a person) according to the nature of the wrong, the king must re-establish the person on the performance of Swadharma:" "राजा यथा पराधं विनीय दण्डयित्वा यछिस्यधर्मे स्थापयेत"[13]

VYAVAHAR AS JUDICIAL FUNCTION

Positive law, that is, the law enforced by sovereign authority like that of the king, has its roots in the usages and institutions of pre-jural society in which man begins to have a social life, and a need to delimit his interests to preserve the interests of the society. In the absence of political power restraints are exercised first by magic and then by religion through which customary law in the absence of kings and judges is enforced.[14]

It appears that the Vedic society, as represented to us in the Vedas must have had a need of stable social order. We have seen that in early Vedic society, the concept of Rita represents the concept of right and wrong in the same manner as the concept of Greek physis or physika (physi in English) represents the principle of order in the universe in early Greek society. God Varuna is said to be the upholder of this Rit and he punishes the person who does un-rita and he forgives one who prays to him and performs the appropriate ritual as a penance. He has the power of magic with him called 'asu'. This shows at first authority had magical or mystical source. But in practice, the Rit devoid of this magic and mythology is the law of the community. It obliges one to perform the ritual penance and to expiate for the crime or sin. Then, people begin to specialise in the knowledge of Rit and they begin to prescribe proper rituals and punishment. They are the Brahmins, learned in the Vedas, the repository of all wisdom. The king was at that time only a leader on the battle field. As a military chief, he was considered to be the protector of people and it was not considered to be his business to administer justice.

In the later Vedic age and the Brahmna period, king's power was used in punishing the wrong doer. He executes punishment but wrong is adjudged by the community. Manifest wrong doers or notorious offenders' were simply punished by the might of the king to right the wrong.

After a great interval of time when we come to Dharmsutra period, we find that king is mentioned as a judge and to deal with Vyavahara becomes his important function. But the disputes which the king decides are almost offences which are considered by people of the age to be grave transgressions of socio-religious conventions. Practically, the only civil disputes which the king deals with, are debt, deposit and pledge, on the principle, no doubt, that non-payment of a debt is as great an offence as theft. All the other disputes are still settled by the various Kulas, (कुल) Srenis (श्रेणी) and other organisations which do justice among their members.[15]

In early days we find that the king is advised and assisted by Purohit (learned Brahmins). At the next stage the king is enjoined to have sabha of learned men which advise him in the administration of justice and also to perform various other tasks. Then we find another functionary the 'Pradvivaka', originally, probably a foreman of the Sabha but eventually emerging as a Judge. These Sabha Sadas (members), the Pradvivaka and the Purohit were all learned Brahmins, fully conversant with the secrets of Dharma and who, between them, share the bulk of the administration of justice which, it was always presumed, was to be done according to Dharma. These classes constituted a body of experts and specialists in law and performed functions nearly analogous to those of the college of Pontiffs in ancient Rome,[16] and a precursor of modern legislative assembly or parliament.

But the king had no monopoly of the administration of justice as we find that in ancient India, administration of justice was a function, completely decentralized among Kulas and guilds. It was at a later stage that the king was vested with the power to administer justice. According to Sen Gupta the king had not acquired so much might and personality in Vedic times as to be considered a God. His respect depended upon his service, i.e., performance of his duty. The concept of divinity is an innovation and seems to have been the result of foreign ideas. However, Kane holds the contrary view. In view of the fact that judicial authority of the king is not founded on the fiction of divine personality, the only plausible explanation of this controversy is that the king was only a protector of the people from the enemy and an upholder of dharma, i.e., the social and moral order. He wields danda (*Sceptre*) to maintain dharma. In a different way danda is described as 'dharma' and 'dandniti' as the education of the king. King is not looked upon as the source of law, for the duty to impose law is laid down by the law itself. Further the essence of ancient law is that king should place himself under the guidance of sages. In later times, the power of the king increases. Hence, Manu goes so far as to give him the power to legislate and to coerce the subjects to obey him. Manu's Rajakrita laws or royal decrees, however, provided that they be not opposed to dharma or sacred law. This legislative and administrative power of the king, however, grew immensely which will be commented upon in the next Chapter of this thesis. Suffice it to say that this power which grew gradually was more of an executive and political nature than judicial.

As judicial function called for day to day administration of justice, permanent judges were appointed and the Pradvivaka, a reference to whom has been already made becomes lateron an independent judge. So was the case during the time of Yajnavalkya and in the time of Brahaspati where we find four types of Courts. Those that are stationery are called 'Pratistha' and they are permanently seated in a town or a village. Another type having itinerant nature are called 'apratistha'. Those that are empowered to use royal seal are called 'mudrita' and the courts which are personally presided over by the king are called Sasita. The first seem to correspond to the Kulas, Srenis etc. The second seems to be special jurisdiction for populations living in forests, for soldiers, and complements of caravans. The last two refer to royal courts. Kulas and other analogous bodies are not institutions specialising in the administration of justice. Their function as judicial organs eludes us completely. We can only presume that they played the role of an arbitrator, and tried to bring parties to an agreement. Failing to arrive at an agreement, the parties could move to the court of the king.[17] The king had two jurisdictions, one resembling the civil; the other the criminal. Kautaliya mentions two types of courts (1) *Dharma-Sthiya* which dealt with contentious matters between the litigants. The proceedings here are initiated by the parties. (2) *Kantak-Sodhana*, whose function is to do away with thorns or bad elements of society, is a court in which action is initiated by the King. For deciding cases in Courts of Dharma-Sthiya the procedure and law are laid down in dharmasastras. *As for the courts of second kind, i.e., the Kantak-Sodhana, the procedure is found in the Arthsastras in detail.* Dharmasastra deal with 'Prakirnaka' in negligible manner. It means that in this field the king had a free hand. However, Manu and Katyayana, Narad, Yajnavalkya devote some verses and offer advice to the king in this regard.

EVOLUTION OF LAW

We have now to consider as to which law was applied for the purpose of administration of justice. The concept of Rit in early times and its subsequent form, Dharma, later, both go to explain the nature of law. The content of law and the sources of Rita or Dharma, in theory, were said to be the Vedas, as they were assumed to be the 'sum total of all knowledge'. However, as per Apastamba 'Samyacharika', the rules agreed upon by the learned men in the assembly were also a part of the law, based upon a presumption that such rules were derived from the Vedas. However, this presumption that the Vedas were the ultimate source of law, seems to be more of a myth than a reality. Such a myth is descernible even in the common law of England where the doctrine that judges do not make law but only declare it, is a myth. Sen Gupta compares this law of ancient India with the "Fas of the ancient Rome which was also declared for them by the learned. Step by step after the king began to administer justice, some of the rules of this Dharma or Fes came to be enforced by the king with the advice or learned men".[18] This law, then, is incorporated in dharmasutras and dhramasastras by Smritikars and is further interpreted by the commentators of the medieval era who believed in its religious sanction and had faith in its divine source. It was to be enforced and administered by the king as dharma, in Vyavahara or litigation, with due allowances to customs and usages of families, castes and countries.

At first, a very few disputes came before the court of the king. There are various reasons for it. In the beginning, "family law which was mostly connected with religious and ritual law as well as with the authority of domestic tribunals was not included in the laws of the king's court".[19] Certain transactions, as disputes between Guru and pupil, father and son, husband and wife, master and servant (or slave) would not give rise to Vyavahara. They were at first disposed of by domestic tribunals. So is the case with disputes about land and its cultivation, about trade, disputes between herdsmen, usurers and artisans. They did not go to the king's court. The concerning guilds and respective village authorities decided those disputes. But disputes between such guilds of authorities and between them *inter se* could be and usually were decided by king's court. From the beginning of the jural society, we find provisions in earliest law for disputes between "creditor and debtor, herdsmen and owners of cattle or persons whose crops were destroyed by cattle".

Obviously, the number of cases which constituted the earliest topics of king's jurisdiction was very small. As they are dealt with by Gautama, Apastamba and Baudhayana, they are mainly the offences against the society of those days and are considered so serious violations as to deserve punishment by the king. Such is the case of theft which was punished by the king as it was considered to be the duty of the king to protect people from robbers and thieves. The wrongs of 'hurt, abuse and adultery' were dealt with and punished by the king's court only when they were considered as 'grave violations of social proprieties and caste privileges and decorum. There was no general classification for offences. Apart from these punishable offences, the only, apparently civil action which came to the king's court from the earliest times was probably an extension of the law of theft. Withholding payment of money or thing borrowed was only a step removed from theft and analoguous to theft because whereas in theft possession of a thing or money is taken by the thief without the consent of the owner, in debt it is taken by consent. We here clearly see a common element viz. possession of the thing or money. "The rigour of the law of Debt, even down to the days of Manu and Yajnavalkya shows that a defaulting debtor was looked upon as a sort of criminal against whom creditor might take any means, fair and foul, in a manner slightly rigorous than the Nexal-Creditor in the twelve tables".[20] According to Manu, "A creditor can realise his dues by dharma (i.e., by gentle moral appeals) by litigation, by fraud, by fasting at the debtor's door or by force".[21] Again, Vajnavalkya says, "The king must not forbid (or stop) a creditor who is attempting to realise his debt, and if the debtor pursued by a creditor doing so, applies to the king, the debtor will be punished by the king and made to pay the creditor his dues" (II-40)"[22]. In ancient Rome also debt which was contracted by Nexum, left the debtor completely at the mercy of the creditor or creditors who could enforce payment by means of self-help. In ancient India, Creditors would do so without suing in king's courts. With the emergence of king as a judge 'debt' was included in Vyavahar in dharma-sutra period. After the recognition of debt there was a consequent regulation and formulation of rules on the related matters like interest and payment (e.g. by service, or by instalments). Similarly, 'pledge', 'suretyship' and liability of heirs and other matters were regulated and recognized.

In early law the development of king's jurisdiction took place in three ways: "Firstly, there was the natural development with increasing complexities of social relation and logical extension of principles. Next there was the extension of the king's jurisdiction to matters which were originally matters for domestic or guild tribunals. Lastly, the laws also developed by infiltration of custom and usages of alien society, either due to adoption or adaptation by the Aryas of foreign customs or to the survival of alien customs in such communities after their adoption of Aryan Culture".[23]

In the words of Sen Gupta the first development was a 'natural development'. This took place when the law of deposit arose out of the law of debt. In the same manner the law of Asvamivikarya developed out of law of theft. Receivers of stolen property, harbourers of thieves, their servants, and other accessories were made liable. Nevertheless the Court had to face the problem of one who had with him the stolen property but who proved that the property was purchased from the 'market-overt'. Obviously, he could not be dealt with as if he was a thief or a receiver of stolen property. He was then recognised as the bonafide purchaser without liability.[24]

The law, on liability of hardsmen towards the persons who were owners of cattle or whose crops were destroyed, was recognised early but with the development of society and economic progress it gave spur to the evolution of law regarding free servitor and their wages.

Next development of king's jurisdiction was the result of absorption of that jurisdiction which was originally vested in domestic and guild tribunals. Thus the sphere of Vyavahara extended by means of encroachment upon domestic tribunals. At first, sexual offences and adultery were outside the jurisdiction of king's court as they were religious offences and fell within the purview of domestic tribunals. But they were brought within the sphere of kings jurisdiction. Gautam's law is a rudimentary attempt to do so. He says that they come within king's jurisdiction for they 'were a type which grievously offended the sense of social properties of the community'.

Similarly, land and boundary disputes which were matters to be dealt with by village tribunals were brought within the jurisdiction of the king's court and in consequence elaborate law on the topic was developed by jurists of king's court which we find in Narada and Brihaspati. Disputes regarding guilds and communities began also to be contested in king's court in later times which, at first were the matters for autonomous social units to decide. These topics developed under the head "Samvi-dvyati Karma" or Samayanapakarma.* Inheritance also was brought under the topic 'Vibhaga'.

The last method by which king's jurisdiction grew was by way of absorbing foreign laws and usages in spheres like 'family law' by developing the law on marriage, sonship and kinship. Sen Gupta believes that on these lines it is possible to imagine a course of development of the topics of Vyavahara. This was accomplished by the learned men who "from the earliest times specialised in the knowledge of law and with the introduction and expansion of king's

* "It deals with the enforcement by the King of the resolutions and decision of quasi-corporate groups, of village (grama), Desa (Country) or Samghas or guilds" (Sen Gupta).

justice, grew into a body of practically professional lawyers and who had the duty to advise the king in the administration of justice and also assisted in solving problems of law for the people who appealed to them,–as the Romans appealed to the Pontiffs or to the juris-consults".[25]

VYAVAHAR AS PRIVATE LITIGATIONS

Litigation, in Ancient India, was of two kinds: one was initiated by the king and the other by a private party. In the first case, the motive was to protect the interests of state, as in the other it was to recompense the individual or to punish the wrong-doer, at the instance of the complainant. This included those called civil as well as criminal cases instituted by the parties. This is what is meant by the term private litigation which is analogous, in a way to the modern civil as well as criminal cases that are initiated by the parties. The wrongs were classified by Manu under eighteen heads or titles[26], and were called *Vyavahara-pada* or *Vivada-padas*. The classification of Manu is usually followed by most of the writers with a few variations. The list given by Narad and Brahaspati re-classified the topics and some more are added for example matters relating to non-service of pupils and apprentices etc. It then becomes a full topic titled 'miscellaneous'. In fact, it is stated, that the eighteen topics can be sub-divided into as many as 132, and the general rule formulated by Yajnavalkya seems to be the last stage of development, which provides that any person injured by any act of another, contrary to the law or usage, may appeal to the king and that in itself amounts to a topic of litigation. This widens the scope of the subject litigation.[27] These topics neither had anything in common with 'formulae of actions' in classical Roman law nor were comparable to 'procedural differences' of real and personal actions of the continental jurisprudence nor was it similar to a case in panchayat or civil court or any matter relating to revenue in British Indian Law.[28] The rules of procedure given by dharmasastras, with a very few exceptions, are rules of general application to all cases. There are no limitations or definitions of actions and the plaintiff is entitled to bring a case when it is such as to be dealt with under the Vyavahara-pada. According to Yajnavalkya, a Vyavaharapada arises when a person is injured contrary to Smrities achara, and submits a complaint to the king. Three elements constitute Vyavahara-pada viz. (1) violation or duty prescribed by the Sastras or a customary rule,

(2) damage, (3) complaint. Violation of a rule of dharma does not suffice by itself to constitute a case. Unless particular (or special) damage has ensued from it. Likewise, infractions of rules of conduct, making up what we have called 'good customs' do not, as a general rule, damage any one. The culprit is bound to expiate his sin which is another matter. He can be compelled to do this by special pressures. The king, for his part, can intervene to secure the performance of penance and even add to a penal sanction if he thinks appropriate. On the other hand, every case presupposes an injury unjustly suffered by the plaintiff. In other words, the plaintiff acts in his own interest to obtain satisfaction and not in the interest of social and moral order. To use the style of the interpreters, the cause of action, started by the plaintiff, is not the invisible effect of the adharmic (opposed to dharma) act complained of but its visible effect.[29] Litigation is thus 'interest-oriented'. Litigation, under specified Vyavaharpada, is different from *Prakiranka* where the apprehension is that public order is threatened or disturbed. But infringement of private rights can also be treated as infringement of public order and the king, if he has already intended to punish the wrong-doer, can join the plaintiff separately, by a proceeding carried on in the name of the state and tending towards the application of a penalty. But these two cases, though simultaneous, will remain governed by their own separate rules.[30] This shows that ancient law never substituted crimes for tort as such the theory of Henry Maine "that the penal law of ancient communities is not the law of crime. It is the law of wrongs or to use the technical word, of torts,"[31] did not apply here. The injured party, in a tort, could be allowed to claim that a penalty be imposed by the State. If a fine was imposed the money would go, as a general rule, to the king. An action of tort, i.e., claiming monetary compensation, could also be brought by the king. Thus, the plaintiff could demand reparation for two kinds of injuries: to claim what is due and to ask for penalties. In such a case the civil and criminal remedies were both allowed. The punishment of the wrong-doer could be demanded by the injured party by way of reparation of the evil of wrong done to him. We can compare it with the exemplary or punitive damages awarded to the plaintiff in common law in certain torts. Sastras do not separate public wrongs from private wrongs and both are merged in togetherness. For all litigation in ancient law "was then considered as resting upon damage suffered by the plaintiff, indeed, what we call a tort; to repudiate a debt or to refuse to return a deposit (Katy. 28. 35) are

torts, just as are misappropriating the goods of another or offering violence to his person".[32]

In the ancient Indian legal system the king alone had the power to punish as he was 'danda-dhar', i.e., entrusted with the power to punish in order to uphold dharma. The jurisdiction was[5] decentralised and disseminated' among Kulas, Sreni, (to which reference has been made earlier) and Gana or puga etc. These jurisdictions were customary in their origin. Dharmasastras recognised them and brought them under the control of the king and there could be an appeal from one forum to another as provided by the earlier dharmasastras and ultimately to the king for review (which is like an appeal), by which method these jurisdictions were united with the legal system established by the king himself. Dharmasastras only deal with the jurisdiction of king's court, its composition, its law and procedure. The king is here the supreme judge and his court is composed of Pradvivaka as *adhyaksa* and three judges or assessors (*Sabbhayas*). The first three are appointed by the king preferably from the class of Brahmins, and no one is chosen from the class of Sudras as described by Manu, Yajnavalkya and Katyayana.

It was directed by dharmasastras that the king should not decide a case alone and should take the opinions of his counsellors. It means he can only decide the matter falling within the scope of private litigation when he is in open court. According to Brahaspati (1.6) "the president pronounces (the sentence) the king Chastises, the judges look to the merits of the case"[33]. According to the theory of dharmasastras, if the decision is unjust, then the sin falls upon the culprit, the witnesses, the judges and the king. It was considered the bounden duty of the judges to persuade the king and make him resile from a viewpoint which they considered to be wrong. King was also morally obliged to follow the percepts of Smritis. As such the secular act of justice acquired a religious significance, and verily for this reason, the act of dispensing justice was treated on par with religious sacrifice. A high degree of impartiality was required of him and it was prescribed by Yajnavalkya and others that the king, free from anger and greed, should give justice assisted by learned Brahmins in conformity with the precepts (Yajnayalkya II.1). King had no liberty of decision when a case was between his subjects. But when the matter related to the safety of his kingdom he had full liberty to take decision according to *artha*, and follow his own policy. With this exception, he was supposed to pay the greatest regard to dharma in

'Vyavahar'. The object of judicial injury that was specified here was to seek the truth of the matter and desist from the pitfalls of hasty decision. The king was asked to reject all 'chala' (deceit or fraud) or chicanery and give correct decision. All the same, though the judgment was to be based upon the texts of Sastras alone, he had to take account of the circumstances to see that the decision did not lead to loss of dharma or accrual to sin. The king was asked to be cautious and be aware of the fact that the plaintiff always works for his personal interest and profit and may try to invoke the aid of Sastras on his side, in derogation to the superior interests, the interests of the throne or State. When "the conflict is no longer merely between a rule of dharma and a rule of artha, but between two opposed orders of interest one can only imagine that the rule of dharma would remain in suspense".[34] In many a case an action could not be started. Brihaspati mentions three cases: firstly, when it was opposed to (the interests) of a city, a village, or high personalities. Secondly, when it is directed against the interests of the inhabitants of a town, of all the realm, or of one of the constituent elements of the State; finally it is barred by the king".[35] It seems that the king could bar complaints which interfered with peace or injured the interests of the State called 'Arth'. Of course, there is no clear guidance as to know what were the interests of the State. The texts are not clear when they point out to be the considerations of Arth i.e., what was useful or expedient or opportune. Manu's verse (VIII. 24) emphasising 'arth' is also enigmatic. Some commentators like Kaulka emphasise that it should be first determined–what is earth and what is dharma? Then, they direct that dharma should be followed. Medhatithi, on his own meaning, directs the king to look to the arth when it is necessary and go against dharma, then perform expiatory acts. According to Brihaspati also, the pure literal interpretation of the texts need not be resorted to, but decision has to be given after a complete acquaintance with the facts of the case. Manu (IV. 176) and Yajnavalkya (I.156) recommend to go against the precepts of texts if they direct to do what is "odious to the world". But it is for the king to determine what to do. Nevertheless, they do not give a clear answer. In such circumstances, the dynamic role of king comes into play and it is beyond the reach of reason and judgment to formulate any precise theory. General inclination of writers is to ask the king to follow the dictates of dharma in preference to 'Arth'. So the Brahmins who assisted king were required to be versed in the science or arth as they were in dharma. The problem of reconciling Dharma and Arth or of choosing one instead of another is too subtle and fluid to be solved for all times and in all cases. But, inspite of their failure to give clear guidance, the writers are aiming at meeting the demands of justice without ignoring those of equity and expediency.

Brahaspati points out that there were two cases in which the king himself would decide. In the first place a case where adequate proof was wanting. Secondly, the king could decide the case when there was a conflict between the precepts of Sastras and the views of the members of court. The verse 52 of Katyayana has been commented upon by Vachaspati Misra to mean that he (the king) should decide when there is conflict between the two texts or between two principles.

A judgment was considered to be complete when it decided the issue and penality was inflicted. The king would not rehear the case. If a party considered that the case was decided wrongly, it was permissible for him to get a fresh trial but if he failed in his review he was obliged to pay double the amount of fine. On this condition, prayer for fresh trial would be granted by the king and the case was brought before the king. In the case of appeal being successful, the judges were made liable to pay fine because they had not correctly judged the case. Again, the king could order a fresh trial on his own accord if he suspected foul play land was of the view that the decision was vitiated by partiality, cupidity or fear (Yajnavalkya II. 305). King's own judgment was open to review. It was a declaration of dharma for the litigants. All his orders were to be obeyed as it was thought that intelligence of kings excelled that of other mortals. So said Brahaspati.

There was no doctrine of precedent. The judgment was considered as an order for the parties and it was not meant to fix the law for future. Commentators do not cite any judgment given by any historical king. Robert Lingat supports this view. As against this, there is another view according to which, the decisions must have served the purpose of precedent and principles--however rudimentary--for guiding the tribunals. The learned author relies upon the expression used in commentaries etc. like: 'This is the settled rule of law', 'this is the settled law', 'the decision is according to the rule established in judicial proceeding' etc. and thinks that these expressions substantially corroborated his view point.[36] But, it requires further research and unearthing of material evidence to strengthen this viewpoint. It is submitted that the doctrine of precedent, as stare-decisis is a peculiar historical product of common law which arose out of judicial decisions only because there were no written laws and so it seems to this humble author that it could not have been developed where written texts like dharmasastras were present from the very beginning. The king could revise the judgment of his predecessor if he believed it to be contrary to reason. King's office was more of an administrator than that of legislator. Rajasasana, therefore, was the expression of royal policies. The king's decision was dharma for the parties but it cannot be said to have created law.

There are definite procedural steps in a law suit. The sequence of states in a law-suit is as follows: First, the plaintiff makes averment, then the defendant makes his reply; when this is done, the members of the court speak (or deliberate among themselves) and after them speaks the judge (Katyayana. 121.9 commented upon by Apararka, p. 611, Parasara III, p. 58). The four stages (padas) of a law-suit, according to Yajnavalkya II-6-8 and Brihaspati are named Bhasapada (the plaint) Uttarpada (the reply), Kriyapada (the adducing of evidence), Sadhya Siddhi or 'Nirnya' (the decision).[37] It was also called Jaipatra.

There are rules of law concerning resjudicata, defective plaints, pleading, preference of evidence and proof; classification of documents, forgeries, or copperplates etc. This should not be surprising because a legal system, in order to serve as an effective organisation for society, has to evolve laws and rules which may seem similar to those of other systems because they arise from the need to meet common and incidental situations in legal business in general.

The classification of suits is also to be noticed in Ancient India. According to Brihaspati "law-suits are of two types; those which originate in demands about wealth and those which originate from injuries. Yajnavalkya speaks of 'arthvivada' which originates from wealth and divides it in fourteen kinds. Those which originate in injuries he classifies in four kinds: as Vakparusya (defamation and abuse), dandaparusya (assault and battery), sahasa (in murder and other forms of violence) and Stri Sangraha (स्त्रिसंग्रह) or adultery. Here, according to Kane, there is clear distinction between civil disputes (arthmula or dhanmula) and criminal desputes (himsa-mula). Katyayana also points out the suits to be of two kinds. One arising when not rendering what should be given, and the other out of himsa.[38]

The procedure in both these kinds was the same with minor

differences, and the same courts dealt with these kinds. There were not two sets of courts like that of common law and that of equity in Ancient India.

Vyavahar is said to have four feet, (Chatuspad) viz. dharma, vyavahara, charitra and rajasasna. This is the view of Narada who seems to have used Vyavahar, to identify the law recognised by the king's court. Yajnavalkya and Brihaspati give the four feet of Vyavahar as the plaint, the reply, the proof, and the decision. *Aparaka* the *Commentator*, of Katyayana enumerates–plaints, reply pratyaklika (determination of burden of proof, or the method of proof, etc.) and Kirya. It seems, according to Kane, Dharma is the sole of the decision and others are really the feet of Nirnaya or decision. A decision is considered to be based on dharma when the wrong doer admits his guilt and the injured party gets wealth or relief without the need of a trial. The decision arrived at by ordeal is also said to be according to dharma. This is a testimony to the fact that ordeals, at some time or the other, were prevalent, in some places. As dharma and Satya are identified, the decision is also treated as by 'dharma'. When the case is decided by Vyavahara or litigation, in the court, with the application of its procedure it is called Vyavahar. A decision is based on Charitra when it is founded on usages and customs, or on presumptions or inference (Anumana) which is also 'Charitra'. Similarly, a case may be decided by the Ordinance of the king or by royal policy and it is called Sasana.

In Vyavaharasara of Narada, it is said that a decision in order to be without grievance all the judges should be unanimous in decision. According to Jaimini, the opinion of majority should prevail. According to Gautama, in case of difference of opinion among the judges, the king is to seek the advice of persons who are learned in the three Vedas viz. (Rig-Veda, Yujur Veda and Atharva-Veda)* alongwith other sciences. Katyayana counsels that the court of justice should associate, with the task of deciding disputes, some good merchants of guilds. In the *Mircchakitika*, a *Sresthin* and Kayastha are associated with the judge. It is enjoined that the Chief Judge and Sabhayas (members) should hold no private conversation with the parties. There was always a court of Chief Justice established by the ruling power and final appeal lay to the ruler himself. In this way Vyavahar had all the basic concepts of a developed legal system.

*** Sam-Veda, being musical, has been excluded.**

PRAKIRANKA AND KANTAK SODHANA AS MODES OF CRIMINAL JUSTICE

In ancient legal theory king has his own duties to perform which are discussed in the texts as 'Rajdharma'. His main duty is that of protection of his subjects from internal disorder and external aggression. However, this protection from internal dangers has four-fold character. He has to avert the danger caused by people forgetting their duties. It is his duty to ensure that the penances enjoined on sinners or wrongdoers are performed regularly by them. Again, he is a surety for peace and order in the society and has to eliminate bad elements, and lastly he has to be an arbitrator in the disputes as surety between the subjects by securing to them a means of administration of justice. In this sense, king has a comprehensive task to perform and for this reason 'rajadharma' prevails over all dharmas. The penultimate to function is important from the point of view of criminal justice. According to *Vardachariar* the "general theory of king's duty to protect his subjects involves the recognition of a king of residuary or miscellaneous jurisdiction in him–somewhat on the analogy of the king being Paren Patriae. The miscellaneous jurisdiction so called because it is not comprised in regular Vivada-pads (titled of law) is discussed under the head of Prakirnaka in Sanskrit books."[39] In this sense the king exercises criminal jurisdiction properly so called. After dealing with the eighteen topics of litigation, Manu (IV. 252 ff) enjoins on him to root out thorns (Kantaka-Sodhana) of his realm. He means by this that the king should take care to render harmless those of his subjects who are proved to compromise public order by their action, or to prejudice his authority. Manu enumerates, in no special order, a certain number of reprehensible acts, more or less grave, for which he provides varied punishments, and recommends recourse to some unusual means for the king to keep himself informed. This part of 'rajdharma' has been given the name of 'Prakirnaka' by other writers of dharmasastras. The literal meaning of Prakirnaka as "scattered diverse, miscellaneous is superficial" because actually the topics contained in 'Prakirnaka' signify a separate aspect of the function of the king. He is not considered here as a judge or disputes between litigants but as one who has to seek and weed out wrong-doers who disturb the peace of society. As such he has to perform the function of a chastiser on behalf of the State. This is what we call criminal law, even if in certain aspects, Prakirnaka resembles rather the police activity of government than criminal justice as we know it today, in which the adversary aspect is usually maintained.[40] The king can thus take action even when there is no plaint. The procedure of Prakirnaka for its initiation depends upon the king. The king is the master of the case. Various lists of offences are given by Smritikars. Katyayana gives three groups of offences. A similar list is found in Brahaspati and Narad with a little more variety of offences. *Pitamba* gives in the first list 22 offences which range from high treason to dismembering of animals. There is a second list which includes offences like breaches of etiquette in king's presence as well as acts injurious to the realm like destroying a cistern or causing obstruction to a public way. The Prakirnaka-law was developed outside Smriti literature, and as it deals with "up-rooting the thorns" which was the sole concern of the king was deliberately neglected by Smritikars. So none of the lists which deal with offence under Prakirnaka is exhaustive. The implication of all this seems to be that it is totally king's jurisdiction to decide whether a particular act or omission is of the nature of 'Prakirnaka', i.e., an offence of the nature of being punishable on behalf of the king to keep peace in the kingdom. It is for him to decide and apply the means to safeguard the interest of the society or of the realm and to secure respect for his officers by efficient exercise of his powers. The whole subject is not the subject of dharma which is mainly concerned with law, but of Artha which deals primarily with politics and with law, in a secondary sense as such the authors of dharmasastras left it to be expounded by the authors of arthsastras. Miscreants are prosecuted under the orders of the king, and he is interested in being informed about the improper activities of his subjects who are suspected of criminal tendencies in them. He has got means of inquiry and investigation justified by expediency. The king can adopt all useful and expedient methods to vindicate his authority and uphold social order and preserve peace of the society. The king has no duty to protect those who are the bad elements or to use the Kautaliyan expression "the thorns of society" for achieving this object the king may resort to tricks and bribery in order to discover and arrest such persons. Manu himself advises for this purpose the employment of spies. Katyayana gives three groups of such offences to be dealt with by this extra-ordinary and exceptional method. For the first group of ten 'aparadhas' he recommends the king to deal with or enquire into them by himself. Those of the second group, known to him, through spies he takes preventive measures. But the third group of offences are to be repressed by four expedients of royal policy which are pointed out by Kane as conciliation, corruption, division and force. King can, for his purpose, use 'stombhaka' part-time informer as well as full-time informer 'the Suchaks'. He is a functionary entrusted with police duties. For deciding such cases, the king can use special service of advisers who are different from ordinary judicial officers and are not dependent upon, or involved in, judicial administration. These matters which are almost extra-judicial are left for the science of 'Arth' to explore as they are considered outside the scope of dharma. In Kautilya's Arthsastra, therefore, we find two types of courts. One is *Dharma Sthiya,* a court which deals with contentious matters according to the dictates of Dharmasastras, and the other is 'Kantak Sodhana' where the king exercises criminal jurisdiction and acts on his own motion to 'extirpate thorns'. Its functionaries are–'Pradestr', the agents of the executive. In criminal matters and in those of the fixing penalties, the king enjoyed a large amount of freedom, whereas in matters dealt within the dharmasastras the penalties were fixed. The sastras incorporated in a special advice for the king not to abuse his power. He should neither appear like a tyrant nor should he show himself very lax and weak. It is recommended to him to consider the motive, the period (काल), the location of the offence the capacity of the criminal to endure penalty, his/her age, and gender etc. He is expected to change sentences or penalties according to the circumstances of each case. Manu, Yajnavalkya and Brahaspati distinguish four kinds of penalties viz., simple imprisonment, severe admonition, fine, and corporal punishment, e.g., disfigurement. The punishment of imprisonment was not unknown but was rarely given in those days. Prisons were used for torture and disfigurement, and were open to public view. There is no precept here analogous to the maxim 'nulla poena sine lege' to restrict the jurisdiction of the king. The king had more freedom and discretion to deal with criminals–He was, both; the Prosecutor and the judge–in the matter of crimes.

As has been stated earlier, the ancient Indian mind views 'Vyavahar' as sacred ritual expressing the sense of sacrifice. It thus glorifies it (Vyavahar) to be a search for truth and a manifestation of impersonal objective and eternal dharma. In Vyavahar, which we have described as litigation or law in action, we witness a display of basic ideas and values of the culture and life of people of ancient India. The Indian Vyavahar does not suffer from the exhibition of individual ago which has been assiduously built-up in Western legal thought of American Realism where the judge is an ego-centric individual Swayed by inhibitions and obsessions due to the ideological influences and psychic complexes resulting in absurd and grotesque decisions. Unlike this, the judge in Ancient India, is an individual free from the limitations of his ego and all earthly attachments. He is a sort of Vairagi (a detached person), cut off from all endearments, passions and possessions. In delivering his judgment he aims at truth and objectivity. His decision is a result of thorough grounding in the basic tenets and values of dharma. The fact that these ideas partook, in a measure, of the religious and cultural heritage of ancient India does not, in any way detract from the superiority and worth that it possessed.

The concept of Vyavahar is so dynamic that in it are realised and assessed the purposes and needs of society. The dislodging of Indian mind from its ancient heritage and culture, as represented by the legal concept of Vyavahar, is regretted all the more when we see the split in our legal system (Indian) by polarisation of judiciary and parliament. It is evident that absolute exercise of authority by either branch is deleterious to the interests of the people. If in a spirit of sharing and sacrifice, our parliament articulates and lays down the 'Dharma' of the time as conceived by the ancients and manifested in the ancient law–with such modifications and changes necessitated by science and technology, but without making any change in the basic structure of dharma, much of the ills that have taken root in Indian society will be remedied. This is not an easy task as gaps of centuries will have to be filled up. However, if earnest and honest effort is made to give the jurisprudence of today a basically Indian base and orientation, it is quite possible to produce a legal theory which we could call as our own. We have already seen how justice was administered without fear or favour and men were happy and secure. This was achieved by a happy blending of judicial and administrative functions of the political authority. Parliament, today, if it desires to enact social and other welfare legislation and law to extirpate bad elements in the interest of the laity, it may very well do so. In the case of legislation of such significance and utility, the judiciary will have no reason to veto it. But if parliament is playing an ideological game and is experimenting with foreign ideas and exotic doctrines, and is cut off from vital source of law, i.e., people and their aspirations then it is certainly disowning its duty and for that matter ceases to represent the Indian spirit and its dharma.

In Vyavahar we have an intermingling of the advantages both of tort and crime because of the unified procedure that it possessed.

At the same time it has not neglected to give recognition to wrongs against society or state, which it does by arming the king with wide discretionary powers. It recognises fully the responsibility of judges to do real justice. The negligence of judges and the king, in case of miscarriage of justice, holds them liable like any other citizens and has its sanction both in law and in religion.

In the Indian concept of Vyavahar, we see the judicial process and legal transaction in its health and vigour. On the other hand we know how formalistic, complicated, expensive, and dilatory is the modern procedure, giving rise to disappointment and harrassment to the litigating public? Today in the industrial age we are witnessing disintegration of society and dehumanisation of its members for the benefit of only a few members of the society. The interest of the bulk of the population is sacrified for the sake of these few, alienating them (bulk) from the mainstream of our lives. Either social and legal engineering have to bring in a society where the poor and downtrodden are raised from the present status of semi-serfdom, to that of dignified human beings and made partners in social process or it will make its devastating effects felt at all the levels of human relations and organisation.

The limitations, if any of Vyavahar are the limitations of legal process itself. A legal procedure can be self-sufficient but it is very difficult to attain the perfection. Modern Psychology has thrown light upon mental processes. But as yet modern science has not invented an apparatus to X-ray human motives, and intentions for the detection and investigation of facts which are relevant in every judicial enquiry. Till then judicial process is bound to be a gamble, and greed of wealth, violent passions, and fraud cannot be checked completely by it. Unless modern science makes investigation and detection certain, morality lends its spirit, religion inculcates faith and economics provides security, to us, law and the judicial process are bound to be uncertain guides to human happiness, and social order will continue to be secured through coercive impositions by the rulers.

Even the doctrine of the rule of law which is said to be the highest development of procedural law in Anglo-American jurisprudence has no magic in its words and may work as a mere legal conceit. In theoretical sense, it vainly implies the yardstick by which it measures the so called 'good law' against the so called 'bad law'. Its ideological content is as vague and sentimental as the content of natural law.[41]

All the theories of law, if at all they are theories are guides for action and not insurance schemes. Law, with all the force at its command, and its procedure succeeds in controlling only the baser aspects of human nature and our projects for the welfare of a civil society are likely to be frustrated. In order that judicial process, and with it law, achieves a greater success it must have an ideal content. In ancient Indian Vyavahar we find an amalgam of elements–idealistic and realistic, judicial and administrative, with an emphasis on Dharmic-Duty, and on both the disputing parties and the judges.

The greatness of Indian juristic mind lies in its realisation that reality with all its multifarious forms is one and the same. The governing principle of Indian culture asserts unity in all diversities and comprehension from within and without. Vyavahar, with its faith, in revealed texts articulating dharma and reliance on irreversible course of Karma, with tacit assumption of distributions of functions in society and awareness of responsibility and duty, proved a very reliable method in ancient times and inspired faith and hope of justice in the hearts of litigants to such an extent that it has kept alive the spirit and authority of dharma, which is very life and soul, of the ancient Indian people.

Vyavahar, the law in action has got all the basic elements of ancient Indian legal theory. It recognises the authority of dharma, the impersonal, eternal, mystic force, as a guide to human beings. It treats law-business as solemn as religious sacrifice. It accepts defacto aspect of life by recognising traditions, conventions, customs and usages; it incorporates virtuous conduct by accepting the '*Sadachar*' of Sisatas as law. It gives due regard to necessity of social, legal order by recognising Raj Sasana, and exercises at the same time a check on royal absolutism in civil laws. While trying to do its best in eking out solutions to problems in courts, Vyavahar assured dignity to the judges, but with responsibility. It invests them with power but not arrogance. It enjoins on them to do justice according to the law laid down in the texts but allows them full freedom to base their decisions on dharma through the agency of interpretation based on reason and equity. In sum, it binds together the individual and the society of that time to re-live in each other as one whole.

Notes and References

1. History of Dharmasastra, Vol. III, p. 247.
2. The Hindu Judicial System–By S. Vardachariar, p. 150.

3. History of Dharmasastra, Vol. III, p. 247.
4. *Ibid.,* p. 258
5. Dr. Jolly Elucidates Narada–Sacred Book of the East, Vol. XXXIII, p. 7.
6. (a) Hindu Judicial System–By S. Vardachariar, pp. 121-22.
   (b) *Ibid.*, 122.
7. U.C. Sarkar, 'Epochs of Hindu Legal History, p. 21
8. Kane, History of Dharmasastras, Vol. III, pp. 245-46.
9. The Classical Law of India–By Lingat, p. 249.
10. Quoted in the Classical Law of India–By R. Lingat, 249.
11. The Hindu Judicial System–By S. Vardachariar, p. 81.
12. *Ibid.,* p. 82
13. *Ibid.,* p. 83.
14. Dr. N.C. Sen Gupta, Evolution of Ancient Indian Law, T.L.L. 1950, p. 325.
15. *Ibid.,* p. 327.
16. *Ibid.*
17. The Classical Law of India–By R. Lingat-p. 248.
18. Sen Gupta, W.C., Evolution of Ancient Indian Law, p. 327.
19. *Ibid.,* p. 332.
20. *Ibid.,* p. 332-33.
21. *Ibid.,* p. 333, Manu Quoted.
22. *Ibid.,* p. 333, Yajnavalkya Quoted.
23. Sen Gupta p. 333.
24. *Ibid.,* p. 334.
25. *Ibid.,* p. 335.
26. *Manu's List is thus—*
    1. Debt.,
    2. Deposit,
    3. Sale without Ownership,
    4. Partnership,
    5. Revocation of Gift,
    6. Wages for service,
    7. Violation of the decision of guilds and other associations,
    8. Rascissions of Sale or purchase,
    9. Dispute relating to herdsmen,
    10. Boundary disputes,
    11. Defamation and violence by words,
    12. Injury,
    13. Theft,
    14. Sahasa or violent of offences,
    15. Strisangrahana (illicit relation with women),
    16. Marital relation,
    17. Partition and inheritance, and
    18. Gambling.

27. Comparative view of law in Ancient India; Contribution by N.C. Sen Gupta in Studies in Cultural History of India, edited by GUVs. Metraux and Franc vis Crouzet, UNESCO, p. 73.
28. The Classical Law of India--By R. Lingat, p. 243.
29. *Ibid.*, p. 244.
30. *Ibid.*
31. H.S. Maine--Ancient Law, p. 370.
32. The Classical Law of India--By Robert Lingat, pp. 245-46, Foot Note 88.
33. *Ibid.*, p. 249, Brahaspati--quoted.
34. *Ibid.*, p. 250.
35. *Ibid.*, p. 251--Quoted.
36. Epochs in Hindu Legal History--By *U.C. Sarkar*--p. 35.
37. Kane--History of Dharmasastras, Vol. III, pp. 297-98.
38. *Ibid.*, p. 258.
39. The Hindu Judicial System--S. Vardachariar, p. 87.
40. Classical Law of India--By R. Lingat, p. 237.
41. Friedmann: Law in a Changing Society, Indian Edition, p. 374.

7

Law as an Ordinanace of The King–'Raj-Sasana'

We have considered the view of law as expressed in 'dharmasastras' and have seen that law is 'dharma' laid down by the Vedas or remembered texts (Smrities) or inferred from the virtuous conduct of the learned. Law to some extent, recognises also customs and conventions of the people. The King has no authority over this law. *He is its promulgator but not creator*. There is another view of law which is not so much represented in Dharmasastras as it is in Arthsastras.This law is that of administrative nature and is designated as *Rajsasana* having its direct source in King's power and authority. It is in a way the ancient counterpart of modern administrative law.

Arthsastra of Kautilya (Book III Ch. I) enumerates four legs of law, i.e., sources or bases of law as: sacred (dharma), evidence (Vyavahara), history (Charitra), and edicts of Kings (Rajasasana). In this order of enumeration it is said that later is superior to one previously named. Whatever be the controversial interpretations of this view of Arthsastra one cannot deny that law as an Ordinance of King is one of the most important sources of law. This is a sequel to the recognition of the power and authority of King which had its seed in Manu and its fruit in Kautilya. Verily, the role of administration increased enormously with the needs of the Moryan empire.

The source of the administrative authority of the King lies in the duties of functions enjoined on a King. As we have already noted that "the general theory of the King's duty to protect his subjects involves the recognition of a kind of residuary and miscellaneous jurisdiction in him somewhat on the analogy of the King being 'Paren Patria'''.[1] If we have a total view of the Smrities we find that "the King appears to owe his authority neither to the divine will, nor to his birth, nor to any social compact, but solely to the force at his disposal".[2] On this authority, to use force effectively, is founded the theory of King's functions and duties. As 'Paren Patria' he has the duty to protect his subjects that is summarised in the expression: 'Prajanam Paripalanam' which consists in providing protection from dangers to peace and security from without and within. He has to meet effectively the external aggressions and become a 'surety for the peace and order in the realm'. For performing the latter task, the King has to secure a good administration of justice and must also perform the function of maintaining peace and order by sternly dealing with those who cause disturbance of peace in society by their anti-social and criminal activities. It is in this context that Rajadharma (duty of the King) is said to take precedence over all dharmas because without performance of it all other dharmas cannot be performed.

We have already seen that in the field of Vyavahara the King as a judge is governed by the dictates of 'Dharmasastras' to a very great extent. Even his discretion has to be exercised in the interest of justice or Dharma. In this field he has no legislative power. He cannot substitute his will for divine commandment. If at all he is allowed to interfere with good custom, it is only to re-establish dharma. He is also permitted to abolish customs which are repugnant to reason or logic of the Sastras. Even in the case of such customs as are anti-Sastric but which have become popular, the King is warned that he need not interfere with such customs, if the interference causes disaffection among the people. This, it is submitted is giving concession to political expediency or 'Arth'. King is thus performing a double role as an upholder of dharma and as a Keeper of peace and order in society. While doing his dharmic duty he is not free but while doing the other he has got administrative discretion and initiative which is largely a matter of royal policy. A discussion of the aspects of this administrative power of the King will be our purpose now.

It has already been pointed out that administration of justice is one of the four important functions of the King which is purely concerned with 'Vyavahar' (private litigation) and is judicial in nature. The rest of the functions relate to the administration of his realm. It is his administrative function to see that penances prescribed by religion are performed so that people remain disciplined and follow the path of right (rightful act). In this sense he, in a way, extirpates the thorns of society. Thus, it is his duty to see that his subjects do not forget or neglect their duties which are prescribed by the sacred law.

As already noted in the last Chapter, the King has no power to legislate in the field of 'dharma'. Even where the King allows such rules as are contrary to Smritis, he does so on grounds of expediency, and they cannot be designated as legislation even indirect. But he has no power to impose his own interpretation of the texts. At the most he can patronise or favour certain commentator so that the dictates of Shastras are better explained and the subjects may be well informed about their duties. Even if the King, in the manner of Justinian, directs the compilation of digests and forbids any more interpretation he cannot withhold future interpretation. Such compilations at his request cannot be called legislation because after all commentaries and digests have no more value than that of opinions and no one can be forced to bind himself by these opinions or views of commentators and digest writers. But the King's real legislative activity is restricted to the sphere of administration. "Because of the large sphere reserved for *dharma* the legislative activity of the King was limited very seriously, but there did remain a vast field in which it might operate. The majority of the topics which come within what we now call administrative law fell under royal authority. The *dharma-sastras* confine themselves to indicating, for example, the qualities which ministers should have. But it fell to the King to divine among them the task of administration, to define the scope and the powers of each ministry. In Book 11, Kautilya presents a long list of rules for the conduct to be followed by the different heads of the public services (adhyaksas), and such rules were clearly intended to be formulated in the shape of edicts".[3] Though local bodies and groups had their autonomous status, the rules were framed by which King's officers exercised control over the transactions of such local bodies or groups. Public Finance, which deals with rates, taxes, custom duties, needs a large number of officers whose powers, duties and liabilities are governed by rules which are framed at the behest of the King. Power to legislate is here delegated to officers and his (King's) instructions in this regard have the effect of laws. Again, in the field of organisation of judiciary and in the organisation of proceedings e.g. in matters relating to appeals, the formulation of rules were necessary and the King here exercised legislative powers. "Even in the sphere of private litigation, the *dharmasastras* give their attention indeed to formulating rules for the solution of disputes, but rules dealing with judicial organisation and even legal procedure are in need of completion. For example, appeal properly so-called, i.e., the right of the litigant who has lost his case to take the decision before a court superior to that in which he was successful, is barely outlined in the Sastras, which do not specify the conditions, the periods, and the effect of an appeal. Once again, the reason is that here we have to do with a matter solely within the royal authority, pertaining to the means employed to give true justice, of which the King is the sole judge. Finally in the sphere of economics, if the dharmasastras enable us to catch a glimpse of King's intervention in supervision of markets, prices, and wages, it is only if we read 'Arthsastra' works that we can form an idea of that encroaching quality which could regulate so many branches of human activity. We could say that the royal edicts penetrated substantially into the daily lives of individuals and communities''.[4] Though most of the royal legislation is now lost to us, it was the expression of the will of the king and its object was to secure the government of the realm. Here we seek law as positive law (as law made by human authority) or law which is enforced by the king's agents and is the expression of king's will. In a different manner from that of dharmasastras, this law also controlled the various activities of the society.

These ordinances or edicts of Kings could be modified, supplemented or abrogated by the succeeding King at his convenience. The extent of this administrative law can be judged from the different activities of the Moryan State as described by A.S. Altekar in these words: The activity of the State ''was to embrace the whole of human life, both here and hereafter. The State was to offer facilities to religions and sects to develop on their own lines and foster and inculcate piety, morality and righteousness. It was to improve the social order and to encourage learning, education and art by subsidizing learned academies and extending patronage to scholars and artists. It was to establish and maintain rest houses, charity halls and hospitals and relieve the distress due to flood, locusts, famines, pestilences and earthquakes. It was to see that the population was evenly distributed and encourage colonization of fresh lands. It was to enrich the resources of the country by developing forests, working mines and constructing dams and canals in order to make agriculture independent of rain as far as possible. It was to offer active help to trade and industry, but also to protect the population against capitalistic selfishness, if merchant princes sought to corner the market and raise prices. It was to regulate the vices of the community by appointing its own officers to supervise wine booths, dice halls and prostitutes".[5] In Arthsastra of Kautilya we get the impression of the widespread activity of the State. In the time of Ashoka, the welfare activity of State further developed and he appointed *dharma mamantras* to look after the morality of the people. In the time of Imperial Guptas these officers were called *Vinaysthitisthapakas*.

The administrative law of the Kings (Raj Sasana) did not stop at merely dealing with welfare and other allied activities but was also extended to facilitate proper administration of criminal justice in which sphere the King had a free hand and complete discretion. It resemble more with police activity and is quite different from Vyavahar or private litigation and is merely classified in *dharmasastras* by the name *Prakinka* and is left to be dealt with by Arthsastras. The aim of criminal justice according to Manu (IX-252) as already stated earlier is to root out the thorns– 'Kantaka Sodhana' of his realm. It is part of King's duties as a guardian of people to keep the society secure from those persons who disturb order and peace of the realm. King does not appear here as a judge "charged with the task of ending a dispute between two litigants but, as a magistrate who seeks out wrong-doers and applies chastisement to them in the name of State". It is King's own sphere and he takes action *ex-officio* in any manner he likes. There is also no fixed procedure and no limitations as regards the time to proceed against them. The miscreants or thorns of society or offenders are prosecuted by the orders of the King. He is to keep a strict watch upon such persons who have criminal propensities and are likely to commit offences. They are to be suppressed as if they are external enemies. Any method of inquiry and investigation is a good method if it can accomplish this task with expediency and efficiency. *A mention has earlier been made how the King could employ tricks and resort to bribery to arrest and entrap them.* For this purpose there must have been a special service quite different and independent of ordinary judiciary. For dealing with the thorns of society, there are special courts, as mentioned by Kautilya called *Kantaka Sodhana*, a reference to which has been made earlier, where ordinary law and procedure do not prevail. The dharmasastras have no say in this matter. The King looks more to artha, i.e., interest of the State than to dharma to perform this task. This work is entrusted by Kings to three functionaries called *pradestr*, who are agents of the executive. *Again, King was more free in fixing penalties in criminal matters.* Even when dharmasastras prescribe fixed penalties for certain crimes they often give choice between penalties and neglect to mention the amount of the penalties. The King can deal freely with criminals and there is no application of the principle like nulla Poena sine lege (no penalty without the authority of law).

The criminal jurisprudence, evolved out of the English legal system may appear to have been built upon extra-ordinarily merciful principles such as ensuring fair trial to the accused, imposing entire burden on the prosecution to prove the guilt of the accused, giving benefit of doubt to the accused, presuming always the innocence of the accused till the guilt is proved beyond reasonable doubt and permitting acquittal of ten persons alleged to be guilty rather than to convict and punish one innocent person, is a mere chimera and a creature partly of delibrate design and partly of the errors and accident of historical development. In the result, however, the English criminal law, till the 19th Century remained barbarous and reactionary and it was for the purpose of mitigating its rigour and severity that the above principles were resorted to in order to make it more humane and liberal. We know how a theft of 40 shillings was considered felony and deserved capital punishment. Women were whipped and institution of pillory existed and criminals were hanged in public. Judges and jurors committed pious perjury to save the people from such a criminal law. These principles as evolved are certainly laudable but lead to dilatory, complicated, and expensive procedure which the developing countries functioning on the common law (including India), can ill afford. It is no gainsaying the fact that the present criminal law and procedure has failed to deal effectively with the problem of crime. In contrast to this the ancients succeeded amazingly to deal with this problem. It has become proverbial that in the times of Kautilya when Chandra Gupta Morya reigned there was peace and plenty and people used to go out without locking their doors. It seems that it is a gigantic task before our present law reformers to attune our criminal law and procedure to suit the conditions and needs of the times.

Unusual expansion and popularity of administrative law in democracies to cope with the commitments of a welfare State, create two grave dangers for the inhabitants of the democratic world. First, by giving upper hand to the executive and by taking recourse to extra-ordinary procedures, and also by making matters non-justiciable, we are liable to increase the interference of State too much and to whittle down the essential freedom of the individual to the extent that the so-called welfare State may turn out in fact to be a despotic state. Second, in order to check the excesses of administrative agencies we have to invest judiciary with extra-ordinary powers of review of administrative actions which is turn may further prove to be a set-back to all our schemes of social reconstruction and planning. It is very difficult to meet these two horns of the dilemma without having a sound grounding in democratic values which consist in developing a high degree of civic sense and responsibility. In ancient India the King, inspite of his large powers in administration, was held in check by the doctrine of Dharma, the doctrine of Karma, and the diversification of society in different Varnas where the ruling political Ksatriya power was subordinated to the religious power of enlightenment and knowledge. There was no need of such a constitutionalism as we have today which is devoid of moral and spiritual base. The ancients had a complete constitution in the concept of dharma. There was no need of judicial review when the doctrine of Karma as the inexorable law or eternal justice, religous sense of duty, spirit of Vajna and morality–all aimed at the welfare of the people and exercised a complete control upon the executive. Today, mechanical civilisation and materialistic culture bred in atheism, self-interest, distrust and greed are trying hard to transform these spiritual values and moral principles into sociological norms but it seems certain that it will not only take long time to accomplish this task, but even when accomplished, the task will still remain unfulfilled. In the view of this humble author the only panacea for these ills is to revert to the spiritual and moral base of the ancient jurisprudence which helped the ancients to usher in a golden age.

Notes and References

1. S. Vardachariar, Hindu Judicial System, p. 87.
2. The Classical Law of India, by Robert Lingat, p. 215.
3. *Ibid.*, pp. 230-31, Ghoshal cited.
4. *Ibid.*, p. 231, B.P. Sinha, J.B.R. (1954, 277-308), cited.
5. Quoted in Indian Thought Through the Ages by B.G. Gokhale, pp. 155-56, Published by Asia Publishing House, 1961.

8

Mimansa–The Interpretation of Law

The theory of the interpretation of law in Indian legal philosophy has its origin in the theory of language and the theory of the origin of this world. Modern semantics asserts that words are not things in themselves or vehicles of meaning, they are incomplete symbols, as language is not a perfect medium of expression. Therefore, arises the need for Interpretation of law (a function of the judge) has become so important that some jurists have begun to hold that real law is not what is enacted by the legislature but that which is the product of interpretation done by judges. This has been reflected in juristic thought in two ways. One is seen as the operation of judicial discretion used for the higher end of justice of which law is only a mere instrument. The other dimension of thought, which is modern development called American Realism has evinced a distrust in judicial function, wherein interpretation of law is seen as the net result of dynamics of extra-legal influences. It is thus hold that irrational, personal and ideological factors and brought to operate on the letter of the law through interpretation and a chasm is created between the law which is laid down and the law which is adjudicated upon.

In Indian legal theory, interpretation has its beginning in the Vedic theory of language put forward by Dirghtamas. According to this theory, "language can be divided in four quarters, and it is only the wise poets that have known it. Three quarters of it remain concealed in a cave and only the fourth part is in use among men".[1] Only the wise who are Rishis and have vision can see these three parts. In this mystery of language lies the magic, or 'maya' or 'lila' of law to recreate itself. Legal interpretation is then an aspect of cosmic lila or maya or '*kama*', of dynamic reality, as extended to the sphere of human actions controlled by law. Interpretation then becomes necessary to know the meaning as far as possible which is contained in language.

Another theory which is associated with the theory of language is that of *Mimansa* (literally an enquiry is a system of Indian philosophy), which is Vedic in its orientation. It takes the 'realistic position' for the understanding of the world. World is real and real is what can be known. "What is absolutely beyond knowledge is not what can be called a reality; what is spoken of beyond the sphere of knowing in an absolute way, is a self-contradiction".[2] The question, that is important thus is: What is knowledge? In reply, it is said, Vedas are the knowledge itself in their real as well as literal meaning. The main aspect of the Vedas relates the great moral law that governs the movements in the dynamic world.[3] *Mimansakas* come forward to establish the authority of the Vedas and to ascertain dharma which is defined 'as a command or injunction which impels men to action'. It (Dharma) is the supreme duty, the 'ought' or the categorical imperative. Arth and Kama which deal with ordinary common morality are learnt by worldly intercourse. But Dharma and Moksa which deal with true spirituality are revealed only be Vedas. Dharma is supra-sensible and consists of the commands of the Vedas. Vedas command us to do certain acts and to refrain from doing others. Dharma then become identical with Vedic injunction. Vedas alone give us the standard of what is wrong and which is right in life. 'A good life is a life led in obedience to Veda'. The revealed truth or dharma of Vedas comes through the medium of words. But the explorations of words is not so easy, as according to the theory of language as stated above; only one part out of three parts is visible to the ordinary human beings. Hence, one has to perform the difficult task of interpreting the language and of the Vedas in order to get the right knowledge of its prescriptions. The main aim of Mimansa, is to perform this task of interpretation and ascertain from the Vedic expressions, that element of dharma which is seated in it by establishing co-ordination between thought and expression. The sole aim of Mamansakas is to uphold the authority of the Vedas and dharma which is revealed in it. This authority is determined through reason and logic. It is thus rightly claimed that Mimansa is not merely an Updesha-Sastra (didectic) but is a reasoned enquiry, i.e., a Pariksa-sastra. It is thus that he (the Mimansak) enters the arena of logic; and though he may not be a rationalist in the full sense of the term, he cannot at the same time be described as a more dogmatizer. The Vedas, according to the traditional theory, are not the creation of any person as there is no author of the Vedas. Vedas are revealed texts. There is no possibility of any essential truth or dharma revealed by the Vedas, to come in conflict with common experience. What they teach is to be supposed to be only the matters which are beyond life and are, therefore, not empirically varifiable. But what they (the Vedas) prescribe are injunctions to be obeyed by men. They are ritualistic in nature. A ritual is to be performed just because the Vedas command us to perform it. Some of these rituals, it is true, are to be performed in order to enjoy heaven hereafter or to obtain worldly benefits, such as rainfalls. But there are some of every day routine (e.g. nitya-naimittika karmas) which must be performed just because they are enjoined by the Vedas. Here the Mimansa-ethics reaches through ritualism, the highest point of its glory, namely, the conception of duty for duty's sake. Like Kant, the Mimansa philosophy believes that an obligatory action is to be performed not because it will benefit the performer but because we 'ought' to perform it. Like him, again, Mimansa believes that though an obligatory duty is not to be done with any interested motive, yet the universe is so constituted that a person who performs his duty does not ultimately go unrewarded. The difference is that while, for this purpose, the Mimansa postulates in the universe the impersonal moral law of Karma, Kant postulates God. Again, whereas the source of obligation for Kant is the higher self which commands to the lower, 'thou oughtest to do what is good' for the Mimansakas it is the impersonal 'Vedic authority,* which categorically enjoins duty''.[5] Dharma, according to *Mimansaka*, stands for rights and duties of religious kind. It is dharma seen in the light of ritualism. When sacrifice or rite is performed according to the injunction of the Vedas, it is believed that a capacity which did not exist before is produced, either in the action or in the agent. This capacity is called *apurva*. As a result of this 'apurva', the performer

* Vedic literature consists of two parts—one dealing with prayers in the form of verse called in Sanskrit 'mantrast'; the other of 'Brahmanas' or ritual texts which consist of prescriptions or procedures for performing rituals. For the purpose of 'Mimansa', i.e., interpretation of 'dharma' which could be attained through rituals, the second part, i.e., that relating to 'Brahmana' is more important and this consisted of injunctions.

attains heaven. "This apurva is like a potency or faculty which resides in him until desired results follow". As a result of the operation of moral law the performer attains heaven. Later the end of heaven was replaced by Moksa.

Injunctions, according to Jaimini, may be either positive or negative. The positive injunctions are of four types. Apurva Vidhi, Niyama Vidhi, Parisankhya and Anuvada. Negative injunctions are of two kinds–Pratisadha or Nisedha and Paryudasa. Apurva Vidhi is an order which enjoins some thing not otherwise known, e.g., the grains should be washed. Even those expressions which give reasons for performance of certain actions are to be treated as 'arth vada'. They should be interpreted as forming part of Vidhi Vakya (injunction) or be rejected. Apurva Vidhi is a sastric rule which creates a duty of original nature, of which the sanction is absolutely unattainable by the senses and for which there is no earthly cause and is thus obligatory. We could not have known that this part of the duty was necessary for the sacrifice except by the above injunction. Niyam-vidhi is that where though a thing could have been done in a number of ways, yet an order is made by the Vedas (it is a rule, making one of two alternatives obligatory). It is a direction only partially spiritual, and is thus only directory. It restricts us to follow some definite alternatives (e.g. though the chaff from the corn could be separated even by the nails, the order, that corn should be thrashed restricts us to the alternative of thrashing as the only course acceptable for the sacrifice). In the Niyam-Vidhi, that which is ordered is already known as possible, but only as an alternative, and the injunction insists upon one of these methods as the only one, to be followed. In Apurva-Vidhi the thing to be done would have remained undone and unknown had it not been for the Vidhi, i.e., injunction. According to Dr. *Siromoni*, – 'parisankhya' is an apparently positive rule implying negative precept, for example, the rule that the flesh of certain animals may be eaten, prohibits the eating of the flesh of other animals, better opinion seems to be that mentioned by Babu Kishorylal Sircar that it is merely a rule of convenience depending on experience and observation. 'Anuvada' is merely a rule which is a statement of facts. Of two types of negative injunctions the pratisheda is one which prohibits the doing of that which might be done otherwise, either out of natural inclination or on account of some positive ordinance prescribing the doing of an act. The other called the *paryudas* is an exceptional clause in a vidhi creating an original duty.[6]

This prescriptive Vidhi is different from 'anuvada' on the one hand and 'arthvada' on the other. The former is merely a description of facts, the latter, however, states reasons or explanations which may be interpreted liberally.

MIMANSA AND ITS FUNCTION IN VYAVAHAR

Originally the rules of Mimansa were developed to help in the understanding of those Sruti texts which were 'obscure, uncertain, and conflicting'. We find that earlier writers like Sabara and Kumarila apply their rules solely to Vedic texts inspite of the fact that Dharmasastra literature had begun to grow considerably in their times. But in later times, as A.S. Altekar observes, the Smriti writers were canonised, and it became as delicate and difficult to differ from their views as from Sruti. The number of Smritis became much larger than those of the Vedas and Brahmanas and their texts were often contradictory with one another. It can be only an apparent divergence of opinion which can be explained with the help of Mimansa rules. Thus the latter were useful in establishing how the Srutis really laid down a harmonious body of rules about the Vedic sacrifice, inspite of their apparent divergence in some cases. They could be equally useful in proving how the Smriti literature as a whole was free from any literal contradictions. Medieval commentators like Dharesvara, Visvarupa, Vijnanesvara, Madhavacarya, Kaluka, and Raghunandan often resort to the rules of Mimansa, when confronted with conflicting texts. There can be no doubt that Nyaya and Mimansa indirectly gave considerable scope of reason in deciding obscure and conflicting points. In theory they were not to overrule the sacred texts but in practice they did so though indirectly.[7] Thus by the ingeniousness of the Indian mind the rules which were to be used for making Vedic injunctions of ritualistic nature were transplanted for the interpretation of legal codes. Such application did not appear unnatural to the Indian mind because there was intermixture of 'right' and 'rite' in the sastras. Further Vyavahar or legal trial was also seen by Smritikars as a religious sacrifice. Thus it became very easy to apply the rules of ritualistic interpretation for deciding legal disputes. Colebrooke explains the technique of Mimansa thus: "It will be observed as has been intimated in speaking of the members of an Adhikarna in the Mimansa, that a case is proposed, either specified in Jamini's text or supplied by his scholiasts. Upon this a doubt or question is raised and a solution of it is suggested which is refuted and a right conclusion established in its stead. The disquisitions of the Mimansa bear, therefore, a certain resemblance of juridical questions, and, in fact, the Hindu Law being blended with the religion of the people, the same modes of reasoning are applicable and are applied to the one as to the other. The logic of the Mimansa is the logic of the law; rule of interpretation of civil and religious ordinances. Each case is examined and determined upon general principles; and from the cases decided, the principles may be collected. A well worded arrangement of them would constitute the philosophy of the law; and this is in truth, what has been attempted in the Mimansa. Jaimini's arrangement, however, is not philosophical....''[8] Mimansa literally means ''enquiry'' and with this enquiry and investigation a 'true juridical' science began in India. Interpretation, in ancient India, was understood as was understood by the Romans. A study of ancient Roman Law has revealed to this humble author a great similarity in this respect. It is a matter of satisfaction that this author is in good company as he has been able to lay his hands on the views of an eminent writer viz. those of Lingat who is also of the same view. The relevant portion is quoted here:

> ''I take the word interpretation in the sense given to it in Roman law. The commentators and digest-writers have, in effect, a task analogous to that of the jurisconsults. They are not expected to state law properly so called, but to propose solutions to disputes; solutions which they approve and which they certify to be conformable to the texts. They prepare the way for the judge and they simplify his work, but they do not take it on. There were in order respects, several notable points of resemblance between the role of prudents and that of our Hindu 'interpretors' (as I shall call them) which explain the high opinion which both groups had of the significance of their function. They both regarded it as a veritable priesthood.''[9]

With respect to interpretation the assumption of Indian jurists (Mimansakas) is that dharmasastras were the expression of eternal law and a rule of law is to be deduced not from a particular Smriti but from the whole of the written tradition–i.e., the Vedas, and Smritis etc. According to them, Smritis were founded on the Vedas which were the great truth in themselves to serve as the source of all the rules of conduct and precepts of law. This doctrine was the necessary means by which Indian society lived in its own 'ideal image' and "has ceaselessly sought itself, and has always aspired to its own rediscovery. The role of interpretation amounts to this: it offers society the means whereby it can rediscover itself in fact".[10] They used the technique of interpretation to exercise choice between alternative views and rules coming before them. In this way by rejecting or accepting texts they comprehended and fixed the totality of known texts and measured their scope. Inspite of the fact, that through this interpretation the arbitrary element has entered into their constructions. They thought that they did their work honestly and sincerely and by various citations of diverse texts not available to us now in original. We hope that lot of lost and forgotten literature has been reclaimed in the process of interpretation.

The aim of interpretation is the search for truth, and Mimansa literally means the same. The truth is the norm or 'ought' or dharma which is the task for the interpretor to determine. Here the intention of human legislator is not sought for. What is sought for is divine commandment of dharma, which is revealed in texts. Mimansa tries to discover the true injunction and determines its significance. Dharma here has reference only to ritualistic direction and to know its correct execution is the sole aim of Mimansakas. But the transposition of ideas was easier for the fact that under the orthodox doctrine the rule of conduct which conforms to dharma takes its own source as it is directed and presumed in the Vedas. Likewise, the Mimansa rule of interpretation found a domain of application ready made in the sastras and precepts, concerning good customs and penances. But even in what concerns rules of a specifically juridical character which go to make up the Vyavahara, the extension of this method to the texts of Smritis was in no need of justification. The regulation of disputes is presented by dharmasastra authors as a sacrificial act, or as if it were a sacrificial act, the rules of which must be scrupulously observed under pain of sin.[11] Further, when rituals in the age of dharmasastra period, had fallen into disuse, the transplantation of rules interpreting rituals into the field of Vyavahara gave rise, at times, to subtle cauistry in absence of the true object of interpretation of rules. But on the whole the rules of interpretation were the rules of good sense and served as good latin tags and axioms of Western jurisprudence which any other jurist could have appreciated and applied. Some times their use exhibited originally verging on the bizarre. With all the embellishment or ornamental use which the jurists resorted to, the commentators had also the capacity to go deep into the discussion and exhibit all the formalistic and linguistic considerations. The commentators had but one aim, i.e., the employment of interpretive art to accomplish their end of escaping from dilemmas and reconciling conflicts. In this way by the use of logic they endeavoured to give rational solutions. The art with which they worked out and employed their method could be an envy of subtle sophists, casuists or semanticists of all ages. When reading their commentaries one is reminded of the "different solutions which an analogous problem has called forth in Roman law and in the older and modern common law".[12] They took their work seriously and wanted to search out reason amidst diverse texts. No one need deny that they might be rationalising their preconceived opinions but they worked in the furtherance of the cause of legal science. It is also true that the art of interpretation in those time is handled differently by different writers to reach different solutions. Due to voluminousness and variety of texts which constitute Smriti "the commentators and digest-writers had a good hand to play. But interpretation as such played a large part than did juridical theory as we know it. . . . . Each of them is conceived that the solution he proposes is the one which emerges from the totality of the *Smriti*, and which consequently expresses the rule of *Dharma*. One may well say that the Indian mentality is not so sensitive to contradiction. . . . However, that may be, it is certain that each of proposed solutions was an authority. . . . . Thus if we wish to envisage a general evolution of ideas–in default of an evolution of law, which remains beyond our power to achieve–it is upon such solutions as these that we must rely".[13] Though opinions differed from place to place all the solutions were treated equally valid. These solutions they thought were fit to pass as rules in actual practice. To a very great extent they fulfilled the needs of the times, what they did was to give religious sanction to practices which had already got social sanction. In case of conflict between Smritis the reasoning and practice were to be the guide. This is sanctioned by the text of Yjanavalkya. Immemorial usages were treated as conformable to the teachings of sages. Interpretation was used in general to justify different solutions for the subcontinent which had in it the varied ways of living, and it had wholesome effect as the commentators were guided by a desire to validate those practices and customs which appeared to be blameless.

Eventually, it gave rise to different juridical systems which, Colebrooke, for the first time, called schools, i.e., the schools of Banaras, Mithila, Bengal, and so on. Robert Lingat observe that to understand "what happened in India as a result of this recognition of 'Schools' we should take for comparison politically autonomous countries which have adopted the same laws. France, Belgium, and Holland for example, have what is virtually the same civil code. The very same article of the code can be, and sometimes is, differently interpreted in each of the three countries. In India where local populations have always had the benefit of measures of autonomy, and where a great variety of tribunals used to co-exist, the real diversity of customs must have involved a diversity of laws".[14]

The commentators and digest writers had neither the intention to give recognition to customary law, indiscriminately nor could they do so as none amount of 'text-torturing' would legitimise certain customs. It was necessary for the customary rule to have certain characteristics on account of which dharmic rule could be seen in it. In fact, interpretors exercised choice between customs they rejected, amended, adapted them and thus, 'aryanised' them. In this way they not only harmonised texts but provided legal foundations for an institution which was originally customary by deducing the principle from the 'Sastras'. By interpretation, and correct formulation they could fill in gaps and thus created a legal framework for the customary rules to fit in. This systematisation of custom also gave rise to divergent doctrines of Dayabagha and Mitakashara. Both of them claimed to be founded on Smritis. In fact, the two systems correspond to two types of family: "the one resembles a patriarchal family in which the father is the sole master of the estate; the other a joint family where the assets are the collective property of the members. Debate continues on the question which is the more ancient. But any one who places himself in the period when these two systems were worked out cannot doubt that both types of 'family' involved were co-existing; and that Vijnanesvara and Jimuta-Vahana, in succession to others, have simply tried to give structure to them, offering thereby a valid intellectual organisation of their family customs to different social groups (which were, perhaps very dispersed originally)."[15]

Interpretation then made its way from immutable text of Smriti to mobile traditions and customs of the community and facilitated passage from one to other, fixing the latter with the indispensable aid of the former. Interpretors were the real intellectual organisers of

Hindu Law. Even their defects of interpretation worked for a constant renewal of jurisprudence giving it strong foundations in the life of the community with all its multifarious variations, according to time and place.

THE ROLE OF RATIONALISM IN THE EVOLUTION OF ANCIENT INDIAN LAW

Rationalism has a potent influence to mould ancient Indian law from the beginning. People were in the habit of periodically setting their house in order down to the 13th Century. It is only as a result of Muslim contact that Hindu society became static and conservative. As theoretically Smriti or Vedas were considered as the source of law so the whole truth of law was believed to reside in the Vedas. But as a matter of fact Vedas are not legal codes. "Very few among the topics dealt within the Dharmasastra was treated in details in Vedic literature". The very Asram is foreign to Smhita literature and four castes were mentioned only in solitary passage in Rig Veda. . . . laws of debt, pledge, sureties, contract, etc. are hardly over touched upon in Vedas. A question is bound to be raised in case as to why then Sutrakar and Smritikar excel each other in recognising Sruti as the supreme source of authority. The reasons can be given for this Altekar gives the following reasons:

"(1) The supreme authority of the Sruti was a kind of legal fiction like the overriding authority of British Parliament till the beginning of 20th Century. The Parliaments of the colonies like, Canada and Australia had virtually acquired supreme power by the end of 19th Century. . . . The Sutras and Smritis profess to bow down to the authority of the Vedas, even when they were actually departing from the theories enunciated by them".

"(2) The scope of Sruti was widened by including not only the Vedas, but also Brahamanas, the Aranyakas and the Upanisads in them".

"(3) It was further laid down that not only the Vedic Mantras, which lay down definite rules (Vidhis) were to be utilised for tracing authority from Smriti injunctions but inferences were also to be drawn from descriptive passages and stories (arthavada). Early writers like Apastamba were no doubt of the opinion that only mandatory passages (Vidhis) in Vedic literature could be utilised as sources of authority for the Smriti rules, but the Mimansa school of Jaimini advanced the theory that all Vedic texts could be utilised to infer the provisions of the law. Thus the story of Manu dividing his property among his ten Sons, narrated in the Taittiriya-Samhita was utilised to maintain that Vedas recognised the son's right by birth in ancestral property; the same conclusion was drawn from another story narrated in Kathaka-Samhita when we find a father allotting shares in the patrimony to his two quarrelling sons. The story of Naciketas, narrated in the Kathopanisada will attest to the unlimited power of the father over the person of his sons. The reference to the old maiden getting her share from her father's property contained in Rig Veda (II.11.7) will prove that unmarried daughter could get a share from her father's property contained in Rig Veda (II.11.7). While the exhortation in another Rig-Vedic Verse (III.31.2) to the son that he should not give any share to a married sister would show that married daughters got no share in father's property. By recognising *Arth-Vada* as equally authoritative with Vidhi, it thus became possible to trace Vedic authority for a number of Smriti rules and regulations".

"(4) There is no doubt that the Vedic literature was much vaster than what is preserved. . . . . in course of time the later Smriti writers developed the theory that Vedic texts were numerous, that many of them were lost and that no Vedic authority can be found for some Smriti rules, it is because the particular Vedic works in which they were originally enunciated, were lost in later times".

"(5) Kumarila has amplified the point further in a very interesting manner. Vedic authority for a Smriti rule can be given either by quoting actual words of the Sruti text or by giving its gist, when it had been lost. A Smriti rule of the latter category is as valid as the Smriti rule of the former variety. . . ."[16]

From Sutra and Smriti period (C. 200 BC to 500 A.D.) Vedic religion of ritualism waned and the mantras were then not intelligible.

Even to educated people, Vedas were a sealed literature. Very few persons could know the meaning of Mantra and Brahmana. Still Vedas were respected because they were regarded as revealed. The rituals of the Madhuparak or the Sautramani sacrifice were out of the tune of prevailing practices of the new emerging society which suffered a change of belief. The jurist did not intend to give shock to the contemporary society by vetoeing new beliefs and theories. The Smriti-society suffered a change in jural ideas. "Smriti society was gradually veering round to the belief that adoptive son was better than a son born of Levirate; it could not, therefore, be induced to accept the latter one in preference to the former even when quoting the Vedic passage, which clearly disapproves of an adoptive son born of another.[17] Smriti were later canonised as they were considered to be rememberance of traditions of revered and Veda-knowing Rishis. Later on digests came into being and the digest writers profess their view to be based on sacred texts.[18] As they flourished in modern times from C. 800 A.D., they could claim no superhuman authority like Manu and Yajnavalkya, or as being in conflict with the texts of the Srutis and Smritis. They had to profess all along that what they advocated has based not on their personal view but upon the express provisions of the sacred texts.[18] Commentators and digest writers knew changed views of the people. They wanted to legalise the changes which happened in society. They were like *Responsa Prudendum* who worked upon the law laid down in the XII Tables all the time professing to comment upon the law in the XII Tables. All the commentators in India as at Rome, adjusted themselves to the undisputed assumption that the text of the code remained unchanged. The authority of the Smriti texts was Supreme.[19] None of them could avowedly overrule a Sruti or Smriti text. But in fact they 'modified, extended, limited and even overruled the provisions of the Smriti law' like *Responsa Prodendum* in Rome. They further evolved the doctrine of Kaliyuga to perform the negative function of prohibiting certain practices, permissible in Krita, Treta, and Dvapara Yugas. Modern scholars consider digest writers as authoritative. Privy Council pronounced customary practices to be more authoritative. According to the Privy Council a clear proof of usage could outweigh the written text of law. In this way smooth development of law took place without any legislative activity before the British period of India.

SOME RULES OF INTERPRETATION

The first important distinction which Mimansa formulates is between Vidhi and Arthvad. Vidhi incorporates the command of Veda which lateron was equated with the rule of law for purposes of interpretation. It is quite different from arthvada which is the explanatory material e.g. giving reasons, praising Gods and people who follow law or relates facts and other things. This distinction is similar to that between ratio decidendi and obiter dicta in English common law. One the authoritative quality, having legal binding force, the other is only persuasive having no causal relation with the decision because it is only descriptive and is an historical source of law.

The general rule of interpretation of Western common law jurisprudence is that of literal interpretation. According to this rule the statutes should be construed literally in order to ascertain the intention of the legislator. In Indian theory of interpretation, the Vedas are impersonal. Interpretation is not concerned with the relation of words expressed with the idea contained in the mind of the legislator. Here the rule of law has not its origin in the psychology, i.e., the intention of legislator but in metaphysics. It says that there is the eternal relation between words with the reality itself, and their authority need not be doubted. Further, it is said that no part of Veda is without meaning. That means, Veda has to be known and understood by the words used in Veda. From the metaphysical point of view they also prescribe literal interpretation. It is said that "the text of the Veda must be accepted as it is and should be interpreted according to its tenor यथा वचनहि वाचनिकम्.[20] This is enforced by another rule that a far fetched interpretation is only to be allowed when it is supported by authority प्रमाण वन्त्य दृष्टानि सुवहम्यपि .[21] Jaimini considered the literal construction as the most important rule of interpretation but he also makes provision for clear, logical and distinctive rules which permit departure from the literal construction. If the language of a text is clear that unequivocal then such language should be accepted as decisive. When the meaning of a text is not clear, it should be gathered by applying the rule of necessary implication. Logical method should be applied which gives flexibility to words of doubtful import. Accordingly, Mimansa says that when doubt arises about the part of a statement, it has to be resolved by depending upon other parts of the statement. सन्दिग्धेण वाक्य शेषात् (पू.मी.सू.) (91-4-24). According to Maxwell "the true meaning of any passage is that which (being permissible) best harmonises with the subject and every other passage of the Statute''. (Maxwell, 11th Edition, Page 28). Again, ''it is the elementary rule that construction is to be made of all the parts together, and not of one part only by itself''. (Maxwell, 11th Edition, Page 27) Heydon's case permits historical interpretation in English law which has also been called social-purpose-interpretation, in disguise. As a matter of fact, the theory of Kaliyuga, rejecting certain practices as not suitable for the Kali age, because of the decline in the morality of the people, serves as a public policy or social purpose theory of interpretation through negation. Accordingly, the view was that certain rules laid down in the Smrtis have become out of date and should not be followed in the Kali age. Another theory of 'Lok Vivista', i.e., 'intolerable to the public' was also propounded by virtue of which certain texts were said to have no binding force. Yajnavalkya said: 'if one practices that which is abhorred by the public, though it is sanctioned in law, it leads not to heaven; 'similar views were expressed by Manu. Here Indian jurists incline more towards progressive interpretation and for that they have considered reason as their governing principle. The judge is quite free to accept that construction which is supportable solely by the reason of the law. This is more so when the rule of law does not appear to be mandatory. According to Kane, though some of the rules of Mimansa about interpretation of Vedic sayings are similar to those of Maxwell's rules of interpretation of Statutes, yet, he believes that it is not proper to stretch this similarity to a very great extent. These observations were actuated by what Kishorilal Sircar said, during the course of his Tagore Law Lectures in 1909. Sircar equated the Mimansa rules with Maxwell's interpretation of Statutes. It is humbly submitted that such an equation may have been well received at the time when it was made but now, in the present times it is sufficient to assert that the Indian mind was well aware of the need of interpretation and had developed a science of interpretation which was adequate for the purpose and fulfilled the task admirably. Some important rules may be stated, here. . . . without giving into this fruitless controversy we may now state some of the important rules so that we may get a clear idea of the purpose and scheme of interpretation in the ancient times. The science of interpretation starts with a classification of rules into Vidhi and Niyam which as expressed in the English language are what we call mandatory and directory. Vidhi is described as ''a Sastric rule creating a duty of an original nature of which the sanction is absolutely unattainable by senses. A Niyam is a rule making one of the two alternatives obligatory. It is a direction only partially spiritual and is thus only directory".

Mimansa lays down many rules for the interpretation of words which are common to most or the systems of law.

Most important rules in this regard are:

(1) the popular meanings of the words be preferred. Words of Jaimini Sutra and Veda should be understood as far as possible in the sense they have in current usages.
(2) When words can be said to have primary and secondary meanings in relation to some act, they be understood in their primary meanings.
(3) Words should have been contemporary meaning according to the context of time in which they are used.
(4) A word used twice in a sentence should not be taken to have two meanings in that sentence.
(5) Words should have that meaning which is given to them by Vedas (or Sastra) or *Sistas*. When words have many meanings, the usage of the learned and the virtuous Aryas should be followed.
(6) The words of foreign origin which have become current in Sanskrit must be thought to have the meaning they have got in respective foreign languages. Grammar and Sanskrit roots should not be looked into, to know their meaning.
(7) In Veda there are provisions for many actions, but all the actions are not of one kind. Some are primary and others are secondary or auxiliary. The actions which are expressed by words like ' प्रयाज ' which do not embellish any matter they are called primary (प्रधान). But these actions which create some matter or are enabling are secondary or auxiliary.
(8) There is a general rule that singular also means plural. It is called "ग्रहै कत्व न्याय" (पू.मी.सू.) ---- ----- 3-1-13 to 15 .
(9) There is also a rule that in many cases words signifying one gender also include another, i.e., words signifying masculine include feminine.

In Purva Mimansa it is also said that in some matters

attention should be given to the gender and number of words and they should be taken in their proper meanings accordingly.

(10) If the thing declared to be used for oblation is destroyed and the oblation is considered necessary or it has started then its representation can be made by some other object.

(11) There are also rules regarding sentences. There are three main sentences:

(i) When sentences are such that collectively they yield a meaning but not individually, then they should be taken together collectively as a whole.

(ii) If separate sentences can, however, yield meanings separately by themselves, they cannot be connected together.

(iii) In case of certain sentences which are incomplete, suitable words from the context of immediately proceeding sentences are to be supplied.[24]

(12) There is also a rule according to which a special rule prevails over the general and when there is an exception provided to the general rule the exception need be restricted and confined within the strict limits.

(13) The doctrine of *Factum Valet*, which is also a doctrine of interpretation, is given expression by our Mimansakas. The doctrine in Latin tag is worded thus: It means that a thing which ought not to have been done is valid when done. Quod Fieri non Debt, factum valet. In Mimansa it was meant to convey that when a fact is established the fact cannot be altered by hundred texts. This is supported by the views of Jimutvahan to propounder of the Dayabagha School. This doctrine is a principle of Western jurisprudence but it was thus not unknown to Hindu jurists also. In administering law the doctrine has been applied by courts in Vyavahar for textual as well as customary law with all its limitation.[25]

As there were many Smrities written by different persons at different periods there were bound to be conflicting texts. Our Smritikars provided rules also to resolve conflicts between Smrtis and between the texts of the same 'Smriti'. Following rules were deduced for resolving conflicts and for reconciling different texts:

(1) It was an established rule that no conflict should be admitted where it is possible to reconcile two texts. In such a case there is no real conflict, it is an apparent or superfluous conflict.

(2) The apparent conflict was also resolved by the rule of law that the less favoured text was nothing but a statement of fact and did not embody any rule of law.

(3) Where conflict was patent and the texts were irreconcilable the rule was that one has the option to prefer any one of them. But it seems that this rule of interpretation was applied to 'Achara and Prayaschitta' and not to "Vyavahara".

(4) The most satisfactory rule of interpretation was that where there was a conflict between two Smriti texts, preference should be given to one which was in accordance with equity and justice and reason. Yajnavalkya and Narada favoured the application of this rule to Vyavahara also.

(5) Another method of reconciling the conflict was to hold that certain rules in Smritis by virtue of their being disapproved by the people at large have become obsolete and so need not be applied. Narad expressed this rule by saying that, custom is powerful and so over-rides the sacred law. This rule came to be established in Hindu Law during the British period. A rule of Sacred Law can be abrogated by evidence of customs in derogation of it.

(6) The reason for apparent conflict in the Smritis seems to have been on account of confusion created by overlooking the fact that the Smritis at first state the opposite view (Purva Paksh) and then give reason against it and finally in their conclusion, state the principle or rule (Siddhanta). This was also responsible for the opinion that there was more conflict in Smritis, then it really was. The commentators and digest writers could not recognise this to avoid the conflict as they were wedded to the traditional view that every text in Smritis is valid. But when compelled by the necessity, of reconciling the conflict they adopted another mode. They made distinction between Vidhi (injunction), arthvada (explanatory material). This is the rule of the Purva Mimansa and it is also adopted by Jaimini. It was by this technique that commentators and digest

writers tried to avoid inappropriate rules. This was further fortified by another rule of interpretation namely that if a rule was stated with reasons in Smriti then the rule was merely arthavada and if the rule was stated without accompanying reasons then it was Vidhi. Dr. Ganganath Jha explaining the rule says that when an injunction is followed as the statement of a reason this statement of reason has no mandatory force. Certainly, this does not vitiate the mandatory nature of the injunction itself.

(7) The Kalivarjya theory was developed as an interesting instrument to avoid certain conflicts and to hold certain texts as not binding. This theory holds the view that certain rules laid down in the Smritis became obsolete and were to be avoided in Kali age.

(8) Another theory of LOK VIVISTA (intolerable to the public) was also utilised to hold certain texts as not binding. Manu also expressed similar views.

There are also rules of interpretation which are specially applied by the Schools. The Dayabagha also lays down the rule that where no difference is found in Shastras, equility is the rule (समस्याद श्रतत्वद्धि शेषस्या). This rule has been applied in the cases of daughters son, illegitimate sons, and Sudras when there are legitimate daughters etc.

There is also another rule mentioned by Raghunandana in the Udvahatava to the effect that what has been enjoined to be done need not be preformed twice (सक्रत कृते कृत: शास्तार्थ). There is a peculiar rule often made use of by commentators to the effect that when a text forbide an act which ought to be done in a particular way, the permission to do it, in another way, be presumed. Whether an injunction is optimal or not, a commentator may always declare it to be so.

The following hints are given by Dr. Siromony in his valuable book on Hindu Law about finding out the true meaning of the commentator:

(1) If two reasons are given in the same clause for any particular proposition the reason last given is by way of Sadhaka or additional support may be rejected.

(2) When in order to establish any particular proposition several

reasons are given in successive clauses, each successive reason being proceeded by such words, as किञ्च यदा etc. then the reason last given to be accepted as the correct one, in the opinion of the author.

(3) When several alternatives are proposed or propounded, in the same sentence with the word वा (or) it is to be understood that the author does not approve of any them.[26]

In this way one can justify the statement of Colebrooke that logic of Mimansa is the logic of law. It is through this logic, and the dynamic use made by our Smritikars of it that Hindu Law could be made alive to the problems of time and place. By the arduous labour of Commentators and Digest writers, the law was made stable or fixed, yet flexible to incorporate necessary modifications and make allowance for special circumstances. Interpretation kept the whole jural process in gear without the aid of law commissions, legislation and condification. In this way the letter and spirit of the law has been kept alive from the era of Vedas to the era of constitutionalism, inspite of all its erosions.

It is interesting to see how juridical logic was applied in order to solve the ticklish problems of law. The process is not too logical to be static and not too illogical as to bring disharmony and uncertainty in law. It came out as a reliable technique to keep in touch with life and its reality all that which works and perfects within and fluctuates, and manifests outside in social action, thought and behaviour, fills the content of law with its time-geist.

SOME EXAMPLES OF INTERPRETATION[27]

There is vedic maxim of black beans called Masa-Mugda-Nyaya. One text says that black beans and some other cereals are not suitable for sacrifices. The other says that on certain occasions offerings must be made with mugda, i.e., green beans. The question if green beans are not available whether offering be then made of black beans or not? In Jaimini, Sutra the conclusion (Siddhanta) is drawn that as the black beans are forbidden in express words one must not use them even when they are mixed with green beans and even when it becomes difficult to separate the green from the black. By analogical extension when this rule is expressed in juridical form it says that every act contrary to law is forbidden. Similar to the Latin maxim 'contra legam facit qui id facit quod lex prohibet', which means "he breaks the law who does that which the law prohibits. The legal problem which was subsumed by scholars under this rule was–whether co-heir, who kept for himself property which was liable for partition, though he believed that the property belonged exclusively to him, can be considered as an offender or not. According to Jimutavahana of the Dayabagha School, such co-heir cannot be called an offender or thief because he converted to his own use what was partly his own property. Vijnanesvara of the Mitakshara School uses the same maxim of black beans and treats such a co-heir as offender and quoted the verse (IX. 213) of Manu according to which "the eldest son who through greed has robbed his brothers of their property is in no manner their elder brother. He must be deprived of his preferential share and must be penalised by the King. From the same maxim it is concluded that what is not expressly prohibited its permitted. Vachaspati Misra, on this basis, reasons out the issue of rejection of testimony of certain witnesses who have been enumerated by Manu (VIII.118) as those whose testimony should not be accepted. In a case, when it is difficult to get persons who are qualified according to the text to give testimony Vachaspati Misra argues out that those persons can be permitted who have not been expressly disqualified, because, what is not prohibited by law is to be taken as permissible.

The verse of Vasistha (XV. 3), relating to adoption, has given cause to diverse interpretations and all the interpreters have shown the excellence in logic, yet have come to different conclusions. The Verse of Vasistha says: "one should neither receive nor give in adoption on only son for reason of continuing the line of ancestors." It is obvious that the phrase "for to continue the line of ancestors" is only an explanatory clause called arthvada and is not to be considered as a reason for prohibition. This clause only emphasises the importance of the only son. The consequence is that–as has been the view of Vijaneswara, Nand Pandita, and the author of Dattak-Chandrika–prohibition is viewed as absolute. On the other hand, if the clause were taken as a reason or condition then giving such a son in adoption would have been a sin on the part of the father but it would not be invalid.

Similarly, interpretation is called for to make out the meaning of Yajnavalkya's Verse wherein he prescribes the conditions for marriage–that the bride should not be affected by any incurable malady and that she should not be sapinda of her future husband, nor of the same gotra (Patrilineage). According to Vijnaneswara percept prohibiting a girl with an incurable disease has visible motive behind it, i.e., to avoid transmission of diseased to the descendants. Consequently, the clause is not obligatory and is in the nature of a mere advice. To marry a bride infected with incurable disease will not invalidate the marriage. On the other hand, prohibition against marrying a girl who is a *Sapinda* or has the gotra of husband, is not based upon any 'visible motive'. It has spiritual effect and its violation is adharma. Such marriage becomes null and void.

Again, there is a verse 35 of Katyana which says "the King having entered the court, shall look into the cases of the litigants, modestly clothed, with concentrated mind seated facing the East". Vachaspathi Misra had no difficulty in pointing out that to be 'moderately dressed' expressed only visible motive. The aim here is that King should not, by dress, intimidate the litigants. But the direction to be stated facing the East has no visible motive and hence the precept being that of dharma must be taken as obligatory whereas the other is merely directory and optional and its violation is not a sin.

EXAMPLES OF CONFLICTING TEXTS

A verse of Narada (I. 81) says "An object given as a pledge, boundaries (Sima), the property of a child, a deposit, a loan, women, the property of the King, etc. does not cease to belong (to their owners) by being in possession of another. But subsequent verse says "only excepting a woman or the property of the King, 'even (अपि or api) pledges, etc. are lost to their owners when they have been openly in possession of another during twice of ten years".

It is quite clear that we are facing conflicting texts, as regards pledge. In one, the right to it is not lost in the other it goes away by prescription, Vachaspati Misra resolves the conflict by treating the later text as arthavada which only lays emphasis on non-liability of pledge. He interprets the word 'api', i.e., even, and cites an analogical saying of Manu "even drinking poison would be better than to dine in that man's house". The phrase "drinking poison" according to him does not give permission to drink poison. In a similar manner Madhatithi argues that comments on a Verse of Manu (VIII. 35) which says that one may kill even a Brahmin in self-defence. He (Madhatithi) considers the Verse to be only a justification of right of self-defence in general. According to him it means that natural inclination may drive one who is under attack to kill a Brahmin to whom he has no right to touch even. Killing of a non-brahmin, however, in self-defence, is justificable. Nevertheless, killing of a Brahmin is a great sin and unjustifiable.

The Verse of Yajnavalkya (BOOK II-24) also presents the problem of conflict.

The text says that "Of him who sees without objection his land occupied by another, a loss (hani) is undergone with regard to that land at the end of twenty years; if movable asset (Dhana), then ten years are sufficient.

In this reference, according to one group of commentators, like Asahaya, the loss is the loss of the property itself and it happens after twenty or ten years. But Vijnanesvara confronts this Verse with the Verse of Narada which says: "He who enjoyes (the asset of another) without title, even for centuries the lord of the land (i.e., the King) should inflict on that sinner penalty denounced against the thieves": Vijnanesvara is conscious that the Verse of Narad applies only to the tresspasser and not to the case of immemorial possession and only a period of ten or twenty years cannot be called an immemorial possession as such the text applied. The result is that property in the asset does not pass to the owner. In this connection Vijnanesvara interprets the preceding Verse 23, in this connection, which is an exception to the general rule that when two contracts have been entered into successively about the same property, the later in date prevails over the previous one. To this the present Verse may provide as exception saying that if as a result of the second contract "if he to whom the asset was pledged, given or sold in the second instance had actually entered into possession and continued to possess it for ten or twenty years in full knowledge of the first without any protest, on the latter's part, he would win the case. The loss (hani) would fall upon the first lender who had received a pledge, or the first donee or vendee. Vijnanesvara refutes this interpretation. He observes that it is not allowed for one who has already disposed of his asset to dispose of it again."[28]

In this connection, Vijnanesvara refutes another interpretation of Visvarupa on Yajnavalkya II. 26, which is based on the text of Narada (II.71) and says "Of him who shows indifference (Upeksa) or who stays silent (tusnin-bhuta), when the time prescribed (for suit) has elapsed, action is no longer allowed (Vyavahara na Sidhyati).

Here Visvarupa interprets that loss would be the loss of judicial remedy and not of asset or right of property. Devannbhatta, supporting this view, contends that loss is loss of proof in court of human means. The owner can get the issue decided by ordeal. Apararaka also speaks of the right of rightful owner. He further says that it is a sin to disown the owner of his property. Though the person cannot be evicted by judicial remedy yet he should all the same restore it to the owner out of fear of sin.

Again, Vijnanesvara severely criticises this interpretation. According to him Manu's and Narad's intention is not to make the loss of a judicial remedy depend upon the simple passivity of the true owner or a simple default on his part in excercising his right but from the absence of causes which would explain or account for his passivity. When none of these causes seems to exist, as for example, when the true owner is neither a lunatic nor a minor, the possessor can defend an action for ejectment. But afterall, the only problem was one of fact, and if the true owner has arguments to persuade or to establish his rights, there is no reason to hinder his doing that Vijnanesvara recalled that it is the duty of the King when a case is before him to decide according to the merits of the action, without allowing himself to be distracted from that task by Chicanery (chala) Yaj. II. 19)[29]

In view of Vijnanesvara the V. 24 is meant merely to induce the true owner not to be without action or he will suffer loss or 'hani'. The loss here is not the loss of asset but that of produce or profits. Possession for short periods like ten or twenty years cannot give to a person proprietary rights. The text of Yajnavalkya should only be taken as direction to owner not to remain silent and inactive. The true owner has judicial remedy and he can sue for getting the asset but he cannot get the profit or produce. This shows how the interpretors tried to give rational solutions to problems. It may be said that they directed reason to support their own views: "Authors who, like Visvarupa or Aparaka, give possession for ten or twenty years the status of a means of defence analogous to the 'praescriptio longi temporis' of classical Roman law, use arguments which render such a solution perfectly valid. As for those who, taking Verse 24 literally, attribute an acquisitive power to prolonged possession by the tresspasser, their arguments do not fail to support their opinion and to dispose of the texts followed by Vijnanesvara. They hold, for example, with Srikara that Verse 24 only applies when the owner is present, while Verse 27 and analogous texts which provide for possession for three generations, only come into effect if the possessor came into possession while the owner was absent or dwells in another region. As for the Verse of Narada (I. 87) which says that he who enjoys without title even for Centuries should be punished by the King, we could believe, with Raghunandana, that it applies only to possession of an asset belonging to a woman (*Stri-dhana*) or to the King; or even with Sulapani, that this text is a rule of *arthasastra* which cannot prevail against Verse 27 of Yajnavalkya which expresses a rule of dharma; or even, again, with Devan-nabhatta and others, that it applies only when there is no doubt that the possessor has no title to the asset. Finally for others Verse 24 has only an even more limited application. It applies only between co-heirs where one of them has obtained at the partition a portion smaller than that to which he was entitled; or between two possessors in succession equally without title, in which case the first, no matter how long he had possession, was evicted by the second after twenty or ten years of peaceful possession; or even in favour of a possessor whose title was affected by some flaw. Pessession for ten or twenty years without protest on the part of the true owner would thus serve to cover the irregularity in the title, etc.''[30]

Skill of the Indian jurists is again visible when we consider their interpretation of the texts relating to marriage with maternal uncle's daughter or paternal aunt's daughter. In Book IX, Manu holds such marriage as blameworthy and sinful. But this type of marriage is very common in South India. Many prohibits such marriages in the following words:

> ''He who has relation with daughter of the sister (Bhagini) or with the daughter of the sister of his mother, or with (the daughter) of his mother's brother (who is) apta, should observe the lunar penance (candrayana)''. Again, ''A wise man will not take as his wife (any of) these three women; because of Sapindaship one must not marry them, for he who marries one of these falls into hell''.

Some other dharmasastras prohibit such a marriage without any qualification. Majority of interpreters agree with Manu. But Madhva who is a Southerner knows that such marriages were prevalent there since very long and are held desirable, considers such marriages justifiable. By interpretation and reasoning he reaches his desired conclusion. At first he evades the Smriti text by confronting some Vedic passages which, in his judgment, allow such marriages and by applying rules of Mimansa he comes to the conclusion that these passages embody injunction (Vidhi) and are not merely of descriptive nature 'arthvada'. The general rule of interpretation is that when there is a conflict between Sruti and Smriti, the former should prevail over the latter. Madhava would have ended the matter here but his anxiety to respect the authority of Manu goads him further. He says that words 'Bhagini' and 'apta' in Verse 172 for paternal aunt's daughter and mother's sister's daughter are used only when father's sister and mother's sister were married in some inferior form of marriage like gandharva and asura etc. In that case alone daughter of father's sister or of mother's sister can be called 'Bhagini', i.e., sister by the bride-groom. When marriage is in higher form the gotra of girl is changed into the gotra of husband and sapinda relation is broken with her 'natal' family and the word 'bhagini' cannot be then used for her. Similar is the case if mother's brother is married in a higher form of marriage. The daughter of mother's brother then cannot be called 'apta', i.e., a close relation of his sister because the relation of her with natal family has changed and cannot be retained. Thus, the prohibition of Manu cannot be considered as general prohibition as it does not apply in cases of children of Brahma or Daiva marriage. But Madhava argues that as marriage with maternal aunt's daughter has not got the approval of Sistas and is condemned by them at all places, a presumption can be made that there was Vedic injunction reprehending such marriages.

But marriage with maternal uncle's daughter though disapproved by Sistas in North is admitted and practised by the Sistas of South. As it is justifiable according to the principles of Mimansa, validity must be given to it in regions where it is an immemorial custom.[31]

Two things are necessary for a society to win the struggle for existence in view of Walter Bagehot. First is, "that it shall acquire a legal fibre, a *jus strictum*, some set of rules, however, elementary, to give it cohesion and strength. This requirement the Romans satisfied when the law of the XII Tables put into writing, and so made more rigid, the already fixed customary law of the people. The other requirement, the same author says, is that when this has become too rigid and too elementary for its possessor, owing to the increasing complexities of civilised life, some method of escape shall be found, so that what was rigid may become elastic, what was primitive may be levelled up to meet more advanced wants. This means of escape the Romans found to some extent, as will be seen later, in '*interpretatio*' put upon the XII Tables by Pontiffs and the earlier jurists, but infinitely more in the work of the practors, to whom they owned the growth of a second set of legal institutions founded largely, by no means exclusively, upon the *jusgentium* which grew up side by side with and reacted upon the rules of the older civil law''.[32] The dualism of fixity and change was also recognised in Greek Law. The hard rigour of the generality of rule was said to be softened by equity to avoid injustice. It worked to soften the hard contours of law. It is called a 'leadian measure' by Aristotle. Equity thus temporises, tempering the wind to shorn lamb, by individualising the treatment of the particular case in a legal system. The law has to be stable as well as progressive. The undue toughness of common law also created in England a separate legal system called Equity which gave to English legal system flexibility which was missing in the common law. In the field of judge-made law, a common law judge would stick to the doctrine of precedents normally but when justice would demand he is able to depart from it by overruling, distinguishing and disregarding the precedent in the name of authority, justice and reason. The history of law is then a give and take offer between 'consolidation and progress'. One must aspire at certainty in justice, and progressiveness too but these objectives are constantly in conflict, with one another. In case of interpretation in English law, the traditional and literal interpretation together with the doctrine of state-decisis gives stability, certainty and unity to the legal system. But any narrow and strict approach is buttressed by many so-called rules of interpretation all tending to operate restrictively. These may be called, grammatical rules, such as the ejusdom-generies rule, or the rule expressio unius exclusio alterius and various presumptions such as those of restricting the construction of statutes, which interfere with existing rights affecting the liberty of the subject, or which are penal in effect. But although the books are full of instances where such rules have been ostensibly applied, they are very apt to dissolve away like smoke whenever the court feels strongly that another interpretation is to be preferred. In such a case the court may invoke the so-called rule in Heydon's case or the 'mischief' rule, which affords a platform for a broader approach.[33] The common law judges also make by interpretation an enactment workable in practice by filling the gaps left by the legislator as far as interpretation allows it. Interpretation is then a juxtaposition land intermixture of law and life. More than that it represents in its cosmic aspect the 'Lila' or the creative urge or 'Maya' of this universe which is working within and without in every action and event of this world land is its sole explanation. It works by its own Swadha or Sakti, which called for comprehensive philosophy of law as may perform various functions in the life of law. The legal energy must be at work constantly. In conflict-situations its work is that of social engineering, or *Samanvaya* (समन्वय), at unconscious organic level it is 'Volksgeist', as spirit of people or collective consciousness of people. For softening passions, to refine men, it is called Reason; To solve legal problems rightly it is spoken as 'justice'. To hold together men by fastening obligation upon them, it is called 'Dharma'. To threaten, coerce and punish people for violating law, it is called 'Danda'. To work for legal, social and moral under, it manifests as 'Rit'. To perform the function of analysing the language of law it is called 'Mimansa'. Mimansa then is not merely a linguistic or semantic diversion of the juristic mind of the Mimansaka or Commentators or Digest writers or the judges but is an undertaking to keep the whole legal system in gear-a task, which has been done well by the interpreters of the ancient Indian law. The commentators used the rules of interpretation vigorously to solve the legal problems, to bring in new concepts and further the evolution of law. They performed the different task of providing a framework of logic and reason to strengthen the legal system as dharma, to endure for the resist its complete demolition.

Today interpretation in India is torn between rival political ideologies of individualism and collectivism and is suffering the pangs of birth, again after the abortive juridique of preserving 'basic structures'. It is waiting for some wholesome synthesis which has not been so far provided by the legal theory of the West.

Notes and References

1. Some Fundamental Problems in Indian Philosophy–By C. Kunhan Raja, pp. 115-16.
2. *Ibid.*, p. 267.
3. A Critical Survey of Indian Philosophy–By C.D. Sharma, p. 236, Chapter XVII, 1964.
5. Introduction to Indian Philosophy–By Datta and Chatterjee, p. 345.
6. Gosh: Hindu Law. Appendix, p. 858-59.
7. Sources of Hindu Dharma–By A.S. Altekar, 1952, p. 33.

8. Quoted in Gosh's Hindu Law, p. 856.
9. The Classical Law of India–By R. Lingat, p. 143 (Foot Note-1).
10. *Ibid.*, pp. 143-44.
11. *Ibid.*, pp. 148-49.
12. *Ibid.*, pp. 165.
13. *Ibid.*, pp. 166-67.
14. *Ibid.*, pp. 170-71.
15. *Ibid.*, p. 174.
16. Sources of Hindu Dharma, pp. 7 to 9–By Altekar.
17. *Ibid.*, p. 9.
18. *Ibid.*, p. 25.
19. *Ibid.*
20. Gosh, Hindu Law quoted at pp. 856-59.
21. *Ibid.*
24. History of Indian Philosophy–By S.N. Das Gupta, p. 404.
25. Introduction to Modern Hindu Law–By Derrett, pp. 211 to 216.
26. Quoted in Hindu Law by Ghosh, p. 17.
27. Robert Lingat, Classical Law of India, Part II, Chapter I.
    Ibid., pp. 151-56.
28. *Ibid.*, pp. 162-63.
29. *Ibid.*, pp. 165-66.
30. *Ibid.*, p. 166.
31. *Ibid.*, p. 170.
32. Quoted in Leages-Roman Private Law, p. 25 (Second Edn.).
33. Dennis Llyod, Jurisprudence (1st Edition, p. 385).

9

Law and Justice–Dharma and Nyaya-I

In ancient Indian legal theory the concept of 'dharma' (discussed in Chapter 3) was all pervading and brought in its fold not only the duty to be performed by every individual comprising the social groups in those times but was also the ideal of those who were charged with the function of administering justice to the disputing parties. It was, therefore, said that to do justice, nothing but justice, and justice in truth as well as in deed was the 'dharma' of the King. If he failed to perform this duty, it was even permitted by the Sastras to ask such a king to step down from the throne or if he was unwilling to do, he could be dethroned by force. It would thus seem that Dharma, on the one hand is the duty every person, on the other it is the duty of the ruler as well. Not only this but all rules of human action were the rules of dharma; putting it differently, they were the rules of human conduct. It was thus understood that 'dharma' is law, dharma is truth, dharma is justice; it is virtue as opposed to vice; it is rightful conduct as against a wrongful one and a moral act in contradiction to an immoral or amoral one. It would, thus be clear that the ancients had no need to propound any theory or concept of justice, as the Westerners have done for the simple reason that 'dharma' itself was a repository of justice par excellence.

However, as years rolled by, it was because of the emergence of Nyaya and Vaisisika philosophy which developed the science of logic and reasoning that the concept of 'Nyaya' found a place in learned treatises and discussions. To the Nyaya philosopher 'Nyaya' meant a reasoned conclusion, a proved conclusion. Nyaya, literally a judgment, became then, a method of deciding learned disquisitions paying full regard to systematic methods of proof. By analogical extension this method was found fruitful for deciding disputes in courts, where also proof was necessary. It was obvious that when ordeals began to fall into disuse and people began to believe in more rational modes of trial through witnesses and evidence, this theory of proof became indispensable. Thus 'Nyaya', which originally was a logical method of deciding a learned controversy (theory of knowledge), became by extension and application, a method of deciding disputes (theory of justice). Basically 'Nyaya', or the so-called justice, is neither the root nor the fruit of Indian thought and culture but an enquiry about truth or knowledge. Unlike Rit, Dharma, Vrata, Danda, Yajna, Karma the word Nyaya has no theological and metaphysical basis in Vedic literature. Yama, who is the God of justice is called 'Dharma-raj' not Nayaya-raj. The equation of Nyaya with Dharma is only due to the usage of language.

The formulation of the doctrine of justice, and subsuming the total philosophy of life and ideals of socio-political existence under 'justice', is a peculiar characteristic of Western thinking. The debate about 'what is justice'? started in Greek thought, is still going on in the West, but without any conclusion and with so much fatigue that modern or present-day positivistic juristic mind is inclined to reject the concept of justice and is constrained to consider it as something beyond the purview of jurisprudence or theory of law. The fact is that the concept of justice is constituted of diverse elements, like ethical, social, political, logical, psychological, and consequently any method or theory which emphasises the one or some of them by ignoring other or others is bound to be insufficient or incomplete. It seems that by discussing justice writers agree to disagree. This disagreement is the direct result of the attitude of distrust or anxiety developed in the west about the government, State and law. This is nurtured by the growth of materialistic culture, together with the separations of social sciences, conflicts of institutions, declarations and the character of demands of populace against governments, birth of democracies, and resistances, revolts and revolutions of people against monarchical and despotic regimes and colonial powers. In this atmosphere of hope and fear or conceit and cynicism, it is very difficult for the doctrine of justice to reconcile or balance the interests of a socio-political atomistic society wherein individuals and social groups are constantly engaged in scuffles for power, position and privilege. As no sections want to be harmed they claim different kinds of protections against each other at the threshold of 'justice'. Due to this, different kinds of justice have sprung up. Social justice is sought after for the protection of social harm, political justice is seen to protect political harm and the legal one protects against the legal harm.

Inspite of the various denials in the western thought justice cannot keep in tact its frontiers. They are bound to be encroached upon and broken into by incursions, and instruisions of the general current of ideas. Justice must then comprehend the whole theory of social and political existence. If it does so it then approximates Dharma which is a synthesis of various diverse elements of thinking, feeling and willing, of stability and change, etc. But it seems that the Western mind cannot see justice as a whole. It is in the habit of seeing justice particularised, i.e., as a justification of some political or social or economic or moral or some other theory. The Western thinkers have failed to measure the breadth of justice. Even in Greek theory when discussion starts with the perfunctory and general view of justice it is immediately directed to its particularities. It seems that Westerners do not want to see the wholeness or oneness of a concept. Perhaps they cannot do so because they try to unravel the mystery only through reason and do not know that by reason alone one cannot know fundamental concepts like justice. Unlike the Westerners, the Indian mind has the capacity to comprehend the whole wherein it can see the form, content and spirit. Devoid of this view Western notion of justice is only a partial fulfilment of dharma.

It would be my purpose now to examine the theory of justice without which no theory of law could be called complete. This would naturally involve a discussion of the Western concept of justice and assessment of its value and viability in the light of its significance and import in the ancient Indian legal theory. A detailed discussion of the latter will follow, apart from what has been referred to briefly above. Inspite of its indeterminacy of meaning the concept of justice has its value. It is only due to its importance and acceptance, on all hands, as having a beneficial sense that it has acquired lot of interpretation, widening its meaning and import. If we look to the etymology of the word justice or go back to its origin and the root from which it has grown, we find a notion of 'joining' (as in the

Latin jungere or the Greek Zeng nunai) of 'binding', or fitting, or 'tying together'. Justice is thus, in its original notion, the quality or aptitude of joining; it ties together whatever it touches. Primarily, it ties men together, by common bond of right and fitting order of relations, under which each has his position in the order and receives his due place–(Suum cuique); each has his rights as his share of the general right pervading and constituting the order; and each owns jura as the examplification and concrete expression in his own case of the general jus.[1] It is just like 'dharma' which has its root meaning in 'holding together' and Rit which has its root in 'binding'. From this idea of aportionment of just or right starts a 'subjective feeling and consequent desire for a fitting order' and Justinian defines it accordingly. His institutes emphasise three aspects of justice:(1) jus as an objective expression of right which is recognised and enforced by rules, (2) living upto one's position, (3) actually and positively respecting another's position and rights.

Justice, then performs the function of 'joining' and fitting together. But there is also a further extension. Justice is joining or fitting together, not only of persons but also of principles. It joins and knits together and claims of the principles of liberty with those of the principles of equality, and both with those of the principle of fraternity or co-operation; it adjusts them to one another in a right order of their relations.[2] Again it reconciles conflicts or joins together not only different principles but also conflicts within the area of a single principle itself. Justice has been called a term of synthesis. "It is the final principle which controls the general distribution or rights and various principles of their distribution". The theory as a balancing of interests in all its purity devoid of standard or measurement is presented by Roscoe Pound who calls it functional justice and emphasises impartiality minus ideology.

It is for this reason that justice is represented as the holder of balance and the visual representation of the personified figure of justice accordingly shows here with a balance in her hand and with eyes blindfolded as a sign of her impartiality.[3]

JUSTICE AS AN IDEAL

If justice is considered as the fulfilment of positive law with all its provisions and procedures it cannot be put forward as a standard. In its ethical meaning justice is considered not in its narrow meaning of legal justice but as some thing which is good in itself. It is then identified with the ideal of human good. It is seen as an instrument of good life. Legal activities can be evaluated by the standard of good life. Law then becomes a means of procuring good life. In this sense justice is just like Dharma. Though there can be some difficulty in determination of the nature of the good life and right method to ensure it yet there is no difficulty in realising that justice is the realisation of good through law and the ideal is accepted on all hands.

But when justice is expressed in terms of any other ancillary ideal, it becomes only a partial fulfilment of life and controversy starts then it ceases to be a 'total good' and 'ought of life'.

In Conclusive Debate about What is Justice

Every theology, philosophy and political or social ideology had speculations about justice. The idea of justice in the Holy Christian scriptures is a transcendental one. Justice is not known through reason. It is one of the mysteries of faith. There are two elements of justice which are found in scriptures and are in opposition to one another. One is the doctrine of retribution which is presented as justice in old testament and another is the doctrine of love which is the avowed doctrine of the new testament and is propogated by Jesus Christ. There is also the difference of approach between Christs and his disciples. Christ's doctrine of justice is denial of recognition to the authority of positive law and state. Whereas Paul recognises such authority. According to Paul, "there is relative, human, justice, which is identical with the positive law, and an absolute, divine justice which is in secret of faith".[4]

In the philosophy of Plato the doctrine of justice holds a very important place. Plato identifies justice with retribution, as retribution is instrumental for attainment of 'good'. The idea of justice derives the whole of its value from the idea of good. But when it is to be determined what is good, the dialogues of the Plato are of no help as he does not discuss but resorts to myth. As such the secret of justice cannot be disclosed, not even in the laws of the best law-givers.[5] In one word it is a divine mystery. For practical purposes Plato considers justice as the proper performance of one's functions. It is expression of harmony. Aristotle takes happiness as the starting point of his ethics. To him happiness is the supreme good. Justice in its general sense is righteousness. In his contemplation happiness is the consequence or reward for virtue but is not identical with it. At first, he rejects virtue as the end of life. But yet according to him, transformation of happiness into virtue can take place by the reason of right performance of activity and one's own function. Then good is happiness and happiness become virtue later in evolution of his doctrine. With some contradictions the moral good is humanised and putforth as a virtue of man. Again virtue is conceived of as a mean between two extremes. He gives the doctrine of golden mean. Accordingly, justice is also the observation of the mean. "Aristotle distinguishes, at first, between two kinds of justice, one is general justice and the other is particular justice".[6] According to him, there are two concepts of justice–lawfulness and equality. The term 'unjust' held to apply both to man who breaks the law and the man who takes more than his due. Hence, it is clear that both the law-abiding and the fair-minded will be just. 'The just', therefore, means that which is lawful and that which is equal or fair, and 'the unjust' means that which is illegal and that which is unequal or unfair.[7] According to Aristotle lawfulness is a broader concept, whereas equality is a narrower one. Every unlawful act is not unequal act but everything which is unfair is unlawful. As a result of this, justice includes whole of lawfulness. It is also whole of virtue, i.e., perfect virtue. By lawfulness Aristotle means conformity to positive law. To him the law-breaker is unjust while the law-abiding is just. Particular justice can divided by him as distributive and corrective. He introduces here the principle of proportional equality. While distributing things like honours, offices, etc., the State was to look to the difference in individuals as it could not be just to treat unequals as equals. In his book 'Nichomachean Ethics', the standard he sets for distributive justice is merit. In democracy, he says, all freemen are considered equal, in an obligarchy, the consideration is made on 'the basis of wealth and nobility of birth', and aristocracy, virtue is taken as measurement of distribution. Corrective justice is concerned with restoration of equality which has arisen due to violation of law. It has application to transactions, like that of selling, lending, etc., which are called voluntary, and cases of fraud and theft which are involuntary transactions, these may also be the cases of criminal wrongs but Aristotle treats them as civil wrongs. In these cases the aim of the judge, according to Aristotle, is not to punish but to give redress. In cases of offences against state (and not against individuals), Aristotle calls for the application of the principle of general justice. Here the principle is that of arithmetical proportion. It makes no difference whether a good man defrauds a bad man or a bad man a good one.

The law looks only to the difference created by the injury, the parties themselves being treated as equal.[8] Aristotle points out a third kind of justice which he calls as 'commutative' justice. This kind governs the exchange of commodities and takes into consideration as its measure the skill of the parties and corresponding value of their products.

Aristole's formula of distributive justice is open to criticism in many ways. He says that if rights are allotted and if two individuals are equal, equal rights shall be allotted to them. According to this formula a capitalistic as well as a communistic legal order is just, and a legal order which confers political rights only to men who have a certain income, or who belong to a certain race, or are of noble birth is as just as a legal order which confers the same rights to all human beings who are of certain age without regard to other differences. Any privilege whatever, is covered by this formula. When a legal order reserves all possible rights to one single individual (the ruler) and assigns only duties to all others (the ruled), such a legal order too is just, since the difference between the ruler and the ruled is considered to be decisive, so that the ruled cannot be considered as equal to the ruler.[9] This concept of justice as distributive, for obvious reasons, has failed to find favour. Likewise, Aristotle cannot solve the riddle of corrective justice, i.e., in what way or in what proportion lies the correction of wrong by punishment. His formula "To each his own", is too verbal and tautological to be of any service for rational determination of the equation. It seems that Aristotle himself was dissatisfied with this formula of justice. In Book VII, of his Ethics, he inclines more towards friendship when he says "Friendship appears to be the bond of the state; and law-givers seem to set more store by it then they do by justice; . . . And if men are friends there is no need of justice between them; whereas merely to be just is not enough; a feeling of friendship also is necessary".[10] Concord, i.e., peace, rather than justice according to such observation seem to be the end of the State. Justice is identified in his 'Politics' as the function of the State. For the law is the order of the political community; where the law determines what is just. It comes to this that justice is lawfulness, and if justice is the function of equality, then justice is only equality before law. It seems that justice cannot be defined by rationalistic or moral philosophy. Augustine puts an end to the rational argument when he considers that justice is christianity and injustice is paganism.

Natural Law Theory of Justice

Natural law theory is also a theory of justice because it considers what is right and wrong in relations between men, in society. According to this view all the natural processes are directed towards some end and they are determined by final causes. Nature is seen pervaded with will and intelligence. This is a teleological view. This implies that nature is a kind of superhuman personal being; an authority to which man owes obedience. At the lowest stage of human civilisation this interpretation is called animism. It is a social interpretation of nature, for primitive man considers nature to be a part of society. Since the spirits of souls animating the natural phenomena are believed to be very powerful and able to do harm as well as good they must be worshipped. Animism is consequently a religious interpretation of nature. At a higher stage of religious evolution when animism is replaced by monotheism, nature is conceived of as having been created by God and is, therefore, regarded as manifestation of His all powerful and just will. If the natural law doctrine is consistent, it must assume a religious character. It can deduce from nature 'just' rules of behaviour only because and so far as nature is conceived of as a revelation of God's will. As a matter of fact, there is no natural law doctrine of any importance which has not a more or less religious character.[11] Natural law theory considers that value is immanent in reality and that value is absolute in character. On this presupposition the doctrine of natural law asserts that law can be deduced from nature and that law is absolute justice. It identifies laws of nature with rules of law in human society. Nature is considered here as a just social order. Nature (like that of primitive animism) is conceived of as a part of society. Natural law creates dualism between natural and positive law and considers that positive law must be subject to law of nature. If positive law is considered unjust, natural law entitles the individual to offer resistance and violate that unjust law. This is another way in which natural law asserts a theory of justice. On the issue, whether private property is just or not, all natural law theories, from Grotius to Kant, support the right of private property. This view seems somewhat surprising when we see that in Holy scriptures as interpreted by the Church enjoin and ordain that God gave all things to men in common. But man through sin and greed, brought private property into existence. Accordingly, natural law is considered as one of the powerful opponents of communism. But natural law doctrine, with specific methods, has disappointed them in this regard. Natural law doctrine is also used to abolish private property which is adjudged against nature and a source of all ills. Morelly, Fourier, etc. consider private property as a monstrous division of products of nature, a universal pestilence and something against wise intentions of nature and God. As a matter of fact natural law satisfied the deeply felt need of human mind–the need for justification. This is also the essential trend of Sociology and Philosophy of history, as developed in the Nineteenth Century. Although these two disciplines are directly opposed to natural law doctrine, they apply the same method and run into the same fallacy as the doctrine they intend to replace–they try to infer 'ought' from 'is'.[12] Auguste Comte and Herbert Spencer who are leading Nineteenth Century Sociologists develop their theories on the assumption that like natural phenomena social life is determined by causal laws. These writers evince a reformative trend of thought and begin to see romantic vision of the future where there will be no idea of rights and people will work on the principle of duty, erasing the distinction between private and public functions with complete socialisation or nationalisation of human life.

Hegel and Marx, the outstanding representative philosophers of the last Century incorporate the technique of natural law in their theories. The idea of teleological universe govern Hegel's philosophy of history which shows that reason is the spirit of the world, which is gradually enfolding with the march of time. To him, 'reason' includes morality, and the laws which are expressions of this world spirit as personification of Reason. Real is rational and rational is real. Man's deeds and acts are expressions of this world-spirit which is gradually progressing towards perfection. To Kelsen, "it is hardly possible to distinguish the will of the world-spirit from the will of God," because he says that "the history of the world is not intelligible apart from a Government of the world. Hegel's so-called philosophy of history is the myth of the world-spirit; it is not a philosophy, but a theology of history".[13] Marx employs the dialectical method of Hegel's, and to him also, evolution works by means of contradiction but instead of spiritualism he turns to materialism. Marx, on the basis of his economic interpretation of history and dialectics of the process of development, prophesies not only the end of capitalism but extinction or withering away of state and the end of private property and the dawn of the just order of society. Natural law philosophy has given us these two contradictory doctrines of justice which are from every point of view, untrustworthy. Looked at from the point of view of these being a quest for truth in a scientific way, they are too Utopian and idealistic to be true. From the point of view these doctrines being concerned with politics, they are lies because they (followers of these doctrines) do not practise what they preach.

The dynamic-theory of natural law represented by John Wild and others is founded on the belief that a universal pattern of action, applicable to men every where, requires its completion. This theory claims to be empirical as it derives its principles from observation of experienced facts. The facts are tendencies inherent in reality or existence itself. Finite existence requires completion and has a tendency towards fulfilment. Here, value and existence are merged into one another. The fundamental norm is that human life ought to be lived. In other words, the life of every human being ought to be preserved and promoted. The life of a human being is considered as the highest value. But this norm is not proved to have been recognised by legal systems in the past and is also belittled in the present times for we know that we are still to assess the worth and significance of human life.

Natural law doctrine, as doctrine of justice, is an expression of law as: 'ought to be' or 'just law' or 'good law'. But it puts forth generally only a formal ideal. It cannot convincingly provide any material standards for knowing what is just. Classical Natural Law doctrine introduces two elements of just law. One is that of 'value' and the other is that of 'universality'. But these have not proved to be very helpful for the determination of what is just law. Universality, as a theory of valid, law is now a lost hope in face of increasing growth of diverse systems of positive law, based upon differences of cultural developments and environmental conditions, together with socio-political and economic considerations of its administration and enforcement. Again, the assertion of universal principles, based on reason, are not true guides for consideration of the problems of law.

Natural law, by fusing universality and value has also given birth to the doctrine of natural rights. It gives reason to the owner of 'natural rights' to defend these rights against the interference of law and State. On analysis this theory of 'natural rights' also proves inadequate. With its foundation in natural human tendencies, these natural rights are frequently conflicting and are 'not competent courts of last appeal' as they are not capable of precise formulation and application. They provide for the protection of known evils and do not work for manifest good goals. Natural law, as the ideal of justice, is only a formal standard and cannot be of any practical use for bringing social justice and social order as it claims, because it does not give answer to what is social justice and how will it be brought about. It is quite clear that there cannot be a priori determination of social justice and the ways of its realisation. According to Saleilles, answers to all these questions, "depend upon certain social facts with which law comes in contact. These facts change, evolve and are transformed. But that depends, in turn, upon conceptions one forms as to justice and order as to authority and liberty, as to right of the community, and the rights of individuals, as to the proportion to be established in the incessant strife between these opposing forces and this proportion varies and alternates".[14] Natural rights only point to the abstract conditions of social welfare. They need to be revised and reinterpreted constantly to make them suitable to diverse circumstances. As a result of the realisation of this requirement, Natural Law itself has acquired a name in modern times as "Natural Law with variable content". It has become how relative to time and place and in a way it has diluted its force. The concept of natural rights obliterates the distinction between legal rights and moral rights; is and ought; and wish and power; Natural Law represents ideal of justice without awareness of practical needs and possibilities. It fails as a complete theory of justice.

Similarly, liberty as an ideal of justice fails to convince one with all its ferver because of its ambiguity of meaning. In one sense, it professes an unbridled freedom which is dangerous and foolish; in another sense liberty grants freedom but with restraints, in such measure as may be necessary for happy and peaceful existence. Yet the important problem still remains unsolved. How to determine the quantum of restraints and freedom? It is obvious that for a good life of a citizen there must be a mean between political or legislative despotism and regimented freedom of anarchy. The ambiguity arises from the fact that the ratio between freedom and restraint cannot be determined for all times to come. The advocates of 'liberty' not only demand more freedom but also, many a time persist in claiming freedom for its own sake. Little do they realize that unqualified freedom cannot serve as an ideal of justice. Freedom by itself is not an adequate ideal unless it is put as freedom to do or enjoy good things. Without this moral element present in it the doctrine of liberty cannot become the doctrine of justice. As this moral part cannot be logically derived from liberty, justice cannot be identified with liberty.

There is one more view of justice which refuses to be assessed by any formula or definition. It is a kind of instinct which, without appealing to the reasoning mind, goes of its own accord straight to the best solution, the one most conformable to the aim of all judicial organisation. In fact, we know that there is no such sentiment in human soul if at all such a sentiment is to be cognized, it is necessarily a mixture of moral doctrine resulting in a moral sentiment. This complex of moral belief is as open to criticism as the belief or doctrines of which it is a composite. To identify such a sentiment with justice is only ones own admission of moral ignorance.[15]

The utilitarian standard of justice is general happiness. The clearest formulations of this view is found in Sidgwick. According to him the main idea of justice is "that society is rightly ordered, and, therefore, just, when its major institutions are arranged so as to achieve the greatest net balance of satisfaction summed over all the individuals belonging to it".[16] Social justice, in this context, is looked upon as a principle of rational prudence applied to an aggregative conception of the welfare of the group. The technique of utilitarian theory of justice is to subsume the concept of right under that of good. Like a teleological theory first it defines good independently of right in terms of happiness and then uses 'right' as right ordering of happiness and for balancing pains and pleasures, i.e., to workout a scheme of net balance of pleasure over pains. According to John Rawls the principle of utility defines good as satisfaction of rational desire and social co-operation is directed to achieve greatest satisfaction of rational desire of individuals. It does not matter directly how one man distributes his satisfaction as long as it gives him maximum fulfilment. Rights, duties, opportunities, privileges, forms of property and wealth, etc. are only measured in this light and no scheme of distribution is treated as valid and right by itself, but is so only in relation to the standard of happiness and as such liable to be changed according to its effect upon the net balance of happiness.

The whole logic of utilitarianism flourishes on the principle of 'rational choice of man to be happy'. Once this position is reached the same man is assumed to become impartial spectator to witness the co-relation of his happiness with the happiness of others. He even extends his goodwill or sympathy to the happiness of others when he finds that this would not unduly minimise his own happiness. Again if he is a legislator, as an impartial observer, viewing happiness from the point of view of the individual, he can direct legislation in such a way that in result it provides maximum quantum of happiness to the maximum number of people.

The nature of the decision made by the ideal legislator is not, therefore, materially different from that of an entrepreneur deciding how to maximise his profit by producing this or that commodity, or that of consumer deciding how to maximise his satisfaction by the purchase of this or that collection of goods. In each case there is a single person whose system of desires determines the best allocation of limited means. The correct decision is essentially a question of efficient administration. The view of social co-operation is the consequence of extending to society the principle of choice for one man, and then, to make this extention work, conflating all persons into one through the imaginative sets of the impartial sympathetic spectator''.[17]

Happiness is the net balance of majority of individual's pleasure over pain. But as to the problem how to distribute pains and pleasures, and what are the justifications for expected pleasures from things which individuals call rights, the utilitarian doctrine resorts to the criterion of merit or desert as the measurement of justice. Again, happiness is an uncertain, variable and subjective feeling and more of an incidental outcome or by product of man's activity. However, it is apparent the adjustment of good and evil is not an easy task. But in the utilitarian doctrine justice is connected with the problems of balance and adjustment which is still more difficult. Not only this the balancing and adjusting of subjective conditions of well being like love, truth, or beauty, though problems of distributive justice may arise and thus we may be led again to square A.

By this reasoning justice has to protect the elementary good in such a way that it provides the conditions for the higher or subtler values. Both Mill and Sidgwick consider that over the above equality and impartiality the notion of 'requital of desert', i.e., good for good and evil for evil is required, but both are not clear on this point. Later moralists and some of the utilitarians and intutionists, reject the theory that there is duty to reward the virtue and punish the vice. David Ross considers the principle of desert relevant only so far as it is helpful in fulfilling the task of producing as much a combination of moral worth and happiness as we can by its use. Rashdall also prefers a combination of virtue and happiness and not happiness alone as a result of the principle of retribution. It seems that principle of retribution has no great relation to the task of human justice, though some times it may seem that it is necessary for making the offender to realise the degree of moral condemnation that his conduct has evoked and thus to motivate him to amend himself. In case of adult offenders and hardened criminals we cannot think that it is effective. Whatever be the appeal of the notion of merit to common man, it cannot be justified to be the basis of justice. Looking to the functions and administration of justice, the doctrine of moral tit-for-tat works as self-deception and fails to bear fruit of justice when the aim is to create a net balance of good over evil.

There is also another view called pragmatic doctrine of justice which, instead of the elusive and of happiness, prefers the more concrete one, as satisfaction of as many desires of human beings by balancing their interests without friction and waste or with least friction and waste. The problem of harmonising the satisfaction of desires and wants is put forth as an urgent need. This is the doctrine of Roscoe Pound who rejects the necessity for any standard or ideology to harmonise the satisfaction of wants and balancing of interests. Justice then becomes ordering of human relations and balancing of interests. To E. Barker this "seems to reduce justice to a mere *de facto* balance of different social wants, controlled by no criterion, but attained by the registration of any actual equilibrium which the clash of equally valuable wants has attained for itself at any given time. It would justify a balance in which the wants of one particular types, if it were the most powerful or the most numerous or both had tilted the scale. It leaves us accordingly with a pragmatic justice of the fait accompli, destitute of foundation or reference."[18] Justice is seen here in its literal meaning of pure balancing adjusting, and ordering. It fails to be conceptualised and understood and seems more of a reaction against different ideologies of justice.

We have already adverted to the Scandinavian realists who are against metaphysics and ethics and who thus hold that there can be no science of values or theory of justice. Lundsted dismisses all that cannot be proved as a fact. All traditional concepts of jurisprudence are to him mere emotive reactions or mirage of language. He rejects completely legal ideologies or the speculation about justice. Hence all those, who looked to the material objectives of law and common sense or feelings of justice, to fill in the gaps in a legal systems are accused of metaphysical non-sense. Lundstedt holds that any attempt to develop law on the basis of the common sense of justice is to assume that natural justice represents a kind "material law".

This he dismisses as non-existent metaphysical construction.[19] To him those who incline towards natural law or justice to gain an objective valuation of law are misled by their subjectivity because all values are subjective to one's own feelings and emotions and as such are incapable of having any scientific objectivity. He considers that even the theory of balancing of interests of the sociological positivists is based upon a faith in natural justice and, therefore, he rejects it as lacking in legal reality. He argues that if a particular act is evaluated by a norm of 'value', it is bound to be subjective and must uncontrollably differ from man to man. In such a case, Lundstedt asserts that there can be no objective science of justice and for this reason he holds that even rights, obligations, relationships, etc. are all unreal. Therefore, in despair, he concludes by saying that legal activities are indispensable for life. It is in this context that he prefers execution of insane Killers or Sexual offenders to the preservation of the lives of such delinquents to ensure social security. He further maintains that to base law on commonsense of justice is same as putting the cart before the horse. "Without the 'rules' of law actually maintained the commonsense of justice would lose precisely the points of support which are absolutely necessary for the indispensable role which it plays in the social organisation in the legal machinery".[20] If legal machinery stopped functioning, the feeling of justice would lose all bearing and control and the social structure would be fully disorganised. He is not prepared to accept the oft-applied dictum to go beyond the law or to go contrary to law by means of equity or natural justice as he holds this to be purely imaginative.[21] Thus in the absence of comprehensive legal theory* the concept of justice has reached its vanishing point in the materialistic and positivistic western legal theory, due to Scandinavian realism.

The modern value-relativism which is also a reaction against absolute principles of justice does not go to this extent but considers that the validity of principles of justice is not verifiable by science. Human ideas about justice, as revealed by scientific method, reveal a great deal regarding the way our mind and our emotions operate in matters of justice. First of all we have to observe that postulates of justice are generally expressed in terms of some desired state of affairs, for instance, whether equality, or 'more' equality would be established, or liberty, or more liberty, or security and order, or obedience to

* The ethical approach called natural law has become unpopular because of its destructive role in politics.

God's will, or all of these are so established. "Ideas of justice, in other words, seem to express an urge for an ad- "just"-ment to some ideal state of affairs that is considered a "Just" one or "More Just" but can be described without using the concept of justice."[22] According to value-relativism there are two distinct levels in thinking about ideas of justice. "Either our thinking moves strictly within the institutions of our present status of civilisation,–this may be called the "traditional" idea (feeling, sense) of justice; or it may transcend the traditional institutions–then we speak of the "transtraditional idea (feeling, sense) of Justice".[23]

The traditional idea considers and recongise the institutions e.g. Monogamy, family, status of parents and children, private property, inheritance, contract, etc. These institutions are taken for granted. As these institutions are established by positive law the traditional idea is a positivistic one. The positivist accepts such institutions; he uses them for the basis of logical reasoning and draws conclusions, accepts laws, and regulations meant for expediency and certainty; and argues against abuses. When there is a clash between the two principles or two institutions of law and contradictory implications are reached by logic, the traditional sense of justice fails.

Transtraditional idea of justice detaches one from traditional institutions in different degrees and makes him to criticise these institutions on the basis of the principles of justice taken from outside the legal systems. The standard is not related to objective factors as offered by traditional institutions but is subjective – i.e. relative to one's personal conviction or creed about what is the most valuable state of affairs or goal or what is the way to realise improved conditions of life. There are various standards which have been set by different writers which intermingle and overlap. Arnold Brecht has pointed out important standards as a result of which the jurist appears as a believer of one or more than one of them. The ideal types are - (1) Equalitarian, (2) Liberatarian, (3) Revelationist, (4) Conservative or Traditionalist, (5) Authoritarian, believing in leadership principle, (6) Majority Worshipper, (7) Hedonist, (8) Group Worshipper, (9) Harmonizer, (10) Pyramid builder believing in aesthetic values of works of art, (11) Man of duty, (12) Peace and order fanatic, upon these top values the most of the concepts of justice in the 20th Century are founded.

Scientific value-relativism considers that values cannot be proved by science. It also considers that man cannot do without values. Certain values have become part and parcel of human thinking. Though science cannot prove or disprove the values chosen by people, it can help in analysing them and show how far these are related to well-known human purposes. It cannot established what goals are valuable but it can draw our attention to such goals which may involve risks and dangers. It can show what conflicts arise while we pursue such goals, what means can be chosen to pursue these goals and how these goals and purposes influence men's minds.

This science of value-relativism refuses to pronounce judgments on moral values for the simple reasons that if finds it difficult to bridge or fill the logical gap between "is" and "ought". Values, according to it, can neither be proved nor disproved by means of facts. Since values are certain beliefs or attitudes of mind or opinions or convictions and are observable, they may motivate an individual or group to act in a particular manner or to hold certain ideologies.

Inspite of all the limitations of this scientific method a tentative list of universal postulates of justice has been put forward as follows :

(1) *Truth* : In the objectives sense (as when we speak of an objectively just action), justice demands an accord with truth: that is, all relevant statements on facts and relations must be objectively true. In the subjective sense (as when we speak of just person), it demands an accord with what is thought to be true; that is, the acting or judging person must honestly think (believe) that the relevant statements are true....

(2) It is unjust to select arbitrarily different systems of values in considering one case and another.

(3) It is unjust to discriminate arbitrarily among equal cases. Here "arbitrarily" means that which is in contradiction to the accepted system.

(4) It is unjust to restrict freedom arbitrarily, i.e., what is contrary to the accepted system.

(5) It is unjust to inflict punishment or moral reproach for non-fulfilment of a law or a command which is impossible of fulfilment.

The first and the fifth postulates, viz., truth and impossibility are independent of any particular system of values.

In setting forth these five postulates, Brecht means to say that

"Justice demands a conformance with all of them. Any law, action or judgment anywhere can be branded as unjust, in an international and interdenominational language, if it violates any of the five. It can be branded as 'objectively' unjust if it actually violates them, and as 'subjectively' unjust if the law maker, acting as agent, or judge knows that he violates them".[24]

By summing up these postulates we would obtain a minimum definition of justice......

If for a moment we look to the Indian juristic scene of to-day, we witness a strange conglomeration of ideas which are neither Western in the strict sense of the term, nor are they oriental. We are faced with a hybrid culture and consequent hybrid juristic system. Having gone through this hotch-potch of legal philosophy during all these centuries, the Indian mind is still clinging though precariously to metaphysical reality, firstly because it has actually experience the unity of existence in its spiritual experiences. This has been manifested through the lives of Indian seers and sages who obliterated the distinction between subject and object. Secondly, in India, unlike as in the West metaphysical principles have not been exploited to suit political ideologies of revolution or depotism. Naturally we are not yet scared of these principles. Thirdly, the popularity and progress of science which has resulted in almost a craze for material advancement in the West has not been able to solve all the problems of life because of the sole emphasis on exploration of matter. This is an ample and irrefutable testimony of the indispensability and inseparability of spiritual aspect of law from the general theory of law. The truth of the above statement, this humble author feels, was completely appreciated and realized by the ancients and the general happiness and peace which reigned in those times is an eloquent testimony of it.

The Functional Role of Justice Through the Centuries

According to Ginsberg the core of justice, when expressed in negative terms, is exclusion of arbitrariness and more particularly exclusion of arbitrary power. This is carried forward by the doctrine of rule of law when it stipulates that no one can be a judge in his own cause. Secondly, it implies that methods are to be provided for settling disputes without the use of force by the concerned parties or litigants. Thirdly, it means that the coercive powers which the law must necessarily have at its command are not unlimited. Those who make the law are also subject to it. The theory of justice, to a very great extent, has been a movement of protest against the law's delays, against arbitrary application of law, and against the inequity of the laws themselves''.[25]

Justice, as impartiality was recognised in Ancient Egypt and in the land of early Hebrews and is expressed in the injunctions given to judges to administer the law impartially. From these beginnings the line of development of justice can be further traced. First, it is recognised that laws which were judging people equally may themselves be unequal. Law then begins to be changed to remove arbitrary discrimination like that of race, colour, religion, and sex, as far as possible. Thereafter, the notion of impartiality is extended to wider range of legal relations and rights and duties. There is seen a movement from equality in political rights towards equalisation of social and political rights. In ancient Rome equity is equivalent to equality in Aequitas is Aequilitas together with this is the realisation of 'fair exchange' of services as just, on the basis of fairness and social responsibility, for ensuring to the parties at least minimum conditions of physical and mental well being. Thirdly, the notion of justice may be viewed as applicable in relation between states. States are, to put it mildly, expected not to be judges in their own cause, and should not resort to force to settle their grievances. It is also realised that control and distribution of world-resources should be done with justice and the creation of modern economic organisation, is a step towards this realisation. Finally, ''in Western civilisation there are deliberate efforts to define the limits of coercion, to mark out spheres which should be left to the free choice of individuals, for example, the spheres of thought and its expression, religious belief and worship. In all these ways the notion of justice according to law is gradually pervaded by the notion of justice in the law''.[26] Once we have recognised exclusion of arbitrary inequalities we see a necessary direction towards justice. We also look to the exclusion of arbitrary power of one man over another. ''Justice has, therefore, been mainly concerned with the control of agression and of domination made possible by natural, inequalities or by inequalities generated by institutions''.[27] Again the most obvious ways of assuring this is to entrust coercive power to a legitimate authority – the state – and to prohibit its use by individuals. ''In the free societies the most important principles that have emerged are, the division of powers designed to avoid over-concentration, and the principle that the power of the state are derived from the people acting through law and that law itself is subject to limitations. These limitations may be embodied in the constitution in the form of fundamental rights, or they may be 'extra-legal', as is the case in Britain, where the theoretically unlimited legislative powers of Parliament are in practice limited by the freedom of the press and of association and assembly and the habit of responsible government under the party system. These limitations are not purely formal. They rest on the assumption of fundamental rights, and the problem of their validity leads back to the more general problem of the basis of moral rights and duties."[28]

The exclusion of arbitrariness grows gradually also in the sphere of criminal law. The historical development in this regard can be traced according to the principal of justice: (1) At first, early law does not give equal protection, certain groups, like slaves, and serfs, were not having the equal protection of law. The protection which was granted to great nobles and high officials was greater than that extended to poor masses; (2) Punishments were also unequal and varied according to the gradations in social ranks; (3) In authoritarian states the methods of criminal justice were liable to be arbitrary and oppressive. Gradually and slowly the "rational procedure by evidence and argument replaces trial by ordeal, combat, or compurgation. Finally, the conception of punishment is humanised, greater stress being laid on the prevention of crime and rehabilitation of the criminal than on retribution. The advance in all these directions is by no means in a straight line, and there are periods of retrogression, yet on the theoretical side, at any rate, it is unmistakable".[29] In modern times the principle of distributive justice of Aristotle has its use for equitable distribution of means of physical and mental well-being in a 'highly differentiated and, large scale society'. The problem of dealing with payment of services should also be dealt within the principle of distributive justice. The principle of distributive justice which has its administration in proportion to merit to relevant resemblances and differences and what is relevant or not is to depend upon the particular right which is under consideration. "For example, in the case of economic rights, differences in need are relevant, including the conditions necessary for the performance of specific functions and the more general conditions of well-being; in the case of educational rights differences in capacity or interest are relevant; in the case of electoral rights and principle of 'one man, one vote' is adopted in the interest of securing participation by all and in the absence of any agreed method of estimating differences of political capacity. In general, the criteria of relevance adopted by a society vary with the moral outlook prevalent in it and are thus a good index of the level of moral development attained by it''.[30] What differences and resemblances are material for attaining the conditions of well-being, is difficult to decide when we want to allocate economic rights and duties but there is a general agreement that ''gross inequalities are unjust, and the right to minimum conditions of well-being is now widely recognised. But there is no agreement as to the distribution of property or the reward of service as above the minimum. Differences in need, ability, productivity, or effort have been put forward as relevant. But apart from difficulties of measurement, none of these is free from objection on ethical grounds. It is arguable, however, that as judged by any of these criteria the wide differences in wealth now accepted are disproportionate and that there is, therefore, a strong case for reducing inequalities, even if there is no agreement as to what would constitute proportionate equality. In this, as in other contexts, it is easier to recognise injustice than to define justice''.[31] Thus the formal principle of exclusion of arbitrariness, can be linked with distribution of means of well-being. This has been the role of justice in bringing reform in law and in making it more humane. While going through the previous Chapters we must have known that similar role has been performed in India by the concepts of Rit, Dharma, 'Danda', Vyavahara, interpretation, etc., which worked for the benefit and welfare of the individual and society. More of this role will be seen in the next Chapter.

Notes and References

1. Principles of Social and Political Theory by E. Parker, p. 168 (P.B.) Edition.
2. *Ibid.,* p. 169
3. *Ibid.,* p. 170.
4. What is Justice?, Hans Kelsen, p. 81 (1971).
5. *Ibid.,* p. 107.
6. *Ibid.,* p. 116, quoted.
7. *Ibid.,* p. 125.
8. On Justice in Society – By Ginsberg, pp. 66-68.
9. What is Justice?, By H. Kelsen– pp. 127-28.
10. *Ibid.,* p. 132.

11. *Ibid.,* pp. 137-38.
12. *Ibid.,* p. 159.
    From Law of Nature Spencer deduces the moral and political norms of society like a natural law thinker. This he does in the name of Science.
13. Kelsen : What is Justice?, p. 167.
14. Ethical Systems and Legal Ideas – By Felix Cohen, p. 109 (Quoted in).
15. Ethical Systems and Legal Ideals by Felix Cohen, pp. 81-82.
16. A Theory of Justice by John Rawls, p. 22.
17. *Ibid.,* p. 27.
18. Principles of Social and Political Theory – By Earnest Barker, p. 172 (P.B.) 1967, Pub. Oxford Univ. Press.
19. Introduction to Jurisprudence by Denis LLyod (1st Edition), p. 258, Note 64.
20. *Ibid.,* p. 263 (Extracts).
21. *Ibid.*, Extracts, p. 263.
22. Political Theory – A Brecht; Indian Edition, pp. 146-47.
23. *Ibid.,* p. 148.
24. Political Theory by Arnold Brecht, pp. 395-97 (Indian Edition).
25. On Justice in Society – By Morris Ginsberg, p. 64, Pelican Book (Penpaguin) A. 717 (1965).
26. *Ibid.,* p. 65.
27. *Ibid.,* p. 70.
28. *Ibid.*, pp. 70-71.
29. *Ibid.,* p. 71.
30. *Ibid.,* p. 73.
31. *Ibid.*

10

Law and Justice–Dharma and Nayaya -II

Justice, as a legal concept, has been found hard to define. It is a composite of concepts, or an ideal proportion of them which can never be prefixed. More than that, it may be one's own ideological construction, or intellectual preference or critical reflection or emotional reaction. Its appeal to human beings is so great that no legal theory can ignore it without the risk of being incomplete and inadequate. Though justice is not amenable to logical and scientific approach as there is no unanimity about its settled content and meaning, yet it is a sort of demand notice which we direct against our legal systems, social orders, and political institutions and agencies. It is our theory of expectation, the net result of our desires and demands. Justice is also then the theory of the ends or values of law which are assessed by objective determination in the light of the practical working of law. But values, absolute or relative, are also imposed upon a legal system in order to be fulfilled by it. Whatever, be the difficulties that be fall, or encounters made, the search for justice must continue. It should not be rejected as meaningless, chimerical irrational for "there is danger that the human race will fall back into a condition of barbarism and ignorance where unreason will prevail over rationality, and where the dark forces of prejudice may win the battle over humanitarian ideals and the forces of goodwill and venevolence".[1]

The characteristic habit of the ancient Indian mind, which is still within us, is that in order to solve any particular problem it first comprehends it in the context of the whole reality and then draws conclusions or forms judgment or propounds any theory relating to it. In other words, it sees unity in the whole existence with all its phases. All the important concepts are oriented on this basis. This basis provides the key to the understanding of the concept of law as the ancients in India viewed it (law). They viewed law in all its diverse aspects. To them law is positive law as well as ideal law. Law is the nature of this world as well as that of man. It is knowledge of law as well end of welfare. It is textual prescription as well as *defacto* virtuous conduct and practice. It is administration as well as interpretation. It is an ideal norm (dharma) as well as political expediency (Arth). It is the bond, the duty, or that which holds us together, as well as the character of freedom or Right, or which is determined according to one's own reason and conscience. It is relative as well as absolute. It is an intelligible concrete rule of conduct as well as the mysterious aspect of the whole reality. Our concept of justice is included in our concept of Dharma or Law which covers the whole metaphysics, epistemology, and ethics of law. The highest reality to Indian mind is 'Brahman' but it is undefinable. When its aspects are described it becomes 'Sachidanand' which means Existence, Consciousness and Bliss. It is how the indefinable reality, the Brahman, or its human counterpart Dharma, can be described and correlated. As the Indian thought, feeling and will are oriented on this view of reality, it is better if we try to understand justice in the light of the total view of reality. Justice, to the ancients was dharma. According to this humble author, justice then, in deed as well as in truth, to be so, must conform to this reality and is to be studied from the point of its knowledge (Gyana), action or power (Shakti), and Bliss (Annanda). Truth, reason, impartiality, and 'duty' are important from the point of view of knowledge of justice. Order, harmony security, punishment and prosperity are important from the point of view of action of justice; and happiness, freedom, and welfare are important from the point of view of ethics.

1. JUSTICE AS KNOWLEDGE (GYAN)

In order to know the ends of law or realise the theory of justice, we will have to deal with law together with social, religious, moral aspects of ancient Indian thought and values which have a complete correspondence with Reality which is in ancient phraseology the 'Sat-

Chit-Anand'. The discussion has therefore, to proceed on these lines. Knowledge of justice lies in truth, reason, impartial performance of judicial function, and sense of duty.

(a) Satya (Truth) as a Theory of Justice

'Sat' is existence itself, which in itself is a value. When it exists in social, moral, and jural life it exists as (Satya) truth. Ethico-legal norm of truth is then, a derivative of metaphysics. 'Satya' or truth has a practical importance in individual social life. "Satya contributes to the welfare and harmony of society, as a whole. It engenders mutual truth and love, and binds the individuals together. On the contrary if the individuals were to distrust, deceive and betray one another, the unity and harmony of society would be jeopardized. Hatred and discord would take the place of love and harmony. The ethics of 'Satya' is also based on the conception of the unity of self as identical with or at least similar to other selves. Not to tell the truth is tantamount to distrusting the other self. Distrust proceeds from regarding the otherself, as separate from or as opposed to one's self. It results in preventing another person from sharing with one's self a common knowledge which should be the same for all selves. Satya promotes unity. It is at once ethical and social virtue".[2] Truth is thus the end of law. When truth operates upon the facts and propositions of law it emerges as justice. Thus 'justice' is truth in action.

Truth has in itself all the juridical idealism because it is reflected in all the key concepts of Indian law and they can be interpreted or re-discovered in the theory of truth. Vidyaranya, the great commentator of Rig-Veda considers 'Rit' to be the mental perception and realisation of truth. Shankeracharya, commenting upon the text of Brihadaranyakopanished, observes that "Satya is the speaking of truth while Dharma is the observance of truth in action. The author[3] of Hindu Ideals says "while 'Rita' denotes the mental perception and realisation of truth and 'Satya' denotes the exact expressions of words of truth as perceived by the mind, Dharma is observance of truth in conduct of life. In fact, Dharma is the way of life which translates into action the truth as perceived by the man of insight and as expressed by him truly. In short, Rit is truth in thought, Satya is truth in words and Dharma is truth in deed. Hence, the Brihadaranyakopanisad proclaims that which is Dharma is truth. Therefore, according to Indian thinkers Dharma and truth are interchangeable expressions and denotes the fundamental aspiration of man which is the pursuit of truth in thought, word and deed". This pursuit of truth becomes the primary aim of life as it is bound to contribute to the prosperity and well being of mankind. Mahabharat, considers the authority of truth to be even higher than the Vedas. Virtuous conduct of Veda-knowing people and prevailing customs which have become true part of life have been recognised from time to time as law, to a very great extent. The aim of Vyavahar also, as has already been mentioned, is an inquiry into 'truth'. Mimansa seeks only the true interpretation or application of the injunctions of the Vedas. In sum, all the concepts of law and its ideals converge on truth. The Rig-Veda says "By truth is earth upheld"(X.85.1). The supreme Brahman itself is the Right, is the Truth. (Nrisimhottaratapini Upanishad-I. 6).

Truth has great convincing power. It can bring a change of attitude in our view about what is just and what is not just. Men generally base their ideas of justice upon the truth of certain facts, or opinions. But when they realise the untruth of these facts and opinions they easily change their belief about justice, or otherwise of those facts or opinions. It is due to this tendency that some of the evils of history have been done away with because on rational enquiry they were found to be false, i.e., unworthy of our legal system. The Indian mind has reacted against the evils of Karmkanda, formalism, superstitions, mechanical trials, ordeals, etc. It has given the people of those times the advantages of a developed rational procedure in Vyavahar. We, to-day, are again implementing justice by knowing the truth of social life. Through the agency of law we are abolishing discrimination on the basis of caste, creed and colour. We are trying to raise the status of the untouchables, the backward classes and scheduled tribes by restoring to them the true social respect by means of social justice. This is so because we have realized now that their status is not in accord with truth, i.e., it is not worthy of them as human beings, and though at one time it may have been considered as just but not now when we also realize that it is discriminatory between man and man and so it is untruth and hence unjust.

We have still to realize the other untruth on unequal distribution of wealth. We have to do away with privileges and disparity of income because both these are unjust. A great change and transformation will take place if we expose the evils of the day and earnestly pray like the Rig Vedic seer 'Lead me from 'asat' (Untruth) to 'sat' (Truth). Great Indians, from the past to the present, have tried to follow the path of truth in various fields of life. Mahatma Gandhi even identified God with truth. He forged the doctrine of 'Satyagrah', literally to seize or hold truth, to give passive resistance and non-cooperation. He vindicated truth and justice through it and declared: "if a man will only realise that it is unmanly to obey laws that are unjust, no man's tyranny will enslave him. This is the key to self-rule or home-rule–so long as the superstition that man should obey unjust laws exists, so long will their slavery exist. And a passive resister alone can remove such a superstition".[4] He further says that those who believe that they are not bound to obey laws which are repugnant to conscience have only the remedy of passive resistance upon to them.[5] Satyagrah does not amount to cowardice but is the highest type of bravery. The passive resister suffers for the cause of justice and truth by not obeying law which "is against his conscience, even though he may be blown to pieces at the mouth of a canon".[6] Satyagrah is declared by Gandhiji to be the citizen's birth-right (*Young India*, 5 June, 1922). This theory of Satyagraha is almost, nay, a true Indian natural law theory and has proved not only effective in India but has become a powerful weapon against unjust laws throughout the world. This theory proves that there is, in the minds of human beings, a permanent and universal equation between unjust and untruth. In this lies not only the sanity of our mass-mind but also a warning to administrators, legislators and politicians not to depart from the basic concept of truth which is just and not to misuse political legislative, and executive power for their personal ends.

(b) Reason (विवेक)

However, we need not be too dogmatic about truth. It needs to be understood in the light of justice. For this, we should travel into the realm of Reason or 'Viveka' which has been expressed by Manu as 'Atmatusti' (Self-satisfaction) and was enumerated as one of the sources of law. We should seek living and dynamic truth and not lifeless and static truth. For instance, a lie may be stated to a dying person to keep alive his hope of recovery. Political lies may also be told to keep up the morale of the soldiers in war. So falsehood and untruths justified when they serve some higher values like mercy, respect for grief, the good of public or the nation as a whole. Similarly, for the sake of convenience and utility legal fictions and presumptions, are allowed to prevail in the interest of workability of a legal system. But it is too difficult to provide any theory to know how far should these untruths, presumptions and fictions be allowed. It can only be said that they may be allowed to the extent that they serve the ends of justice. In such case they have to be considered as reasonable.

'Viveka', thus moderates the rigour of truth. By virtue of this Vivek, i.e., reason and logic, our Mimansakas made workable that legal system which was oriented on the Vedas and the Smirtis. By this method they kept alive the spirit of justice by de-recognizing obsolete customs and concepts and gave admittance to new ones.

Like truth, Viveka is also an end of law and is a means of justice. Any theory which formulates law has to be refined and purified by reason. To a very great extent, reason has been able to make law a means of justice, because reason is the power of justice. Those writers who use reason in the pursuit of certainty are using it in a narrow logical sense and they find it inadequate. Kelsen considers that justice is not amendable to reason. Alf. Ross seems to see irrationalism in the very idea of justice when he says "to invoke justice is the same thing as banging on the table: an emotional expression which turns one's demands into an absolute postulate".[7] Reason has also its broader conception in which it can serve the cause of justice. In this aspect it embraces the whole field of enquiry and the span of our purposes. It is through this reason that we seek 'convincing grounds, for our opinions and proofs, of our conclusions'; we weigh and consider facts which are relevant to the problem in hand, test it by historical and psychological insights, make the view propounded more persuasive, by giving it the force of reasons derived from varied sources of our experience. All this is done in the spirit of detachment and impartiality to seek the solution of any legal problem; and this we do with all the consciousness of the limitations of human capacities. Reason, thus, becomes a vehicle of Dharma or justice. By this means also, we can discuss and determine the relevance of empirical facts for providing more just solutions. We can also make choices between conflicting values for their viability for social order. The doctrines like 'Kalivarjya, lost sruti, Arthvada, Lokvivasta etc., to which have alluded earlier, served the cause of justice in ancient India. Indian jurists were capable of choosing properly between Dharma and Arth by virtue of Viveka or Reason. In Vedic times women had equal rights; niyoga was practised and widow marriages were permitted; and daughter's share in inheritance was recognised. But due to the deterioration of times these rights began to seem unjust and reason was sought to hold it so. It was because of the fact, that women began to be looked upon as inferior beings. Now in modern India, recognising and realising the worth and dignity of the women, we have given them equal status. This is nothing but the role of reason which has helped us in implementing justice. In this sense reason has the power to change the social situation with the corresponding ideas of justice.

Inspite of the fact that reason can point out the just solution, it is not the only method for implementing justice or Dharma, and we have to look for some other agency in the interest of justice. Some problems of law which are controversial and debatable cannot be resolved by reason alone. The ancients were conscious of it. Many issues, like the abolition of capital sentence, euthanasia (mercy-killing) allowing pariodical contractual marriages etc., cannot be decided on the basis of reason. Firstly, because deepseated religious feelings, cultural influences, and sentiments, prevail over reason. Secondly, reason in such issues cannot yield correct answers. It would thus seem that the justice or dharma cannot be explained or determined by reason alone. So Mahabharat declares that no one can completely know what is dharma. To some extent, it may be mentioned that Dharma is shrouded in mystery. This only shows the limitation of reason to explore the nature of dharma. Reason was to the Indian mind only a means not an end. There was neither an exclusive rationalistic era in India nor was there the need for its antidote, the irrationalism. Ancient Indians had a vision of reality in both the aspects, the Lokik and Alokik; the latter is seen only through spiritual experience. 'Man is a spirit and an integral whole', reason is only a part of his capacity. Rational knowledge is only a part of his being. Purely rational knowledge does not always convince it. Indian mind has always been in the quest of Dharma (Justice) and is ready to advance in the light of new experiences. When dharma is not knowable through other sources; when it is not possible what is justice and what is injustice, the only alternative is to leave it to one's judgment and experience. To this extent, it is submitted, dharma or justice is a dynamic concept.

(c) Impartial Performance of Judicial Function (Nyaya or Positive Justice)

Justice in courts is called *Nyaya.* There it represents the characteristic impartiality and the supremacy of the rule of law which are both the pillars of justice.

According to Manu (VIII. 3) justice consists in application of law to the cases arising between the members of a state. Law is known from customs and from Smrtis (institutes) e.g. those of Gautama, Yajnavalkya, and others. Justice, as interpreted by Sukra, consists of two elements: First, it consists in a discrimination of the good from the bad(of course according to the law). Second, it has a utilitarian basis, in as much as it is calculated to minister to the virtues of the rulers and the ruled, and promotes common weal.[8] According to Kane, the primary duty of the king was to administer justice impartially and to punish the guilty. The king was considered as the fountain of justice. To Manu, protection of subjects was in itself the highest dharma. Yajnavalkya points out that protection consists in punishing internal aggression (such as by thieves and robbers and by persons who invade a man's rights) and in meeting external aggression. Manu "Personifies the administration of justice as Dharma incarnate by representing that when justice is administered the dart of dharma pierces adharma or falsehood taken out from the body of dharma. (Verse VII 12-14). Yajnavalkya declares that impartial administration of justice yields the same rewards as solemn Vedic sacrifices. (I. 359-360). In this way, administration of justice was held to be a sacred duty. According to mythology, Prajapati authorised the king to use force or 'danda' to administer justice. But it does not mean that king can use force arbitrarily . Certain qualifications are enjoined upon the king. According to Manu, a truthful, a thoughtful and a wise king who knows dharma, Arth and Kama alone is entitled to use the power of danda rightfully. In the tale of Judgment Seat of Vikramaditya told by sister Neviditya exemplifies the requirements of a just king. King Bhoj is not allowed to sit on the judgment seat of Vikramaditya by angels. Manu declares that a king who punishes those who do not deserve to be punished incurs great obloquy and goes to hell [9]. Again, in the Mahabharata (Anusasna 6.38 and Chapter 70) and the Ramayana, it is said that the king who does not show up himself for administering justice and suffer the litigants waiting for him would suffer like king Nrga. The quick and speedy justice was thus the aim, though adjournments were also granted in special and compelling circumstances. It was realised by Sukra and Katyana that delay in deciding cases was as good as denial of justice. The purpose of legal procedure, was to ascertain the truth of the matter. Manu States that "the king who decides the causes of people unjustly through greed is soon subjugated by enemies, while the king who is curbing his own temper and desires and impartially decides causes according to the dictates of 'Sastra becomes of one mind with his subjects as rivers merge in the ocean''. (VIII.174-175). Brahaspati and Narad lay emphasis on both the secular and spiritual effects of doing justice, saying that "when the king gives decisions according to Sastra he spreads his fame in this world and secures Heaven''.[10] King should not come to hasty judgment. After rejecting the chicanery (Chala), the king should decide according to the real state of facts, for without proper presentation even a well-founded case fails (Yaj. II. 19). According to Brihaspati, for justice, reliance should not be placed upon 'Sastras alone without taking into consideration of the circumstances of the case, otherwise it may lead to loss of dharma (injustice or sin). "When the king is hearing a case between two litigants the essential quality required of him is impartiality. When the king is seated on the seat of justice (dharmasana) let him be devoid of passion, equal towards all, performing the view of Vivasvat (Yama, the god of the underworlds who fixes the destinies of the dead according to their past actions, good and bad). Yajnavalkya declares: "the king, freed from anger and greed, should give justice assisted by learned Brahmins in conformity with the (precepts) treatises of dharma.[11] The king has liberty of decision only when he has to protect the political interests of the State. It is his duty to see that rules of dharma are not exploited for the personal ends of litigants and in derogation of the interests of the state. The king is expected to know 'dharma' and should be able to distinguish it from a dharma; he should likewise differentiate between 'arth' and 'anartha' and may sometimes, prefer artha to dharma but only in special circumstances. Normally, of course, the king should decide according to the precepts of the Sastras, excepting those which are 'odious to the world'. In order that justice may be done, the king was free to apply simple principles of fairness. Justice, in order to be real, must be reconciled with equity. In the interest of justice the king could revise the decision and could order for retrial.

The above analysis of the concept of justice leads us to say that justice is an enforcement of law which is laid down by dharmasastras or is directed by it. It is that justice which is administered by the court, and is characterised as impartiality, foresightedness and wisdom. Here the problem of justice is not to know law, but to apply it. The decision has to be given by following the Dharma, i.e., the precepts, and by employing the prescribed procedure.

(d) Justice as Performance of One's Own Duties

Dharma (justice) is not merely an attitude of impartiality and detached objectivity with which one must decide cases but is also a duty or obligation. It is swadharma or one's own nature, in which lies one's own fulfilment. Duty is also the expression of sociability, because in order to preserve society it is necessary for a human being, who is by nature nót so self-sufficient and has to depend upon others, to perform his function in order to contribute to the upkeep of the society as a whole. In this way, just order in society is maintained. Swadharma is, them, performance of one's own duties according to one's own station in life. Gita says: "Devoted each to his own duty man attains perfection". (XVIII. 45): "Better is one's own imperfect Dharma, than the Dharma of another well performed"(XVIII.47). In this sense, Dharma or justice is duty in the functional sense according to the Varna-system. This Varna, in ancient times was based on one's own aptitudes, i.e., one's nature. It is only later that Varnas degenerated into hereditary classes and undermined the progress of our society. Hence realisation of one's own duties and performing them is in itself justice. This is doing of justice to one's own self and also thereby to the social whole because if every one will perform his functions well there will be no injustice in society. Justice, according to Plato, also, has this meaning. In reply of the question "what then is justice, and where is the place of its habitation?", it is answered that the will to fulfil the duties of one's station and not to meddle with the duties of another's station, is justice. The original principle, which laid down at the foundation of the State is: "that one should practice one thing only, and that the thing to which his nature was best adapted."(443A).[12] In this context, Plato was of the view that justice in a State is nothing but a manifestation of the sense of duty of a citizen public action.[13] It can be here asserted that in this respect Plato's idea of justice in a State comes nearer of approximates to the functional notion of dharma or justice of the ancients. If this sense develops in our people, there is no need of remedy. Justice of the other type, i.e., corrective justice, is only needed to repair the loss or harm caused by a failure to perform one's own dharma or duty. Gita, hightens this notion of justice by reaching the highest point in morality when it says that duty is the end and it should be performed for its own sake. The same is view of Mimansa which we have referred to earlier in Chapter 8.

This is the epistemological aspect of justice. From this point of view knowledge or source of justice lies in truth, reason, impartial judicial attitude and in our own sense of duty.

II. JUSTICE AS POWER (SHAKTI)

In order to realise justice in life it must perform some active role by establishing peace, order and a state of security by protection of life and property. For this justice becomes a theory of action. For having a better understanding of this role, we will start our discussion with the theory of action, i.e., the Theory of Karma as Natural Justice.

(a) Theory of Karma as Natural Justice

The idea of justice is rooted in the law of Karma, a variation of Rit, and a conception of the whole universe as an ordered whole. The order or law on the physical, social and moral level is Rit. In the same way, the order established on the basis of law, called legal system, has also Rit as its genus. As this universe is dynamic, because of its Swadha (energy or potency), this order works through causation i.e., in succession of actions and reactions. This aspect of Rit is called Karma. A brief mention of it has already been made in the First Chapter. Here we will discuss its importance as a principle of justice. Primarily, the need for justice arises when order is disturbed or violated by the actions of the people in a society which the ancients called the 'Karmas' and on these they built a theory of Karma. Justice,— consists in re-establishing the order or punishing those who have violated the order by their actions (Karmas), recompensating those who have suffered at the hands of the disturbers of order. Justice thus becomes 'Dandaniti' (theory of punishment). Without the theory of Karma one cannot have logical and theoretical grounds for awarding punishment and so administering legal justice. The logical of Karma establishes a link between punishment and the act (wrong) done. The authority or power to punish or administer justice is not an adequate logical explanation. Its logical or theoretical justification lies in the theory of Karma which for this reason becomes a theory of justice.

According to the theory of Karma, the reality which is order as well as existence, is self-sufficient on the natural or cosmic plane and has its own potency. As this universe is conscious and is progressively manifolding itself, it determine our individual, social and moral life. In man, with his free will, it allows him to determine his own moral progress or regress. The doctrine of Karma, as causation, allows our action to determine our future. It appears as a principle of retributive justice which is an extension of the principle of causation in nature and becomes the principle of natural justice. It is expressed thus: "If a man sows thistles, he must not expect a crop of sweet grapes; if he plants prickly cactus, he must not expect to gather juicy apples. This is Karma, and a man knowing, sows the seed of the thing he wants to reap."[14] From this emerges a general principle – 'a man reaps as he sows'. Danda or punishment as justice is an enforcement of this law of Karma which ordains man to bear the fruit of action. This law of Karma was conceived of as so inexorable that man may not escape it even by early death in life. It seems that it was logically necessary that the doctrine of rebirth and transmigration of soul be developed to make the doctrine complete. The doctrine of Karma is not fatastistic. Man can undo the bad effect of Karmas by knowledge, right conduct and thus can reverse the course of regression. Law of Karma, then, is also the law of practical reason which can bring about moral regeneration. The Law of Karma is the universal moral law which governs the life of the individual and society and becomes the moral book-keeping. It is based on the principle of merit or desert and is the incarnation of eternal justice.

This doctrine of rebirth is not mentioned in the Vedas but is only a post-Vedic development. It is found in Brahmnas and earliest Unpanishads. In Brahdarayanka Unpanishad it is said that due to Karmas man's soul wears new body after his death. In Chhandogya Unpanishad (V. 10) metapsychosis is described and it is said that man is reborn in superior womb, or inferior womb like that of a dog swine or an outcast. This is due to good or evil Karmas. Karma then becomes an explanation of men's present status and station in life which is the result of his previous birth. The good Karmas alone can set-off bad Karmas and man is free to perform then to bring about moral regeneration and improvement of his status in the next life, if he fails to get it in the present one. For this purpose, for sins and offences penance or punishment is necessary. After death Yama, the God of justice or dharma, judges men's actions who are brought to his court by his messengers according to which the next birth is determined. Buddhists consider that if an act is not volitional, it is not a free determination and a person cannot be held responsible. By enlightenment, the evil effect of all the accumulated bad Karmas can be undone. According to Jainism, Karmas, which cloud or cover the soul by their particles and obstruct the vision of truth and knowledge, can be removed by austerity, service, instruction and penance. Jainism also takes a volitional and intentional view of Karma.

In the Gita two views of Karma are given to us. In a wider sense, Karma is conceived of as the creative force which brings beings into existence. Accordingly, the whole created world is the Karma of the Absolute. In the narrow view, Karmas are actions done by the individual soul on account of 'Prakriti' and 'Gunas'. The tendency of all such Karmas is to bind a man and he is liable to fall and easy prey to attachment if the Karma is 'actuated by desire or self-conceit' or when 'done through delusion without regard to consequences'. If the action is 'done without love or hatred and without any desire of its fruits and free from attachment', it is a good Karma. As one cannot avoid doing Karma for worklessness or non-activity in life is impossible, what is needed is to work 'with a controlled mind and in an unattached manner' (III.7). If we ask what actions are to be performed, Gita says that a man's obligation is to do his duty enjoined upon him by 'dharma'. He should perform his function well without desire of rewards or fruits. Here, as we have mentioned before, the doctrine of Justice, called Dharma, resembles Plato's theory of justice. It consists in harmony of proper functions which are performed by a man. This concept of Justice is the aspect of Rit or law, as order which, is again illustrated by doctrine of Karma and explained by the propriety of actions on which the order maintains itself. The duty should be done with the sense of sacrifice like Yajna, i.e., 'Yajnarthkarma', without any desire for reward, because in God's nature there is no causal connection between virtue and happiness. In this sense justice is, that Karma or duty which is done or performed by judges, administrators, rulers interpreters, commentators, etc., is the proper and honest performance of their duties, without favour, fear and prejudice and without any desire for reward. This is an impartial adjudication. In this way just order in society is established and maintained. It also becomes socio-economic justice when the individual identified himself and his interests with others. Metaphysically there is the identity of the individual with the universal soul but it has to be realised in consciousness and action. "He sees, who sees, the Lord Supreme existing equally in all beings, deathless in the dying". (Gita XII-28). 'The self is all beings and all beings are in the self. He who sees me in all beings and sees all beings in Me, he never becomes separated from Me, nor do I become separated from him (VI. 30). The social duties of a person are, therefore, a part of his duty to realise his higher self. It is not merely based on identity of interests but an identity of existence''.[15] Gita gives expression to the socialistic principle of social and economic justice when it declares that: 'He who enjoys objects gives to Gods without making offering in return to them is a thief (III-12). The same idea has been expressed in Ishavasyopanished. 'There is the dwelling place of God in every thing that is moving in this world. Enjoy the world with a sense of selflessness; do not hanker after another man's wealth'. In the language of social Ethics, it means that he who enjoys wealth more than necessary for him, is really stealing it because it also belongs to his fellow beings with whose help he has acquired it and it is, therefore, a trust property with him. As every social organism is a body with a soul, it follows that all black-marketeers, profiteers and other persons including in anti-social activities, whether on a small or a big scale, are not merely thieves, but guilty of causing grievous hurt, as by their actions they disfigure and mitilate the collective body of the community in which they live.''[16]

The doctrine of Karma is interpreted by Lokmanya Tilak as a principle of collective justice because Karma does not merely influence individual but also the society as a whole. According to him '' in as much as every human being is born in some family, some community, or some country, it has to some extent suffer on account of the actions not only of itself but also of the community and society such as the family etc. to which it belongs''.[17] On this interpretation, the Karmas of race determine the rise and fall of nations and their analysis becomes a subject of the philosophy of history. The necessary conclusion is then that, because of this idea of collective justice, as applied to nations and countries, the people of nations and countries suffer for the wrong and foolish Karmas (actions) of their leaders. This may appear to be an unusual extension of the doctrine of justice but it does look logical.

Again, Gita gives us the theory of divine justice. This is implicit in the concept of 'Daiva' (XIII. 14.). It means that 'over and above all the materials objects, instruments and means which come into play in the doing of all acts, there is one incalculable element, viz. Daiva. In the view of Dr. Radhakrishnan ''Daiva or super personal fate is the general cosmic necessity, the resultant of all that has happened in the past, which rules unnoticed. It works in the individual for its own incalculable purpose''.[18] It is not to be interpreted as fatalism, as man has risen from the state of pure animalism. He has the capacity to overcome the limitations or heredity and environment by the force of his will. According to this humble author, some amount of uncertainty is part of nature, i.e., 'Savabhava' of this world which can also be called 'Lila' or 'play of the spirit'. Again the law of Karma is so subtle and complicated it is not possible to ascribe or attribute all the innumerable causes which are responsible for the events. It for this inscrutability of Karma that Gita enjoins upon us only to do our duty without any desire for reward.

(b) Justice as Dandniti or Positive Justice

The theory of Karma, as we have seen, has an intimate relation with penance and punishment. We are here concerned with the punishment which can be seen also as mitigation of the effects of Karmas, i.e., wrongful acts. This is a philosophic justification for the infliction of punishment. If an offender does not suffer punishment at the hands of the king, or in this life, he has to suffer the evil effects of Karmas in the next life. It is also stated that if he suffers penance imposed by Sastras or learned men he is absolved from the sins. By punishment a sort of repayment of debt due to Karmas is made. This is sanctioned by dharmasastrakars. According to the view of Vashistha (XIX. 45) which has been re-stated by Manu (VII. 318) and Narad (48), men "who have committed crimes and who have been punished by the king are purified, go to heaven like those who have performed good deeds." The king as this theory shows, seems to possess in addition to the secular power, some religious power. One reason for this is that king has been created to uphold dharma. The other is that punishment is but another name for dharma and by punishment the dharma is restored. "For the (king's) sake Lord formerly created his own son Punishment, the protector of all creatures (an incarnation of), the law, formed of Brahman's glory" (Manu VII. 14). The punishment by the king has the same value as penance has and thus becomes a retributive (expiatory) justice. It is also said that if the king does not punish properly it is he (king) who incurs sin but the sinner or the wrong-doer is certainly absolved from the wrong. However, this aspect of punishment is the implementation of dharma and is different from that which is dealt with by the aim of Kantak-Sodhana and is meted out on the basis of 'arth', i.e., the political interests of the State. Theory of Karma then provides an explanation to the theory of punishment. But punishment can also be explained on the basis of the characteristic human nature and practical needs of social order.

Rita and Dharma are the expressions of eternal order. On cosmic level, this order maintains itself, but on human law it has to be maintained by the human agency of danda. Danda becomes a theory of positive justice. By administering positive justice this order is maintained. The truth is that without justice no order is preserved and without order justice is not possible. Justice and order are complementary to each other. Man, by his very nature, is not always inclined towards the maintenance of order. Our ancient sages were conscious of the evil potentialities of man. They considered coercive force of punishment necessary to maintain order. Order is maintained by protecting the life and property and by securing the performance of duties. When it is maintained through punishment it is called justice which guarantees protection and security. According to Man, "The whole world is kept in order by punishment, for a guiltless man is hard to find; through fear of punishment the whole world yields the enjoyment" (VII. 20). Again without proper punishment the social classes are corrupted, all barrier broke down and men fly at each other without punishment. Without it there will not exist a just social order but will be established an era of Matsya-Nyaya, where the big fish swallows the small one. The king has only been created for the protection of the castes and order which, according to their rank, discharge their several duties (VII-35). Again, according to Menu, the highest duty to Ksatriya is to protect his subjects. Kane rightly observes that Danda is raised to the position of divinity by Manu, Yajnavalkya and Vyas. Danda, it is said, rules over all people, it protects all of them, danda is awake even when (the guardians of law) have gone to sleep; the wise men treat danda as dharma (Manu VII-18) etc. In Bhagavatgita (X 38), Krishna says that He (God) is danda in the hands of those who control others. He is niti, i.e., rajniti (politics) for the conquerors.[19] Through danda, the institutions of family and private property and the protection of the weak is ensured. King then becomes the protector of the helpless, the home of the homeless, the son of the sonless and the father of the fatherless.[20] Manu (VI-27-28) also says that by the proper application of Danda three purusharthas of Dharma, Arth and Kama are advanced. To some, Danda has the status of God, but to many it is indispensable for preservation of society.

Kautilya even declares: "That sceptre on which well being and progress of the sciences of logic, the three Vedas (Rg. Veda, Sama Veda, Yajur Veda), and commerce depend is the law of punishment". But it is also a part of justice to award punishment proportionate to the crime looking to the circumstances of time and place and gravity of the offence. Indian jurists of the ancient have recognised the need of considering various factors in varying the quantum of punishment.

In this way justice becomes the expression of order, peace and security. It is the business of law to secure safety for its people. According to Hobbes, the safety of the people is the supreme law. Security and justice are mutually related. Law or Dharma by its prescriptions, procedures, and institutions preserves and secures the interests of individuals and society. By making available the material requirements the frequent violations of law can, to some extent, be avoided; hence law is maintained by security. Today, we consider the security of the people against certain hazards, risks, and vicissitudes of human life (old age, illness accidents unemployment) as part of justice. Law, today, is justly making provisions for old age pensions, health services, workmen's compensations, insurance schemes etc. and these schemes are designated as social welfare schemes which the Westerners regard as their own discovery. How wrong are they when we find that in Mahabharata the following verse occurs :

Anathan Vyadhitn
Vridhan Swadeshe
Pashayen nripah
(Mahabharata-Anushasan Parva).

The king considered it as a part of his rajniti, his moral and religious duty to provide social security to his subjects. Again, law is not merely an ordering device but also works as a means of social security. Social security was the part of dandniti in the times of Kautilya. The ancients were not only actuated by a desire to adjust their law to the changing circumstances of the times but were also conscious that stability alone could ensure peace and good government. They were also alive to the fact that both stability and change are necessary for justice. Danda performed the one, and interpretation, the other.

Justice, in order to be real and true, and must provide equal opportunities and conditions of life by removing inequalities of wealth and living conditions. Ideal equality is not possible. It was not there in the Greek society of Aristotle who based his doctrine of justice on the principle of equality. In a different way, the ancient legal theory has been the expression of equality before law. The law was considered superior to any human authority. At the initial stage the Varna-system was based upon equal opportunities which were provided to persons according to their aptitudes. In the society of early Rig Vedic period women were equal in rank with men; the king governed by the advice of assemblies; republican form of government was also popular; widows were free to remarry; daughters got a share in father's property. There were inter-caste marriages; people were free to preach and adopt any doctrine, religion and could adopt any mode of worship. It is only due to historical reasons and later, social deterioration, that unequal conditions of life began to prevail. It is the task set for the present legislators of repair that harm which has been done to us by Centuries of political enslavement and social stagnation.

(c) Arth as Justice

Ancient Indian mind was not only concentrated on dharma alone but also looked to arth which was also recognised as one of the important ends of life. There are four ends of life : Dharma, Arth, Karma, and Moksa. The ideals of dharma and moksha work for spiritual benefit and are related to the other world but arth and kama are more concerned with the world which is here and now. We are here more concerned with arth which includes within its range all the economic functions and material conditions and objects of life, e.g., attainment of riches, wordly prosperity, material advantages, wealth and all that which concerns commercial life, business affairs, work, prices, etc. Arth in the sphere of law means plaint, action, petition; in politics it is the interest of the state, i.e., expediency. In life in general it is utility, that is, what is useful. "It means the whole range of tangible objects that can be possessed, enjoyed and lost work we require in daily life for the upkeep of the household, raising of family and discharge of religious duties, i.e., for virtuous fulfilment of life's obligations".[21] If Artha is considered as an end of the individual life, it certainly has an important bearing on doctrine of justice. The sources of 'Arth' are economic activity, commerce and agriculture all of them were called 'Vrata'. This Vrata was thought necessary for the state of further the advancement in the economic sphere. The Kamandaka, Nitisara declares "when Vrata is destroyed this world is surely dead though it seems to breathe.''[22] According to Mahabharat, wealth has been given an important place. This is evident from the fact that he who robs another of wealth robs him of his dharma and poverty befalls one who is sinful. (XII Ch. 8). Kaivalya, it was thought, could not be attained by proverty; Arth was also declared to be the source of the whole world; wealth, and wealth alone is important (Kautilya) because lack of wealth is the root of all evil. Wealth had its enchantment. All these views shows that in Ancient India material aspect of life was not neglected. There was harmony between Dharma and Arth. Though arth was important yet it was not allowed to violate 'dharma'. According to Manu wealth should be acquired for livelihood. If in pursuit of arth, one causes harm or loss to others, then it is not right.[23] It was considered unjust for the state of rob individuals of their wealth. It was also considered unjust for the individuals to amass wealth without giving a portion of it charity. This dictate of justice was nothing but a boosting of the socialistic principle and we have evidence enough to show that the ancients did not neglect the welfare aspect of justice in their legal theory.

Thus, on the basis of social ethics, Mahatama Gandhi developed economic idea of a just-economic order in society. He has brought about a perfect synthesis of 'Dharma and Arth' by his concept of trusteeship. "Gandhiji, rejects class war and pleads for class conciliation. He argues in favour of a concept of 'trusteeship' whereby the owners of the means of production would regard themselves more as trustees of their property rather than absolute owners. His ideal, he stated, was 'equal distribution' of nation's wealth but since that is not possible he would accept 'equitable distribution' as the next best''.[24] To Gandhi, true economics harmonises with ethical standards. He condemned Mammon worship and propogated the concept of non-acquisitive society in his theory of Sarvodaya (literally dawn or betterment of all). These ideas of justice are in line with our ancient legal philosophy. Again, when the Indian constitution has wedded itself of political, social and economic justice, all of which seem to coincide with the aspirations of our ancient culture. On the one hand, it is an avowal for minimum economic conditions for a healthy citizenship, and on the other, it implies checks on economic activity and accumulation of wealth which are in tune with the Upanisadic enjoyment of the wordly goods, without selfishness, greed and avarice.

III. JUSTICE AS FELICITY (ANAND)

(a) Kama

We have considered the necessity of justice for maintaining order and peace in society, whereby security of life and property is ensured and minimum material wants are satisfied. Now we will consider the highest end of law, i.e., Bliss. Life, without this bliss, cannot realise itself to the full. This bliss or happiness has been also understood as comprising grades and degrees, depending upon variations of culture, material advancement, individual or personal aptitudes and values. Broadly, the ancients termed them as 'kama' and called it as a characteristic of this world. According to them, the philosophic justification for any theory of justice, which takes into account the welfare and happiness of the people, lies in the view that 'kama' is a part of reality, because from it ensue desires, satisfaction, pleasure, and happiness and welfare. There are the very ends of life, the legitimate activity. 'Kama' is the 'lila' or 'maya' or manifestation of reality in its varied forms. It may manifest itself in joy, in the enjoyment of pleasures, and in the satisfaction of one's desires. If this happens to a man he experiences joy. This joy is something which can be distributed to others and in this distribution the distributor also feels joy. Thus happiness is not an individual, selfish, and momentary happiness, but that which has correlation with others. It, then, becomes good or welfare. In the aspect of law and justice or dharma, as securing the joy or happiness, the beneficial aspect is revealed in welfare (Lok-samgrah or Kalyan), happiness (Sukha), Bliss (Anand) etc. All these are the aspects of the reality which in its pure form expresses the joy of Kama. Man, who is the part of this reality and partakes in its process cannot be without happiness or 'Anandam' or 'Anand'. Kama is then, the content of this world, the aspect of the reality and the recognised and legitimate and of human life. Inspite of the fact that due to the prominence given to spiritual side of life and due to its identification with Coarser pleasures of life, the importance of Kama cannot be belittled. At the lowest stage this Kama is sensual or animal pleasure, and at the higher state it is aesthetic enjoyment and delight of artistic experience and at the highest, it is the bliss, beauty and englightenment, i.e., of God realisation. Kama is said to be one of the 'Vibhutis' of God. It is not inconsistent with Dharma. It is grounded in the very nature of man. Manu considers human nature not free from desires. The inclination towards pleasure is recognised in

Chhandogyopanisad (VII-22,1-23) thus : "When (the jiva) obtaineth pleasure then he engages in action; never doeth he enter on action without obtaining pleasure. Only when he hath obtained pleasure doth he engage in action". Yajnavalkya gives the theory of self love which means that man loves the objects and persons simply because he loves his own self आत्म कामं. Hence, self-live is the foundation of reflection of all other loves and is inborn with man (Br. Ar. II. 4. 5). Happiness, then is the demand of humen nature, it is the attribute of the self and is sought for its own sake. Mahabharat also upholds this when it says that all acts have their and, the attainment of happiness (Shantiparva, 190, 6-7, 9). Even Dharma can be looked upon as an instrument of securing the ultimate happiness. To the ancient Indian thinkers "the world was too real to be ignored persistently. The needs of the body and the mind were too insistent to be completely supressed and it was recognised that such supression would finally lead to serious disorders in the patterns of organised social life. The inclusion of Kama as an ideal of life was a sign of this recognition".[25] In order to make this pleasure or the grosser happiness permanent and enduring, it has to be sublimated into higher type of pleasure which is not the satisfaction of body but of soul. This happens by proceeding from what is pleasurable (प्रेय) to what is good (श्रेय). Man has to proceed progressively from the physical, the biological, the mental, intellectual and to the spiritual well-being which is infinite joy and Bliss and is called the 'Anand-Maya-Kosh' of the self (Taittirya-Upanisad III). Again self-live, at the higher stage becomes love of others. All the ideas of welfare and good of others are the refinements of this initial self-love of man. If this welfare is the expression of this happiness (Kama), the dharma itself becomes the aspect of Kama, because it is said that one who knows welfare of others knows dharma. Thus 'Kama' in its purest sense was an embodiment of virtuous living but due to historical circumstances it acquired an inferior status. The Indian concept of Kama as happiness is quite different from that of sensual and quantitative happiness of Bentham which is illusive and is the by-product of the satisfaction of desires. It (happiness) can be justified only as reaction against natural law and historical theories of law, and served only as theory of law reform in the 19th Century England which has suffered a long period of legislative stagnation. Real happiness is not animal, sensual and momentary pleasure or the finite happiness. It is not the greatest good of the greatest number. That which is infinite, that is (the true pleasure) happiness; there is no real happiness in the finite sense. The infinite alone is happiness. "Joy and consciousness, a limitless ocean of joy greater than which there is no happiness–such is Anand".[26] This happiness has to be realised at the initial stage by intelligence and rational discrimination. In it lies the knowledge of the one who controlleth all, the inmost self of all beings, who maketh many forms of one form–they who see that One in the self, only to those rulers of intelligence belongeth the Eternal Happiness, unto none else".[27]

The knowledge and realisation of Reality of happiness is not only the personal, subjective, and limited consciousness; it is not also the individual consciousness unaware of the good of humanity. It is saturated with the sense of service and the will to do good to others. The urge for common human welfare and service is the natural outcome of such realisation. This concern for common human welfare ensues from the concept of the brotherhood of man and common parenthood of God. Brotherhood of man is the voice of Indian spiritualism. By "knowing the supreme to be all beings, the wise extent love to all creatures undeviatingly", says the Puranas. For the large hearted people the whole world is one family. Atharva-veda says that God who is the common father urges us to come together. "Freedom form hate I bring to you concord and unanimity".[28] Yajurveda expresses the need for common concern and co-operative effort thus : "may our bodies, together with all their organs of sense and action, brothren be for your benefit; may your wealth be your service; may our action and our intellectual pursuit conduce to your happiness; may our studies and our knowledge promote your well-being; and may all that you have promote our welfare".[29]

It is thus seen that the ancient Indian Literature is full of the expression of the need of welfare and service. The service and welfare is expressed also by nature. "The trees bear fruits for others, the streams flow for the good of others and so do cows yield milk for others. The human birth is likewise meant for doing good to others".[30] It is our duty to do good for its own sake. "A righteous man is likened to a sandal tree which affords scent even to the axe that cuts it". Lord declares : "He who hates no creature and is friendly and compassionate towards all is dear to me."[31]

This is the cultural foundation from which Indian theory of justice arises, which means that one cannot deny the need of minimum joy or happiness of human existence. This happiness has three sources. At the political level it is the theory of justice. The King, being the fountin of justice, is asked to "bear himself towards his subject as a mother towards the child of her womb–as mother disregarding those objects that are more cherished by her, seeks the good of her child, even so, without doubt, should Kings conduct themselves (Shantiparva LVI).[32]

On the social level, this happiness is the result of the co-operative effort, co-ordinate and goodwill of other members. On individual level, it is the submission of one's own desire gradually by rational discrimination of different kinds of pleasures. The life of individual then becomes "a confluence of two principles that make it a continuum of inner conflicts and man's natural endeavour is to resolve and transcend them. This may be achieved by (Samsiddhi) of the individual and the welfare of the world (lok-Samgraha). The two together contribute to the realisation of the individual's freedom. There are the values whose pursuit is worthwhile, for in them is enshrined the supreme good of man. The search for other goods is secondary. The identity of perfection with world welfare is important".[33] The society, in ancient India, is an organisation which supplies these two needs, i.e., of the spirit and of the body and the State is ordained to satisfy them. The entire literature of the Dharmasastras and the Arthsastra expresses it primary concern with welfare.

The concept of Yajna is oriented on the idea of sacrifice, service and welfare. Yajna, for this reason is identified with God, because welfare aspect is the necessary aspect of the supreme . On this basis Vinoba Bhave has started two movements called the Bhoodan-movement and Sampatidan movement (Ref. 1st Chapter), the aim of which is to do justice to the landless and the poor, by making available to them land and wealth. The concepts of Rit and Dharma, as we have seen, are also oriented on welfare. The concept of authority–called Vrata also has its basis in welfare of the world. Punishment is also wielded for the good of the individual and the society. In this way all the important concepts lead to this one view of welfare.

(d) Freedom

Man is a free-willing agent. He is free to choose the path of Good or Evil. Under the influence of Western Culture man exercises this freedom by controlling nature, development of technology, satisfaction of wants, acquisition of property, entering into contractual relations with others, etc. Hence, there are pleas for freedom. It was considered by the theory of justice as a natural right. But when it was known that individual freedom is liable to be abused by unscrupulous individuals and groups the theory of justice allowed limitations on it. But synthesis between freedom and responsibility is not yet complete and its proportion is variable according to different men and their ideas. The net result is that what is available to the Western man is limited freedom but not full freedom. There is no denying the truth that the essence of freedom consists in allowing man to develop his personality. But this truth must be rightly realised. This development does not consist by entering into conflict with others but by self-realisation which has the course of inward journey. The Indian mind seeks freedom by higher spiritual realisation and in fact experiences unbounded freedom. The freedom carved by Western mind is the evil effect of exaggerated individualism, or a means of exploitation of other individuals and their property. On true analysis, this freedom is the rationale for giving sanctity to property. The Indian concept of freedom is negation of one's own ego. In this sense freedom becomes more real and true.

This freedom is bliss and is more positive in its content and has more intensity in its actual experience. It is of a higher kind and is not tainted with exploitation of others. It provides opportunities for human development to the point of perfection. It is not acquisition but realisation. This freedom is not expressed in rights but services; not in accumulation but distribution, not in competition but co-operation, not in agreement but understanding; it is not the civilisation of the ways and means of living but the civilisation or culture of the ways and means of realisation of the very worth, and significance of life and its potency for perfection.

NOTES AND REFERENCES

1. Jurisprudence, E. Bodenheimer (1974), p. 168.
2. The Cultural Heritage of India, Vol. II, p. 289.
3. Hindu Ideals – K. Balasubrahamania Iyer (B.V.B), 1969, Bombay.
4. Hind Swaraj or Indian Home Rule–By M.K. Gandhi– (1949) (Navjivan Pub. House, pp. 46-47).
5. *Ibid.*
6. *Ibid.*
7. Bodenheimer, Jurisprudence, (1974) Quoted, p. 203.

8. The Cultural Heritage of India, Vol. II, p. 518.
9. *Ibid.*, p. 242.
10. *Ibid.*, p. 386.
11. The Classical Law of India -- By Robert Linget, pp. 249-50.
12. Greek Political Theory--By Sir Ernest Barker, Pub. (Methun, London) 4th Edition) (1951), p. 176.
13. *Ibid.*, p. 177.
14. Sanathan Dharma – p. 37, A Text Book Published by Central Hindu College, Benaras, Printed at Indian Press, Allahabad.
15. Art of Life in Gita –By H.V. Divatia, 1970, Bhartiya Vidya Bhavan -- p. 104.
16. *Ibid.*, pp. 105-06.
17. *Ibid.*, p. 89 (B.G. Tilak quoted).
18. The Bhagvadgita - By Sarvepali Radha Krishnan, p. 356.
19. History of Dharma Sastras, Vol. III (1946), p. 22.
20. *Ibid.*, pp. 22-23.
21. B.G. Gokhale, Indian Thought Through the Ages, p. 51.
22. *Ibid.*, p. 55.
23. Hindu Ideals – K. Balasubramania Iyer, p. 20, B.V.B., Bombay : 1969.
24. Gokhle, B.G., Indian Thought Through the Ages, p. 72.
25. *Ibid.*, p. 77.
26. Sarasaropanishat.
27. Kathopanishat (v. 12).
28. Vedas and Allied Scriptures--by B.B. Doyal, (Jaico) 1966, p. 58.
29. *Ibid.*, pp. 121-22.
30. Quoted in Spiritual and Moral Values of Mankind (Macmillan) (1961) pp. 19-20.
31. *Ibid.*, pp. 19-20.
32. Quoted in Vedas and Allied Scriptures, B.B. Doyal, Jaico–1966, p. 108.
33. Indian Mind Edited by Charles Moore, East-West Centre Press, *Honohihi*, University of Hawaii Press (1967), p. 377, contribution of Tarachand.

11

Important Concepts of Law

As we have already seen that the basis of Indian legal philosophy is rooted in religion and mythology, it does not enter into critical analysis of legal concepts. We cannot hope to see modern conceptual analysis of law in ancient India. Dharmasastras were more prescriptive than analytical and, in the circumstances, they suited the Indian society which was plain and unsophisticated. In the absence of organised legal profession, and reporting of precedents, no scientific analysis of law and its concepts was necessary. Culture was sought to be directed towards integration and synthesis. Isolated treatment of concepts of law did not call for attention of leaders of society. Administration of justice, in the beginning, and at the end, i.e., in Gupta period, was decentralised. On the whole, there was not an atmosphere of doubt. People had great faith in inexorable course of Karma which was considered to be operating as an irreversible law of moral causation through birth and death.

Crime

The aim of criminal law was stated to be the protection of people. There was a developed mode of administration of criminal justice. It has been wrongly said that Hindus did not know of a genuine system of criminal law. According to S. Vardachariar,[1] this type of criticism is unjustified. He quotes Holdsworth to show the condition of English law. Holdsworth observes that "even the statutes of Edward III's reign show that the boundary line between the criminal and the civil liability was as yet uncertain. Many offences the commission of which would, in our time, be repressed by a criminal prosecution, were then remedied either by civil or by criminal proceedings and some times only by civil proceedings. There was as yet no organised police force nor there were armies of inspectors of different kinds. Except in the central courts, the administration of justice was in the hands of amateurs whose purity and impartiality were in many cases justly open to suspicion......" According to Vardachariar, Hindu Law looked to the duty aspect rather than to that of right. Right was not considered the sole expression of law but duty was. It was for the king to maintain moral order as well as social order. Though compensating the injured party was the part of the legal process yet mainly, the aim of king's justice was looked upon by law books as "to put wrong doer back in the right path, to correct and reform him, to make him penitent and purge him of sin of his wrongful act".[2] As such no unequal emphasis was put on the civil liability of the wrong doer to compensate the injured party, or penal liability to undergo punishment but both of them were current. Yet criminal law served its end of protecting and preserving social life.

Dr. P.K. Sen, in his Tagore Lecture on "Penology, old and new", has expressed his view that the Hindu Law was oriented on the idea of criminal wrong as causing alarm to the people and the end of Hindu criminal jurisprudence was from the very beginning to preserve the social order. The fact is that the theory of retribution on vengeance was not the ruling doctrine of Hindu criminal law. Where punishment is severe it is very difficult to say whether the end is retributive or deterrent. Because both retributive and deterrent punishments are severe. But this much is certain that Hindu criminal law was not oriented on the ideas like "Breach of the king's peace". The idea of 'king peace' was only a means to increase the power of the king in political society. One cannot deny that criminal law has its basis in the 'natural desire of mankind to avenge a wrong'. If justice is to be done, the law must provide some procedure which will enable the injured person to come forward and seek justice. The king alone cannot have the total concern of criminal law. His work is supplement and incidental and is based on the task of upkeep or policing of society. King's rule was not overpowering in so called private criminal litigation of ancient India. The power of the king was limited as Medhatithi in his commentaries on Manu puts it "in disputes relating to debt, gift, etc., the parties may come to settlement, the king has no right to interfere with their doing so.....but an offender has to be punished by the king even though the other party may like to come to some arrangement with him''. It means civil and penal redress could be had at the same time, in the same cause. The king was only a partner and not master or owner of criminal justice. In political field where security of the state was at stake he was allowed to deal with the enemy as the sole master. The modern development of administrative law and the provisions for declaration of emergency, in emergent circumstances, can be said to have a justification in this functional distinction between law as a means of adjudging conflicts between the individuals, and law which holds the society together by weeding out thorns ''Kantak Sodhana''. In serious criminal wrongs which were wrongs against the political society the king could take immediate action without delay. Modern disquisitions about administrative law are only rationalisations for this need of society which was recognised in ancient Indian law.

Systematic presentations of doctrines and intellectural discussions of legal ideas were not totally absent in ancient India, but there was not a separate branch of legal knowledge. Unlike the Western modern juristic thought of today there was a tendency towards integration and synthesis. The notion of individual moral responsibility was always mixed with social responsibility, punishment and expiation were the two sides of the same coin of 'dharma'. As late as Katyayana (472), 'Prayaschitta' (expiation) and 'danda' (punishment) are spoken of as the twin modes of purification of the wrong doer. According to the 'Svadharma theory', a crime, being a deviation from the offender's dharma, involved not merely harm to society but also degradation or loss of caste to the offender and thus made him: (1) unworthy of social communion, and (2) unfit to perform spiritual acts. Hence arose the necessity for expiation. Penance, expiation and post-mortuary punishment were logical parts of a system based on the religious and philosophical theories in Vogue during this period of history and sincerely believed in by the ancient Hindus. Hiaun-Thsang records 'they dread the retribution of another state of existence'. The position may be compared with what prevailed in Europe during the Middle Ages''.[3] Robson observes ''The Church required penance for homicide, wounding, way-laying, treason against the Lord, prejury, incest; for some offences, penance formed the only penalty in other cases it was reinforced by secular punishment. Those who refused to undergo penance were liable to be sentenced by the secular authority to fine or imprisonment or to be outlawed......it suited both state and Church in those days to identify crime as sin and hold that the secular law had a religious purpose as well as a punitive function''. (Rob. pp. 78, 79 and 93). The 'Prayaschit' (expiation) also served the purpose of modern reformative theory because the conditions of prayaschit were Anutapa, i.e., contribution and Uparama, i.e., resolution not to commit the wrongful act again. According to ancient legal theory, Dharma had social, religious and legal aspects and emphasised all the three aspects as Duties and King could enforce all these duties. That the offender was expected to surrender himself voluntarily for punishment (Gutama S.B.E. II, p. 244; Apastamba S.B.E. II, pp. 82 and 90) though the idea was based on fear of punishment in the after life, yet it emphasises the recognition of the principle of responsibility.[4]

Somewhat privileged treatment of Brahmin-offenders is visible in ancient law of Dharmasastras. In this, it exhibits the essential trend of all other ancient laws. The immunity of the Brahmin from capital punishment is only a concession given to the truly religious mode of life of the Brahmins and the important role they played in Vedic culture. Such privileges are not absent in modern times also in the case of certain dignitaries.

The emphasis upon justice and considerations of the circumstances of time and place show that distinctions regarding international wrongs and unintentional wrongs must have been prevailing in the minds of early jurists. Punishment, not only for hurt but also for attempt to hurt, was inflicted.

Ancient Indian legal theory of punishment is mainly preventive. According to mythology Brahama created, out of his own essence, 'Danda' to protect all creatures. This shows that like modern positivists the Indian jurists were aware of the evil potentialities of human nature. They considered that men by their nature were prone to evil and would fly at each other's throat but for fear of punishment. In the state the king was armed with the power to punish. Without the institution of State, anarchy would prevail which is described as a state of Matsya-Nyaya wherein the bigger fish swallows smaller one. This view is expressed by Manu, Kautilya and the other jurists and is also incorporated in the epics. In order to prevent a condition of society in which the strong are prone to bother and trouble and weak, punishment was made not only preventive but deterrent as well. It was for this reason that Manu directed that such offenders ought to the punished and even disfigured at a conspicuous public place. The purpose of severe punishments like those of death, exile, or mutilation, etc., seem to be not only preventive but deterrent also. Of all these we have ample proof in Manu. Manu, in another place, advises the king to cut off the offending limb of a thief to prevent him from stealing again. This is also the opinion of Brahaspati who recommends that in the case of taking by force women, men, gold, gems, the property of a deity, or a Brahman, Silk and (other precious) things the fine shall be equal to the value (of the article stolen) or double the amount shall be inflicted, by the king as a fine; or the thief shall be executed, to prevent a repetition (of the crime). Sukra is definite on this point when he opines that "the punishment of the wicked means prevention of wicked action by them. This is being quoted with advantage by P.N. Ramaswami, J.,[5] to indicate the severity of punishment. The end of punishment is also recognised to be corrective. Commentator like Yajnavalkya and others consider punishment as a means of placing on the path of dharma those who have deviated from it. The aim of the law-giver is also considered to be one of reforming the character of the offenders. Mahabharat gives expression to the same sentiment, when it advises the king to reform or correct the miscreants by punishment. Sukra advocates reformative end of punishment when he says. "The king should punish such bad men and also those who have been vitiated by bad company and teach them good ways of life".[6] Punishment is also considered as a purifying agent so when a thief is punished he is absolved of the sin or guilt. If the offender is wrongly forgiven the sin falls upon the King[7] (Ref. Chapter VI).

It is worth-mentioning here that the classical penologists and criminologists emphasised the need to treat the criminals more kindly and humanely. This philosophy is an historical outcome of a very harsh and severe criminal law in England, where not less then 160 offences were punishment with capital sentences. Such a situation, as it existed then, was looked with disfavour by the judges who, naturally wanted to lessen the rigours of such punishment and perhaps, it is submitted, this philosophy of reform of the criminal and penal law, has been taken to its extreme, so much so that the criminal is put in a favoured position. It is respectfully submitted that an erroneous view of this kind is still being continued today. The main thrust of their (criminologists and penologists), argument is based upon the doctrine of fault which stated briefly is that only that person should be punished whose fault has been proved beyond all reasonable doubt. This seems to be "The theoretical reason behind the many rules of evidence also. But this humble author is compelled to submit that this doctrine of fault is based upon animism and individualism whose influence is now neutralised because of the paternal attitude of the modern state which takes upon itself the social responsibility to deal with the modern emerging problems of criminal law. A study of the modern developments in the science of criminology and penology would show that the fault-doctrine has been completely rejected for the obvious reason that it is a costly luxury and yields results which are disappointing. The ancients took a saner view which was based upon the sole consideration of social and community interest. The ancients never suffered from the loose ends of either the animistic or the individualistic fault doctrine. How refreshing and animating to find this view of the ancients in dealing with the problems of criminal law as ultra-modern and appropriate, in the face of new developments in modern criminology. This practical approach of the ancients to cope with the problem of crime effectively seems more praise-worthy in the light of the fact that modern criminology has completely failed to find a formula and a method for dealing with the problem of crime. It is admitted frankly that it is not "an easy task to evolve a theory regarding 'crime' or 'criminal behaviour' and thus relate it to the other ancillary and allied phenomena and say with confidence or with a sufficient degree of certainty that the theory expounded will apply to a given set of circumstances and will yield results predicted. Nor is it necessary to propound a jurisprudential theory which may be universally applied, —it is not within the sphere of a lawyer".[8] Any theory, if it is necessary for us to evolve or any doctrine which we want to continue in our legal system must have a close relevance to the cultural setting of our country and the juristic heritage of our people.

TORT

Tort, as a civil remedy, though available, as has already been stated earlier, yet did not have a separate procedure. Modern actions of tort and private criminal litigation were both covered by 'Vyavahara'. To the ancients this, perhaps, appeared to be more beneficial for the litigants of India. If this principle is incorporated in our legal system, the poor litigant can get compensation for the injury to make good the personal loss and he can pray also for the punishment of the criminal in his own right. In the amended criminal procedure code some improvement has now been made by virtue of which compensation can be awarded in a criminal case to the aggrieved party. But this is in the hands of the judge who hears the criminal case. He may award a portion of the fine to the dependents of the deceased or to the injured. But still it cannot be claimed as a matter of right. In this way the interest of the society as well as that of individual can be served at the same time.

The law of wrongs, in ancient India had been founded on the concept of Dharma wherein a high conceptual regard is paid to duty. Law of tort on modern lines could not have flourished because of the social and cultural factors in Hindu society here :

(1) Dharma was the general policy which aimed at the attainment of the spiritual as well as the temporal welfare of the individual and, through him, of the community;
(2) Temporal welfare was promoted through the advancement of spiritual welfare;
(3) The Dharmasastras laid emphasis on duties rather than rights;
(4) Violation of duty attracted penal sanctions from the king;
(5) The Dharmasastras did not recognise a right of civil action in cases of tresspass to person, conversion, defamation and injuries affecting family relations;
(6) Dharmasastras did not recognise negligence, which is the most prolific source of tort litigation in modern times;
(7) Generally speaking it was the duty of the king to award damages rather than right of the victim to claim damages;
(8) In absence of proof of damage resulting from violation of duty, damages were not awarded;
(9) The Dharmasastras did not recognise non-physical harm as damage. As a result of this damages could not be awarded; for such non-physical harm.
(10) Provision was made for the payment of only ordinary or compensatory damages and not for payment of the examplary or vindictive damages.[9]

Modern law of tort is progressively going towards social insurance by rejecting the notion of fault or negligence as the basis of tortuous liability. The development of State's liability in tort also makes state responsible for torts. In our country this liability of the state has been recognised, though partially, in case of performance of non-sovereign functions. Thus the emphasis is put more on the notion of duty and less on rights—which was what ancient Indian dharmasastras stood for.

CONTRACT

For the functioning of society security of persons and property is to be guaranteed. More than that security of transactions is also be preserved. Law of contract is the expression of truthfulness – i.e., fulfilling one's own promises and honest mutual dealings with the members of society. In other words the fulfilment of promise is truth or 'Satya'. The metaphysical aspect of 'Satya' is existence and the enforcement of this 'Satya' is the 'Rit', the social aspect of it which is manifested in jural relation. Without this there is bound to be disorder. Truthfulness is then the fundamental basis of the idea of contract. "The purpose of the law of contract is to impart stability and security to certain temporary relationships with one another which men spontaneously enter into for themselves".[10] The development of law of contract is a normal consequence of social life. "The fact of contract is due to the natural conditions of the social and economic life and is essentially necessary in a moderately developed social existence in which the accumulation of wealth and the consequent co-operation, division of labour and mutual reliance are necessary concomitants.[11] The law of contract is a voluntary creation of law, where law to govern mutual relations is determined by the parties themselves. As early as Rig Vedic age we find a developed idea of contract. This will be illustrated by instance which follows. "There was a contract between Bhavayavya and Kaksivan that Kaksivan would prepare stoma for Bhavayavya and for this the later would pay the former hundred 'niskas'. Kaksivan performed his part of the contract where upon Bhavayavya paid him the promised sum".[12] We also find the contract of sale and purchase. There is also the development of law of debt, which holds a prominent place in early law. It was very stringent against debtor, and usurers, 'the Panis' who are condemned in several verses for their greed, hardheartedness, irreverence and niggardliness.

In Dharmasastra-period many of the Vyavaharpadas are concerned with many branches of law of contract, e.g., the contract of debt, pledge, mortgage, bailment, sale, partnership, hire-purchase but the writers do not give us the analysis of 'contract'. Nevertheless they have developed in their books the general principles of contract: They say a good deal about the competence of person to enter into contracts. The ancient writers have mentioned about what persons are competent to enter into transactions (Vyavahara). It is held "that dependent persons, minors, extremely old people, those charged with grave sins, Sannyasins, persons who are devoid of limb, and those who are addicted to vices (like drinking and whoring) are incompetent and agreements made with such people are invalid,[13] in some cases dependent persons are allowed to enter into contract if they are authorised by the head of the family. Kautilya also says that contracts—made by persons who are intoxicated at that time or are under the influence of wrath or are distressed or are of unsound mind or are under duress—are invalid. In view of Yajnavalkya contracts brought about by fraud of force are to be declared by the king as invalid. According to Narada wives, slaves and sons are not independents; Katyayana says that one should not give a loan to a minor, woman and slave; woman is incompetent to contract in the sense that she cannot bind by her contract the head of family or husband but she is not incompetent to enter into contract relating to her separate property. Liability to pay of one's debt and ancestor's debt was recognised on religious grounds. The liability for debt, like all other ancient laws, was very rigorous but Hindu law evolved the principle of 'Damdupat' at an early stage by which 'the amount of principal and interest recoverable at one time in a lump sum cannot be more than the double of the money lent. Ancient Indian law developed rules about pledges, sale, sale in market, overt, surety, deposit, bailment, etc. The doctrine of consideration as evolved in England, due to the need of a mercantile race, was considered as redundant in early law of India, for the simple reason that every human action was regulated not only be legal procedures but by an innate desire on the part of the people to behave morally and in accordance with 'dharma'.

The idea of contract did not take an ideological turn in ancient Indian thought as it had done in the West, where, as we shall presently see, it dominated the whole social and political scene. In India, contract, as a legal concept was recognised, from the very beginning. In India, the idea of contract was born, as has been noticed, a little while ago, in the sacred notion of 'dharma'. Not only this it was deified by even imagining, on the basis not of mere superstition but on authority of sacred texts, that all contracts (promises) are supervised by Vedic Gods, viz. Varun and Mitra (Atharva Veda I, 16.2). No contracts could be made without their knowledge. Considering the Western development of contract we find that the theory of social contract is built upon contract. The doctrine of social contract had its germ in political necessities of Greek life. "In Western political thought the social-contract theory goes back to the fourth century B.C., when the Greek city states were faced with the question of annihilation, first, at the hands of the Macedonian Conqueror, and, then, at those of the Romans. When the Greek philosophers were confronted with the loss of their independence, they turned to the question of replacing civic life by mere happiness which the individual might need. The sophist took the lead by stating that the state was the result of a voluntary agreement among men but that it was a hinderance to self-realisation, and therefore, opposed to nature. The Epicurians maintained, that the state rested upon individual self-interest. According to them law was an agreement of utility entered into by the individuals in order to secure protection against violence. Here was the beginning of the later idea of deliberate agreement amongst men to which the later system of Roman law gave a further impetus, when it developed the concept of obligation by contract. Gradually the Roman jurists incorporated in it the idea of government by contract, when they said that the power of the Roman Emperor was based upon the consent of the Roman people. That this idea was indeed, common to the ancient people is proved by the fact that in the old testament there is a covenant made before by king David and the Elders of Isreal.

"When Hobbes took up the idea of contract, it had already passed the stages of agreements in the feudal system and of the conciliar movement in the Church which had received the concepts of natural rights, social contract, and popular consent. But these ideas were lost in the struggles that followed in the Seventeenth and Eighteenth Centuries, when the theory of divine right of kings unsuccessfully fought against the growing strength of popular sovereignty based on the freedom of the individual and his right to rebel. It was at this stage that Hobbes (The Leviathan, 1651), and Locke (Two Treatises on Government, 1690), and Rousseau (Du Contract Social, 1763) took up the thread of contract shaping it in three different ways which are familiar to students of politics".[14] In the present-day Western civilisation, which has materialistic inclinations we find the gradual dissociation with religion which is a strong unifying influence. If it is so, their without being dogmatic, it can safely be asserted that religion is a unifying force and is valuable not only for the cohesive and corporate living but is also an indispensable factor in uplifting man's spirit and consequently guaranteeing his well-being and refinement. If this is so then, without it, legal theory becomes a partial expression of man's life. Finding themselves cut off from this unifying influence of religion, due to internicine wars and conflicts between the state and religion, the Western legal thinkers, out of sheer necessity started frantic efforts to search for some conceptual compendium which may be capable of embracing all the juristic requirements and found this in their so-called secular concepts.

Contract, Property and Rights are thus mere explorations of this approach and thinking but, let us not forget that these give us a temporary or false sense of security, hope and stability, and lead us to frustration only. From this point of view let us now survey briefly the theoretical basis of contract and the political purposes it served in the West which lent it undue importance.

Aristotle considered the whole legal field as the field of contract and suggests "that, in a general sense, the law itself is a kind of contract, so that whoever disregards or repudiates a contract is repudiating the law itself".[15] Hobbes indirectly identifies justice with contract when he thinks that one of the supreme law grounded on human nature is that man seeks peace and follows it. From this ensues his right to defend himself which is the second law. The third law is that in order to live in civil society it is necessary that men perform their covenants made. He took the position that the definition of injustice is no other than the non-performance of covenant. And whatsoever is not unjust in just. According to him in a state of nature there is not possibility of injustice. Promises can only be assured to be kept when there is the coercive power of the state to enforce them. When there does not exist such coercive power of the State, in the state of nature, covenants in that condition become meaningless. Justice defined as performance of covenant, can only exist in presence of the coercive power of State.[16] Plato linked the idea of contract with the idea of good and subscribed to the intuitional theory when he said that promises should be enforced because by that way good faith is preserved and the man who failed to keep his promises develops an ugly soul and comes to ruin.[17] Hegel considers contract as an expression of subjective will which enters into relation with another will and participates in a common will. The driving force of contract is the real existence of a free personality. It is the process "which expresses and reconciles the contradiction, that I remain an independent (e.g. in contract of sale) exclusive owner of something only identifying my will with that of another and ceasing to be an owner. There is a unity of different wills, a unity in which there is a surrender of differences and pecularities. In a real contract both parties surrender and both acquire property, i.e., an exchange.[18] Kant considers contract as an expression of personal right. "Kant's whole justification of enforcement turned on his idea of a common collective possession. One of the forms of right, according to Kant, is the possession of the active free-will of another person which includes the power to determine it by my will to a certain action according to the laws of the freedom......There must, therefore, be a positive transference or conveyance. But this is only possible on Kant's theory, by means of common will, through which objects come into the power of another, so that as one renounces as particular thing which he holds under the common right, the same object when accepted by another, in consequence of a positive act of will, becomes the property of that other. Kant calls the transference of the property of one to another its 'alienation', and the act of the united wills of two persons, by which what belonged to one passes to another, he terms 'contract'.[19] Kant's theory of contract then is that a man by contract withdraws himself from what is common property and effects his own alienation in favour of another. No theorising for justification of phenomena of contract seems to be convincing. Contract has been viewed only in the light of philosopher's own ideology, and there is no general agreement. About ethical justification on validity of contract, opinions also differ "According to some the ground is that a contract is the expression of a concurrence of will and the 'will is inherently worthy of respect'. The utilitarian explanation is that agreements satisfying the above requirements are likely to promote the interests of the parties agreeing without injuring others, on the assumption that sane adults can on the whole be trusted to provide for their own interests, if secured from interference. A third view appeals to the principle which enjoins the avoidance of injury to others. The moral basis of the law of contract is on this view not that the promiser has agreed to be bound, but that he has by his promise created a reasonable expectation that it will be kept and that it is right that the recepient should not be disappointed or suffer from its breach''.[20]

Moral ideal which is expressed in terms of freedom of contract is difficult to be accepted as an absolute moral standard or ideal for law. Even liberals, like J.S. Mill, have not subscribed to it in toto and have equated it with 'freedom of coercion' where it exists without regulation of law. Henry Maine has idealised this freedom of contract as a characteristic of progressive societies of the past but he has qualified it with the phrase 'hitherto'.[21]

''The right of contract is no more absolute than any other right; and when it comes into conflict with other rights, e.g. the right of workers to minimum conditions of a good life, its claims may have to be balanced in the interest of greater freedom of the whole. Again, it was part of the individualist doctrine of contracts that they were only valid when entered into freely and not under duress. But this implies substantial equality between the parties, and it could be reasonable argued that there was not such equality of bargaining power between a factory owner and unorganised adult workers. In this way legislation governing safety in factories or limiting hours of work for juveniles and woman was justified on the ground that, if it interfered with the freedom of the owners, it protected the freedom of weaker party, and that such protection could not safely be left to voluntary agreement''.[22] Thus 'freedom of contract' doctrine is a legal counterpart of exaggerated individualism which is founded on the notion of individual freedom and free-willing individuals as components of an ideal society, having as its economic counter-part in the freedom of trade, postulated by 'laissez faire' doctrine. The doctrine of contract in the guise of, 'laisse-faire' has created a class conflict between labour and capital and consequent degeneration of society by causing a greater mal-distribution of wealth and its concentration in a few hands. The practical effect is that rich have become more rich and poor more poor, and the whole gamut of human social relations get commercialised and mechanised to an extent that it has become a danger to human values and has brought down human dignity and effaced moral conscience. ''During the hey day of the regime of, 'laissez faire', could be said to run from the beginning of the Nineteenth Century to the out-break of the 1914 War, the idea of freedom of contract was in some way regarded as one of the supreme values of a developed society. State interference, especially in the economic sphere was treated as a great evil, and it was thought that the economy of a free society could best be allowed to develop through the right of the citizen to make his own contractual arrangement....The startling abuses which resulted from so unfettered a system led to a counter-move in favour of state control, even though this could infringe the contractual freedom of the individuals"............................[23] Again: "It was usually overloked by those who regarded freedom of contract as the foundation of a free society that without equality of bargaining position such freedom was likely to be entirely one-sided. To say, for instance, that the factory workers of mid-victorian England were free to accept or decline the terms and conditions of work offered to them by the employers, and therefore, should be left to make their own bargain, was to ignore completely the underlying economic realities. With the rise of the trade unions of recent times something like genuine equality of bargaining power has transformed the character of industrial relations, though this does not mean that there is not still scope of state intervention in these matters......Moreover, the modern state has found it increasingly necessary to recognise that many classes of persons, such as purchases of goods (especially under hire-purchase agreements) are in need of protection against traders and supplier who seek to impose unfair terms and conditions on those who are unable to bargain effectively in their own interests. The widespread growth of so-called 'standard-form' contracts has further exposed the unreality of freedom of contract in the economic world of today. In some instances legislation (such as Hire and Purchase Acts) has been passed to remedy the more palpable of the abuses which have emerged as the inevitable economic consequences of unfettered freedom of contract".[24]

It is quite obvious that Western juristic mind, in the absence of the some common standard of legal obligation which was general as well as specific, had to take recourse at first to express the foundation of political and legal obligation by means of some specific concepts which later proved unsuitable to hold within their circumference the vast implications of general legal theory and hence proved unworthy of themselves. Had there been an all inclusive notion, like that of 'dharma' there would have been no difficulty. The dharma is immanent as well as transcendent. It expresses the idea of a specific rule as well as the general notion of law, Right, Duty etc. It implies the doctrine of 'the rule of law', 'constitution', 'political obligations', 'social contract', etc. as efficiently as none can. This is the reason that in Indian thought there has not been useless and conflicting formulations of juristic and political nature as they are in Western thought with the consequential-confusion, and frustration. The tired Western mind again and again wants to approximate in different forms the over-all-concept like that of dharma but all that it yields in, is limited and provisional concepts which become unserviceable after the lapse of time. The Western concept of contract is, it is submitted, a 'pseudo-dharma' concept and has tried to emphasise the importance of the free-willing individual without reference to social responsibility in a wrong manner because in it lies only a perverted sense of rights of the individuals without an adequate reference to their duties towards society.

Again, in the absence of the concept like that of dharma the Western political theory, when it got secularised, felt difficulty in explaining the idea of political obligation which is also an expression of the notion of constitutionalism and the rule of law both of which have become the basis of modern democracies. It appears that resort to 'contract' was made to explain the nature of legal obligation. To Maine 'contract' essentially expresses the idea of obligation. "The obligation is the 'bond' or chain with which the law joins together persons or groups of persons, in consequence of certain voluntary act".[25] This certainly expresses nearness to our notion of 'dharma' which holds people together for forging duty. Contract property is, pact plus obligation. The only difference that appears to this author is that whereas dharma merges individual and society together, Maine's 'bond' is founded on the mere interest of the individual. In the concept of 'dharma', bond or obligation is duty as a synonym of right of good. This duty is not an obligation arising merely out of contract between parties of an atomistic society in which the parties are sensitive about their freedom and rights. But the obligation in the concept of dharma does not bind the parties because of necessity or convenience. Further this obligation is not an imposed one, only from without, but is also binding from within. It would thus seem that an obligation or duty thus conceived must necessarily lead to well-being and happiness. The Indian concept of dharma is synthetic and integrating and because of this resort to any other theory becomes unnecessary. Indian theory of origin of state propounded by Bhandarkar, even if labelled as social contract theory, is quite different from the Western theory. Here the ruler is not a party to the contract.

The ruler is ordained by God to rule. But this is not what Westerners call 'the divine right'. The Indian king rules but within the bounds prescribed by 'dharma'. In the West the whole emphasis is on the individual and his political rights; in the East (India) there is no such emphasis for the simple reason that the ruler and the ruled are governed by their respective duties prescribed by the Sastras. There is no antagonism between the State and the people because the ancient Indian people never built their theories and concepts on individual, social or political ego. As against this they believed in sacrifice, sense of duty and consequent sublimation of their ego. The theory of constitutionalism, in its essence, is a concept of political framework of society. It is a way of settlement of power, its distribution and structure, controlled by a political mechanism by reference to a higher law. In its popular sense, it is a check on arbitrary exercise of power, a limitation on absolutism and assertion of the ultimate sovereignty of the people. All these ideas ensue from the doctrine of people's consent or volition as the basis of polity—which is the necessary aspect of the contract doctrine. The concept of dharma as Rajdharma fulfils the requirement of constitutionalism. The problems and controversies of modern constitutional democracies are unimaginable from the point of view of dharma, because it has potency to do away with all the contradictions and inclines towards unification. Constitution, as a ground-norm, or some higher law of political society is, in the view of this humble author, an attempt to make it a substitute for 'dharma'. But, owing to the political orientation of constitutionalism, itself, we are facing enormous difficulties in making it a success.

LAW OF PROPERTY

Property is not only 'bhog' (enjoyment or possession) but in its essence, it is one's 'Mamatva' or 'Savatva' (own-ness) which is conceptualised in ownership. The magic of 'own-ness' transmutes matter and idea into property. "To be able to say 'memedam' (this is mins) about something constitutes the very soul of owning or appropriation".[26] According to Mahabharata proprietary consciousness is created only by the existence of state. State by its sanction of 'danda' ensures property. "For it enjoins that vehicles, apparel, ornament, jewels, be enjoyed by those to whom they belong, and that one's wife, children and food must not be encroached upon by others. And it is only through *bhaya* or fear of the state that people observe these injunctions, and the sanctity of property is kept entire. A distinction is here brought out between mere 'bhog' and 'mamatva' as the basis of the difference between the non-state and the state. In Europe the identical discrimination has been made by Rousseau in his social contract. "In the 'state of nature', says he, 'there is but possession, which is only the effect of the force or right of the first occupant'; whereas ownership which is founded only upon positive title, is an incident of 'Civil Society'".[27] Yet property is not considered in ancient legal theory of India as the cause but is said to be the effect of State. It does not justify the thesis of Marxism where state is considered as posterior to private property.

In general, property could be acquired by purchase, partition, seizure or finding and discovery, but there were special modes prescribed by the varnas of society, which are considered as additional ways of acquiring property and ensue forth from the special function performed by the Varnas.

According to dharmasastras the acceptance of gifts and other modes are prescribed for Brahmins as constituting acquisition of property. Acquisition by conquest in suitable for Kshatriyas and husbandary and trade are the authorised modes of property for Vaisyas.

The ancient Indian law of property had reached maturity and is comparable to any ancient or modern law. There we find clear distinction between possession, ownership and prescription. Various ways of acquiring onwership are enumerated in dharmasastras. Law of prescription is quite developed and incorporates various exceptions. For prescription, uninterrupted possession is considered to be very essential. There are many kinds of ownership. The distinction of movable and immovable property is worked out. The law on pledge and mortgage is quite developed. The evolution of law of property also tends from collective to individual ownership.

In ancient India the institution of property was so organised that it could not become as a menance to the society as it is today in the modern materialistic world. The individual ownership, i.e., private property was recognised but the Indian people were so contented that accumulation of property could not bring degeneration to society. Firstly, it was an agricultural society unlike our modern industrial society. It did not concentrate wealth of the society in a few hands. Secondly, the influence of religion was so such that the people could not ignore the injunction of Dana (originally distribution) which proved a security for the poor and the learned people. Again, the theory of ashrams, where men had to retire and entrust or distribute the wealth of their descendants or others, was also a factor which would not allow greed and wealth-mania to grow and take on an anti-social character. As a whole, the whole culture was moving from matter to spirit in such a way that matter or property could not acquire the status of the super-imposing absolute value. The doctrine of duty, had a powerful hold on men's mind, as a result of which private property had no chance to transform itself into a sacred private right. The right of property could not be thought of to be an inalienable one. The Varna system property performed a proper function and the idea of other-wordliness made the substance of property in substantial to a very reasonable extent. It could never create the politics of class conflicts, class ideologies, and capitalistic economy, and police state. The culture was such that there was proper functional integration, so strong and sufficient, as to survive to this day with all its deficiencies. In Varna society Brahmins could not accumulate property, as they were to be occupied with learning and teaching of religion. In early society there was no institutionalisation of religion to hold political power. The Kshatriyas were to be the fighters and rulers. They were to hold only political power. Vaishyas were traders, and they alone, were functionally suitable as holders of property. The Sudras was servants rendering service to all the higher Varnas and due to social status and low remuneration could not accumulate property. As there was harmony in the functions of Varnas and their mutual dependence, property only performed its appropriate social function of integration. It never could attain the status of political power. Under the influence of the-ism and expectation of the prospects of a better life in the other world, property had no tendency to remain concentrated in the hands of the rich, but had the tendency to perform the task of social welfare. A regular distribution by way of Dana and Punya was prescribed by our Shastras. Again property had its centre in only one class and which was only a constituent part of the whole with delegations towards the other parts. Property-oriented ideologies and materialistic approaches to life and its aims never loomed large on the mental horizon of Indians of those days. The wealth of a person could not influence the ruler and pandits of society as it does today when we find that power of money has become the motive force of all our thoughts and institutions. The disintegrating materialistic thinking has accentuated selfishness which undermines synthetic and collective consciousness leaving behind disquiet, distress and frustration.

In India, in these circumstances, no need for theories for the justification of property could arise.

But due to the lack of agreement and understanding on fundamentals of society, and under the influence of pseudo-scientific attitude and inquiry, the Western writers have to render justification for one's own right to property. They have made a search for ethical justifications for property, as a result of which three theories of property have come into being:

(i) The natural law theory considers right to property as a fundamental right of a man irrespective of whatever the policy to which he belongs;

(ii) The liberal tradition, makes property justifiable because of the origin and/or nature of acquisition. Property, to such thinkers, arises due to one's occupation and application of one's own labour. Other factors according to their analysis only contribute to the value of the products of labour.

(iii) The third kind of theory wherein the justification is sought solely on the basis of public good and well-being of society.

Inspite of these theories the modern problems of our industrial age remain unsolved. This is so because as long as the holders of property do not realize their responsibility and are not imbued with a sense of service, the question of property will baffle solution. Ginsberg, however, recognises the responsibility of the components of society towards each other and to work for the well-being of all, with all the concern of society for an integrated one.[28] This, it is submitted, has actually been a directing force of ancient Indian culture where we do not find hard contours of absolutism of state or the individual. Property is never viewed as the end in itself but a means to social welfare. To the extent that property becomes the expression of individual ego, the cultural trend directs one's attention away from it to practice 'Vairagya' or detachment which is only a method of checking property to attain the status of a political power.

The 19th Century political and legal thought has oscillated between the extreme views about property. "On the one hand, the practical foundation of social organisation has been the doctrine that the particular forms of property which exist at any moment are a thing sacred and inviolable that any thing may properly become the object of property rights, and that, when it does, the title to it is absolute and unconditioned''.[29]

On the other extreme the position of private property is attacked in socialistic thought. It is asserted that economic evils of society are mainly due to the institution of private property and its unregulated operation in modern industrial life. The rationale behind the idea of property, it seems and to some extent true also, is that it gives security to the holders of the property. ''Whatever may have been the historical process by which they have been established and recognised, the rationale of private property traditional in England is that which sees in it either the results of the personal labour of its owner, or—what in effect the same thing—the security that each man will reap where he has sown. Locks argued that a man necessarily and legitimately becomes the owner of 'whatsoever he removes out of the state that nature hath provided' and that 'he makes it his property' because he 'hath mixed his labour with it'. Paley derived property from the fact that 'it is the intention of God that the produce of the earth be applied to the use of man, and this intention cannot be fulfilled without establishing property'. Adam Smith, who wrote the dangerous sentence, 'Civil Government in so far as it is instituted for the protection of property, is in reality instituted for the defence of the rich against the poor', sometimes spoke of property as the result of usurpation—'landlords, like other men, love to reap where they have never sowed'—but in general ascribed it to the need of offering protection to productive effort. 'If I despair of enjoying the fruits of labour', said Bentham, repeating what were in all essentials the utilitarian arguments of Hume, 'I shall only live from day to day; I shall not undertake labours which will only benefit my enemies'. This theory passed into America, and became the foundation of the sanctity ascribed to property in *The Federalist* and implied in a long line of judicial decisions on the Fourteenth Amendment to the Constitution. Property, it is argued, is a moral right, and not merely a legâl right, because it insures that the producer will not be deprived by violence of the result of his efforts''.[30]

The rationale of the protection of property was that without it wealth could not be produced and business could not be carried on. In order to counter-balance the power of feudals in England and France the small property owner was protected by the far sighted statesmen. This type of protection contemplates only certain types of property, which may help one to work and may benefit production. It performs a social function. Such property has been designated as 'active property'. Such property as is merely concentrated in a few hands and is not as instrument of production has been called 'passive property'. Property, which results in maldistribution of wealth and vests political power in the hands of the industrialists does not deserve to be protected for it is certain that, in the end, it would prove a menance to society.

Property ought not be allowed to become a sort of limited sovereignty which it is prone to become because the essence of property is power, secured by some individual or groups, as against all others. It may even become the focal point of a private empire as is witnessed today in countries of affluence. The result is that, devoid of proper function, property becomes 'the greatest enemy of legitimate property itself.[31] It creates a reign of industrial absolutism. It is for these reasons that governments, even in democracies, have started thinking in directions in which concentration of property in a few hands be prevented.

They have imposed many restrictions, on the right of property and in our own country where this right is, at present, incorporated in the constitution as a fundamental right, (Art. 31) having many restrictions, is now sought to be made merely a legal right. But there are critics who point out that because of many restrictions, the very property is now vanishing away. It is true that the right of property, when considered in its traditional meaning has suffered severe limitations. But the need is to redefine or reconstruct the concept of property.

We are today living in an age, where due to industrial and technological advancement, huge profits are available to the industrialists and technological experts. These profits, therefore, accumulate in the hands of the few as compared to the vast multitudes of humanity in a country who are deprived of their legitimate share though they contribute towards this amassing of wealth. Naturally, there is justifiable cause for frustration apart from the fact, which is accepted on all hands, that it is a denial of the welfare and interest of the greater part of humanity. It is, therefore, necessary to strike a balance which is possible if we interpret the concept of property in its wider perspective—the perspective in which property is not only an instrument of security of the person but an institution of service. The problem in this case is now to achieve this end. Supposing the whole power regarding property is vested in the State, can there be a guarantee of proper service to all the citizens of that 'State'? The results in the communistic and fascist countries cannot be fully assessed in so short a time. But all that we know is that danger of absolutism looms large in those countries. "Therefore, instead of concentrating property in the hands of the state, what is needed is a system in which property of all kinds is distributed as widely as possible, where nobody is perpetually excluded from having access not only to consumer's property but also to the means of production. This, in one form or the other, is a fundamental postulate of a healthy democracy towards which the modern world seems to be moving".[32]

INDIAN CONCEPT OF PROPERTY

The whole legal theory of the West is in fact the justification of the existence of property and need of its regulation. The whole range of thought is only a debate between individual and social purposes. It emphasises the need to achieve a harmonious relation between the individual interest and social interest. Every developed culture, in order to retain its vitality, must strike a balance between rights and duties or obligations, in regard to property. Ancient Indian culture, with its planned social system based on functionalism, i.e., Varna organisation, pre-fixed the role and functions of classes and individuals by the authority of Dharma. Whatever be its later degeneration, it never witnessed the rise and fall of individualism and, vicissitudes of autocracies and revolutions. Inspite of India's enslavement, she has gained freedom without violence. From the very beginning property had its proper social function and abnormal growth of theories and justifications never had their chance of birth or survival. In the 40th Chapter of Yujurveda it is said :-

> "O Man : God is pervaded in all the objects of this world. Therefore, enjoy all objects with detachment, do not covet others wealth". With a little change of words this again becomes the opening verse of 'isoupanishad'.

One meaning of this verse is that God is everywhere and is the seer of all deeds. Therefore, under the influence of greed one has not to covert another's wealth and involve oneself in crimes, as wealth is of transitory nature and often changes hands. Again, there is great emphasis upon 'dana' which, in its original meaning, is distribution of wealth and not charity. Later, under changed circumstances, charity in the form of distribution, is enjoined upon all the individuals of three Varnas. The individual should perform 'Dana' of wealth for the welfare of men. In Arthaveda it is said, "O man you should earn, with hundred hands but perform 'dana' with a thousand hands".

(शतहस्त समाहर सहस्त्र संकिर–अथर्ववेद 3-2. 4-5).

The role of Dana is very great. It is the performance of Dharma or law. Whatever we earn we should not be selfish in consuming it alone. We should enjoy our wealth together. In Veda it is enjoined. "O men your drinking places be common. You take food together I bind you by the bond of love. You make prayers to God together and live united just like spokes of the wheal of Chariot which are united with the hub or its navel".

(Atharveda-3- 30-6). In this context Paramatman (God) again says : "O men, make you men, who enjoy things together, and become of one mind and take food together". According to dharmasastras if Brahmins, Kshtriyas and Vaisyas do not perform 'Dana' they do not obey law. One of the Vrata or injunctions is to practise 'Dana'—which means not to accumulate property out of greed beyong one's need.

Acharya Priya Vrata Vedasvasechapati[33] points out that according to the Varna system all the Varnas are trustees of the people or nation. This implies that if property is abused, ownership of the property can be wrested from such person. There is no right of property by birth but it accrues only by its right use. In the capitalistic systems property cannot be expropriated because it can be inherited by birth. It is only in Puranic times that Varnas were based on birth and so must have been the case with property. Vedic-Varna-theory considers that he who uses property properly, alone uses it. Any one who abuses property will make it liable to be confiscated by the king. A trader who is not using his property for the welfare of the nation is liable to loose his property by the order of the king.[34]

Both capitalistics and communists consider that property is the result of labour. But capitalism also considers birth as a title to property which is denied by communists. According to Aryasamaj thinkers, Vedic-Varna-theory does not consider that labour alone gives title to property. If a person wants to destroy his self-earned property or wants to burn his purchased house, he is liable to suffer confiscation of his property.[35] In Varna-system property could be inherited from parents the right of private property is not absolute and unrestrained.

There are various restrictions which delimit this right. In capitalism the right of private property is considered absolute and unrestricted, as a result of which evil consequences follow. In case of communism and socialism the restrictions are only physical and have their basis in Law. Because of these limitations the person feels that his property is taken away from him by force. He is depressed, sad and is dissatisfied with the state when his hard earned wealth is taken away from him. Thus, communism gives very limited recognition to private property as the communists believe in socialisation of the means of production but this system undermines the psychological element contained in the idea of private property. Private property is the extension of man's ego and his love of self. This type of ego and self-love is a power to reckon with. It can be utilised for creative purposes and has been the main spring of the development of trade and business without which a nation cannot prosper.

Mahatma Gandhi has not defined property but this theory of property is juristic in essence because he has put forward the legal concept of "trusteeship" of property as an ideal social norm. To him possession or ownership is not so important as its use according to one's need. His dictum as he puts it, is : "I suggest that we are thieves in a way. If I take anything that I do not need for my own immediate use, and keep it, I thieve it from somebody else. I venture to suggest that it is the fundamental law of Nature, without exception, the Nature produces enough for our wants from day to day, and if only everyday took enough for himself and nothing more, there would be no pauperism in this world, there would be no man dying of starvation in this world. But so long as we have got this inequility, so long we are thieving. I am no socialist and I do not want to disposes those who have got possessions; but I do say, that personally, those of us who want to see light out of darkness have to follow this rule......In India we have got three millions of people having to be satisfied with one meal a day, and that meal consists of a *Chapati* containing no fat in it, and a pinch of salt. You and I have no right to anything that we really have until these three millions are clothed and fed better". Acquisitiveness, divorced from need is theft. As regards 'possession' which is the necessary consequence of property, Gandhi says : "Possession implies provision for the future. A seeker after Truth, a follower of the Law of Love cannot hold anything against tomorrow. God never stores for morrow; He never creates more than what is strictly needed for the moment......Our ignorance or negligence of the Divine Law, which gives to man from day to day his daily bread and no more, has given rise to inequalities with all the miseries attendant upon them.[36] The rich have a superfluous store of things which they do not need, and which are therefore, neglected and wasted, while millions are starved to death for want of sustenance.....The rich should take the initiative in dispossession with a view to a universal diffusion of the spirit of contentment. If only they keep their own property within moderate limits, the starving will be easily fed, and will learn the lesson of contentment alongwith the rich''.[37] Gandhiji thought that equal distribution of property or wealth was very necessary but he never wanted to snatch wealth from the rich. He had a great faith in their goodwill. Indeed at the root of this doctrine of property is the idea of the trusteeship of the wealthy for superfluous wealth possessed by them. The rich man will be left in possession of his wealth, of which he will use what he reasonably requires for his personal needs and act as a trustee the remainder to be used for the society. In this argument honesty on the part of the trustee is assumed. The great Mahatma never approved of the idea of privilege and monopoly. Capital to him is not an evil in itself. It is the wrong use of capital which is an evil. In social and economic life capital in some form or other has its own usefulness. Trusteeship of the rich is not a legal fiction. By this principle life will be governed by love. ''Absolute trusteeship is an abstraction like Euclid's definition of a point, and is equally unattainable. But if we strive for it, we shall be able to go further in realising a state of equality on earth than by any other method''.[38] He was aware of the fact that complete renunciation by the rich is not possible. ''All that can legitimately be expected of the wealthy class is that they should hold their riches and talents in trust and use them for the service of the society. To insist on more would be to kill the goose that laid the golden eggs''.[39]

Property in the form of capital is the power of society. It is that economic power which cannot be allowed to be misused by persons who are blind to the interests of society. To extend Gandhiji's idea of service contained in property, Vinoba Bhave declared that society has the right upon the capital. Gandhiji used to say that God has provided air and water for the free use of all. All the persons should have common right upon all things. Common right means the right of those who think of the welfare of all the people of the society—who work for the progress of society with a sense of service.[40]

The persons, the people are also the property of the Nation. To destroy the physique or to wreck the health of a person is not the right either of the greedy rich nor of the labourer. In order to spoil such wealth of the nation, if one uses economic power it is to be a punishable crime.[41] A description of the views of these seers is indicative of the very ideas which were saturated in ancient concept of property.

In Indian culture the collective consciousness of society has been called 'Vishnu'. From the aspect of power its two aspects have been symbolised as wives of 'Vishnu'. 'Shree' is one who has her seat in the person of 'Vishnu'. 'Lakshmi' is one who is not so seated but lives apart from his person. What Gandhiji conceived as economic power is like Shree. According to him economic power is not a thing to be viewed from a distance. It must have common (Samyak) utilisation for social progress. Lakshmi can be called, in the language of the economist as 'dead money'. It is a proverbial saying of ours that if wealth is not utilised properly then it will get destroyed. 'Dead Money' which is not useful for society is not better than destroyed money. When the capital is in social service then alone it can fulfil the function of 'Dhan' or wealth. The persons who help in this cause are called 'Dhanya Purush', good or wealthy persons.
for the security of wealth in a bank Gandhiji says that real bank for wealth is 'public'. Though Gandhiji recognises public right upon wealth but he did not consider correct the view of communism which is in favour of abolishing private right of property. According to him the individual is the defender of the economic power of the society and is its trustee. His duty is to keep secure wealth, till it is not needed by society. Capitalists and rich are the part of society and have no existence apart from it. Gandhiji did not believe in liquidation of capitalists but in effecting the change of their hearts. He did not like capitalism but wanted to give capitalists a chance to work as trustees, as protectors of economic power of the society. He did not want that state capitalism should take the place of individualist capitalism and was not in favour of nationalisation on the lines of communism. He wanted that means of production and labour should be utilised for the welfare of the whole human race.[43] The Bhudan movement is simply an extension of Gandhiji's idea of property as it is nothing but reclaiming the land of the village in the village itself. According to Vinoba Bhave property in land is not private property. As air, water are the gifts of God for all, the same is true in regard to land.

Ultimately all land belongs to God. Earth has been considered by our Vedas as mother. We cannot become its owners. Bhoodan is 'Praja-Suya-Yajna', as it is meant for people. It is a movement for voluntary giving of land for its re-distribution. Land must belong to one who ploughs it. It is a movement for the just distribution of land. The slogan is सबै भूमि गौपाल की; which has social meaning सभी भूमि है गाँव की It is a movement of the liquidation of the idea of ownership which is in tune with Upanishadic wisdom—as told in the first verse of Isavasyo Upanishad in which property or wealth is considered the God's gift which should be enjoyed with Tyag (त्याग) i.e., without the sense of ownership. The theory of Bhoodan is re-enforced by the trinity of दान, यज्ञ and तप. It is further inspired from साम्य योग i.e. to see God in all and to see all in God. Even in Varna-system none except the Vaisya could accumulate wealth. Even the Vaisya is not allowed to accumulate wealth in Ashrams of Brahmancharya, Vana-Prasha and Sanyas. Again accumulation of property of wealth is only meant for the upkeep of other Varnas. The motto of Bhoodan "सब भूमि गोपाल की" and "सम्पति सब रघुपति कै जाही have been taken from our great poet Tulsidas. It has the heritage of our culture.[44] Bhoodan Yajna transforms the two fundamental values of capitalism viz., profit and ownership into 'dana' and Yajna. Dana is distribution of the surplus not needed by the Donor and Yajna is the distribution of wealth for the cause of society. Samya Yoga, as social reconstruction, plans that one who has hunger must have with him the means of producing food. One who is not hungry need not possess the means of producing food. It is a way to and non-productive and anti-social ownership. Vinoba does not want to bring a change by legal process because law as a means of social change is infested with its defects and follows the path of force. Vinoba wants to follow the path of 'Karuna' (compassion).[45] To facilitate the distribution of land, many states have enacted Bhoomi dan Yajna legislation.

Our law in the Supreme Court after retreats and reversions has outgrown the individualistc *laissez-faire* notion bout sanctity of private property which is not so fundamental a right now. Now private property can be acquired by state from private persons and compensation can be fixed by government.

PROCEDURE

The law of procedure as we know, is that branch of the law which governs the process of litigation. It is the law of actions 'Jus quod ad actions pertinet'–using the term action in a wide sense to include all legal proceedings, civil or criminal''.[46] The substantive law is more concerned with the purposes and subject-matter of litigation rather than with the process of litigation. Nevertheless, there has to be a harmony between procedural law and substantive law so that, justice may be administered efficaciously. In order to do so it must have before it some basic or fundamental concept which is capable of expressing the total values and culture of the society adequately. If such master-concept is not available, i.e., if there is no articulation of a broad concept which can co-ordinate and organise all the values, goals and aspirations of people then the ends and values of law are bound to be expressed wrongly or rather inadequately by some minor or limited concept which has no conceptual capacity to express the totality of values. This will lead to failure of that concept to represent all the values. This happens when contract or property or procedure or the rule of law is taken (mistakenly) as it is done today, as the comprehensive and highest values of law and life, they be all and end all of them. In this way uncalled for the unusual importance is given to these psuedo-concepts, and the truth becomes known and their inadequacy and fruitlessness are realised only at a great cost when damage has already been done. Since our laws are administered to-day on the basis of these alien ideas and concepts, we are witnessing a sad spectacle in which man is neither happy nor contented, in which a regular tug of war is taking place between the various organs of the Government–the Legislative, the judicial and the Executive–resulting in a conflict and sometimes a complete deadlock. These pulls create disharmony among the different sections of the society, which cause economic imbalance on the one hand and violence on the other. In the light of this, it is submitted that all these ills and the malaise can be remedied if we have master concept of our own which can give expression to the total spirit of our culture in the modern context. Such master concept of law, in ancient Indian, was 'Dharma'.

The Anglo-American jurists made-futile attempts to express the basic legal urges by making 'procedure' the method as well as the end of law, which has resulted in an exaggerated emphasis on the procedural aspect which is upheld for its own sake. Nevertheless it is an unconscious and blind search for a concept like that of 'Dharma' which they cannot find, Fetish of common law towards procedure created a toughness, and stunted its growth. The procedural preoccupation has been detrimental to the common law jurisprudence. As Paton observes: "Moreover, if we look at the course of history, we see that in the middle period substantive law is inextricably intertwined with procedural formalities. The method by which a right can be enforced naturally determines to some extent the nature of the right. At some periods procedure seem to become an end in itself and 'substantive law has at first the look of being gradually secreted in the 'interstices of procedure'. Even in modern England although the 'forms of action are dead....their ghost still haunts the precints of the law. In their life, they were the powers of evil, and even in death they have not wholly ceased from troubling".[47] The Ancient Indian Law had attained all the characteristics of a mature legal system. It has been recognised that, it had division of civil and criminal cases; it provided special rules for criminal cases; law regarding plaint and summoning of the accused; provisions for arrest even before the filing of the suit, exemption from arrest to certain persons, punishment for disregard of summons; recording of plaint, defect of the plaint; burden of proof, examination of witnesses, amicable settlement or compromise; variety of witnesses, their appointment, limitation regarding minimum number in relation to their special qualities, capacity; desirability of witnesses, their unreliability; method of evidence, taking of oath; punishment for perjury and concocting false evidence, proof by ordeal, witnesses, documents, inferences; Verdict or decision by majority of judges; execution of Verdict; Self-help e.g. in causes of debt and so on and so forth. In short, ancient Indian law had all the requisites of a mature and workable system. The litigation in courts called Vyavahar was never considered as a bout but Vyavahar had its aim in discovery of truth and king or State was not only an impartial observer but also had the responsibility to find the truth and do justice. The whole legal system was geared to this aim. Procedure or legal ritualism was not allowed to be resorted to as an end in itself. In India professionalism–the bane of modern law–could not develop and law was on the whole, the aspect of life in general and its culture, i.e., dharma (Chapter 3). State or King represented law and was also governed by it. Law or dharma was not only the ruler of the rulers but a complete reference to the problems of life, a comprehensive constitution for all the aspects of individual and social life. It is an integrating discipline par excellence to the satisfaction of all, generating all the feelings of respect, participation, andearment, and awe which a legal system as such is capable to do. Conflicts between man and society or between man and state, were settled according to Dharma--Rules which applied to all equally. There was no need to sanctity property against state's interference as property itself performed a limited function in a Dharma-governed society. The scene of struggle of political power was not there between the different institutions, agencies, or classes because power contemplated to be distributed according to the norm and necessity of culture, which was inviolable. The revolts and revolutions which raged in the Western hemisphere later did not haunt the minds of the ancient Indian people.

The Role of Procedure in Western Jurisprudence

It cannot be denied that procedure also gives certain rights like right of hearing and appeal, which are as good as substantive rights. Notwithstanding this, procedure cannot be allowed to acquire such heroic proportions as to superimpose and raise itself to the highest legal ideal. Because, firstly, there is inherent natural tendency of a legal system to express some ideal. Secondly, in the absence of proper mechanism or trusted concepts, this urge towards legal ideal starts experimenting with concepts and tries to accommodate the wholesome view of the supreme value which may not get its fuller expression due to the limitations inherent in the concepts adopted. Thirdly, it may also happen that due to clashing ideologies the culture has not realised its cultural ideals and is trying and testing different values. It seems, in ancient India, its values were settled very early to become the permanent aspects of our culture and consequently of law.

The genesis of great legal values of common law system lies in its procedure. The great Charter, The 'Magna Carta', in truth, asserted only procedural safeguards but that was not a novel development for English legal history. That part of the story which concerns procedural safeguards is generally considered to have begun at Runnymede on the Thames under the leadership of Stephen Langton, the Archibishop of Canterbury, exacted the Magna Carta--the Great Charter--from King John. But the story goes back long before that. The Mosaic Code imposed a number of procedural safeguards, such as public trial and the right of confrontation...

"The Romans too enjoyed certain procedural safeguards now included among the liberties of Americans. According to the Acts of the Apostles, Porcius Festus, Roman procurator of Judea, deemed it 'unreasonably to send a prisoner and not withal to signify the crimes laid against Him'. 'It is not', Fastus reported, 'the manner of the Romans to deliver any man to die, before that he which is accused have the accusers face to face, and have License to answer for himself concerning the crime laid against him''.

"Thus, when King John consented to the thirty-ninth article of the *Magna Carta*–that 'No freeman shall be taken or imprisoned, out-lawed, or exiled, or in any way harmed, nor will we go upon or send upon him, save by the lawful judgment of his peers or by the law of the land'–he was establishing no new precedent. This article itself was apparently taken from an earlier continental source and reflected usages well established in England who the Great Charter was given".[48]

The great Charter was intrinsically a security or guarantee against an action which was without a legal procedure. It got acknowledged that the King can be required to judge, not arbitrarily, but according to 'the law of the land'. At first, this protection was limited to feudal lords, later in 1354 it was extended to all men assuring that no man was to be harmed except by 'the due process of law'. It is very clear that in the absence of a master concept of law like Dharma, which was the concept of a total integration of constitutional, administrative, procedural, civil, criminal law, the whole course of constitutional growth had to ensure from the Charter which was mainly a demand for legal procedure. In fact, Charter is not born so great, but 'greatness was thrust upon it', by thought-begging of Centuries. The real importance of Charter is extrinsic and beyond the province of procedure. It has been observed: "Its greatness was ascribed to it by succeeding generations, and therein lies its real significance. For the Charter, whether as the result of bad historical research, romanticism, wishful thinking, or any other reason, in time came to be looked upon as truly the Charter of liberties of free Englishmen. Through the Centuries Englishmen in trouble with the authorities invoked the Charter as guarantor of rights–such as trial by jury and *habeas corpus*–whose relationship with it was, if not fanciful, then certainly remote and tenuous, English Public opinion was quick to rally around any claim for liberty made in the name of the Charter. By the time, Madison and his colleagues added the Bill of Rights to the American constitution, they had acquired a gloss of centuries that made of it a world of liberties which the barons at Runnymeda never dreamed of, and which would have shocked and terrified them if they had''.[49] Edward Coke gave it such an interpretation that he could champion the cause of parliament in the fight against James I and Charles I, who asserted their royal prerogatives. ''Although neither his history nor his historical interpretations were entirely accurate, his reasoning was brilliant and his arguments impressive--in no small measure--because they harmonized so well with the growing libertarian spirit of Seventeenth-Century England and with the democratic liberatarianism of Eighteenth-Century America. Coke's Institutes, published in 1628, contained a commentary upon the *Magna Carta* in which he showed to the satisfaction of the American colonists the identity in meaning between the Charter's 'Law of the Land' and the prevalent 'due process of law' and that the purpose of these provisions was to protect to the citizen from governmental oppression''.[50(a)] Again ''when Edward Coke contested the claimed right of James I to remove from the law courts and to judge for himself whatever cases he wished the king replied that, if Coke was correct, then the King was 'under the law, which was treason of affirm'. But Coke stood his ground and replied that the king 'Ought not be under men but under God and the law'. The inclusion in the Bill of Rights of the procedural safeguards deemed necessary to insure fair play for accused Americans, constituted a recognition that in our democracy the State, like the king, is not above the law''.[50(b)] Here again it is abundantly clear that the procedural safeguards were heightened to the position like that of 'Raj Dharma' of Ancient Indian law.

After the declaration of American Independence when the concept of fair trial was given a prominent place in the constitution and the Bill of Rights, the framers included the more important procedural safeguards which were transformed into the liberties of Englishmen and Americans.

More specifically to provide safeguards, the framers who drafted the Bill of Rights broadly laid down the procedural guarantee in the Fifth Amendment. ''No person'' it says, ''shall be deprived of life, liberty or property without due process of law nor shall private property be taken for public use, without just compensation''. The phrase ''due process of law'' is more comprehensive than the phrase ''law of the land'' used in the *Magna Carta*, which was its progenitor, and provided that no person be proceeded against unless there is violation of an existing law. It has been observed that 'Due process of law' includes much more than this; "it guarantees that, when a person is proceeded against for violation of a law, the government will act fairly and will accord him all the procedural safeguards comprising fair play, within the concept of ordered liberty. The short phrase 'due process of law' thus leaves unlimited room for the evolution and expansion of the Anglo-American concept of fair play".[51] The Fourteenth Amendment again forbade the status in these words: "No state shall make or enforce any law which shall abridge the privileges or immunities of citizens of the United States; nor shall any state deprive any person without due process of law; nor deny to any person without its jurisdiction the equal protection of the laws"...

At first due to narrow interpretation 'due process' clause in Fourteenth Amendment 'dwarfed and dulled' the protection which was given to civil rights by the framers. It is said that the net result of the narrow interpretation of the privileges and immunities clause was that it was practically made ineffective. Little attention was paid to the equal protection clause and it was casually dismissed by Justice Miller. It is to be noticed that in the 'slaughter house cases' the dessenting opinions are only based upon the due process and equal protection clauses. The doctrine of due process clauses came into prominence in 1880 when the United States was having the experience of a great Industrial Revolution. "The legal system of the country was soon to be affected by big industry, big finance, the continued growth in population clustered largely in emerging urban centres, and the increased interdependence of activities. The new American Corporate interests wanted to expand and grow without fear of governmental intervention. These powerful interests which were represented by brilliant lawyers strongly committed to the *laissez-faire* doctrine, sought to forge the due process clause of the Fourteenth Amendment into a powerful tool for the protection of private property and vested interests against 'unreasonable' social legislation. Of course, a number of difficulties first had to be overcome".[52] The transformation of due process clause into an ideology was not expected by its framers. Though 'due process was not defined, it was understood in its literal and limited meaning of a guarantee for a common law procedure, by the generation who witnessed the civil war.' "It believed that due process was designed principally to provide persons accused of crime with the right to counsel, protection against arrest without a warrant, and other procedural safeguards....The framers of the Fourteenth

Amendment, too, thought that due process of law had 'the customary meaning recognised by the courts', which was unquestionably procedural''.[53] We do accept that the procedural rights, though procedural in nature, yet become substantive, to a certain extent, as instruments of protection of the substantive rights. Even before the civil war in America, the due process clause was used to protect those vested property interests, which were related to the contract clause. But it was something revolutionary when the Supreme Court also began to use due process of law to protect substantive and procedural rights against legislative action. The Court could convert the due process clause of ''into a positive, juridically enforced restriction over state legislation and began to give that protection to corporations which was available to actual ordinary persons or citizens. After 1890 the Court became a 'perpetual Censor' of state legislation. By this method a great curb was exercised upon social legislation''. ''In the period between 1890 and 1937, the court proceeded to read its own *laissez-faire* notions into the due process and equal protection clauses of the Fourteenth Amendment, and trade regulatory legislations of the states were struck down. Under this new constitutional doctrine, the Court invalidated laws regulating minimum wages and maximum hours in employment, requiring workmen's compensation, regulating various business activities, and fixing prices. The major theme of the new constitutional doctrine was freedom of contract. This is demonstrated well in the Lochner Case..., where the court defined liberty to include freedom of contract. Thus legislative interference with freedom of contract constituted a deprivation of 'liberty' without due process of law''.[54] There was again a turn after three years of *Lochner's Case*. The court began to adopt a favourable attitude towards social and economic legislation and it appeared in 1917 that Lochner-rule had been 'silently overruled'. But Lochner Case was resurrected from its grave in Adkin's Case (1923) to invalidate minimum wage-law for women and children in the District of Columbia. Again in 1936 a New York minimum-wage for women and children statute was held void by the Supreme Court as a violation of the due process clause. The due process clause, as protecting the economic rights, or substantive due process clause was consigned to a burial from 1937 to 1946. From the broader point of view the substantive due process clause has two parts. On the one hand it works for the enforcement of procedural as well as substantive rights. It has been able to protect 'a fair share of freedom of speech and association', apart from giving the well-known procedural guarantees and rights of the accused; on the other hand, it has 'substituted the judicial decision for legislative will on many issues of public policy. The American Supreme Court leaned towards the protection of the human rights of the individual even when it knew that such protection will be to the detriment of economic rights of 'the poor, the black, the illegitimate and the women'. But in 'largely unconstitutional area of judicial review of administrative agency decisions', the Supreme Court continued to show concerned for business interests, which is evidenced by its decisions against trusts which had begun to command too much economic power, on par with political power. With great difficulty it then realized that the norm of procedure interfered with the greater norm of justice. It seems that now it has been cut to size. The above discussion into the concepts of procedure become relevant and necessary to illustrate how, in the absence of a 'master-concept' or a controlling concept, the subsidiary or secondary concepts are stressed to perform the role which does not belong to them. Apart from this, the American experience is a pointer to the fact that in the absence of a basic concept incorporating the total values of a people, controversial interpretations become legion and ultimately these pseudo-concepts or subsidiary ones are used only for the exploitation of the majority by a powerful and influential minority. This assertion will find further support, in our discussion of the doctrine of the 'rule of law' which has almost become synonymous with modern democracies.

THE RULE OF LAW

Living, by law is civilized way of living. Law then must provide a complete philosophy of life to the extent that it can control human action externally, according to the desired goals of life. With all the consciousness of the proper limits of legal action, which is bred in coercion, law has an equation with life. Jurisprudence must, therefore, provide a window on life by constructing an overall concept which can progressively translate and express the urges of life in the language of the law, to provide a meeting point of law and culture by its language and phraseology, whereby law can be enlivened. Legal activity is then, a social activity and must have a common ideal. This activity in Western Jurisprudence, could not have a reference to such an ideal norm (for reasons already adduced elsewhere) but the striving Western mind has always been experimenting and testing concepts to express this over-all-relevance of life to law and of law to life. It has tried to raise smaller concepts, to the highest rank and stretched them to express this master urge of integration and cohesion of law and life to reach the highest norm which is a complete referent of our civilised existence. Because of the prominence of materialistic culture with all its characteristic disconcerted atomistic thinking about life, and its problems in isolation, the West has failed to formulate a master and integrating concept. Its jurisprudence is only a search for it and history records its failure to find out the key to life and also to law. But conceptual extensions given by jurists to reach the summit of expression and comprehension clearly reveal sincere attempts, to get at the master key which is for ever lost to them and for which they are unconsciously striving for. However, with their predominantly positivistic and materialistic approach, the Western jurists are trying to see the 'unlimited' in the 'limited'. It is like the 'desire of the moth for the star'. This is nowhere more evident than in the development of the doctrine of the 'rule of law' which has been, in a way, idolized.

The doctrine of the rule of law has also been enlarged to accommodate all the different purposes of law. The doctrine, in its simplest form, is present in the writings of Plato. Though Plato knew all the limitations of the rule of law yet he considered it indispensable. Cairns in his legal philosophy of law, observes, "It is really necessary, he (Plato) says, for men to make themselves laws and to live according to laws, or else they will not differ from savage beasts, a metaphor which Aristotle also employed. He urged this for several reasons : Human nature is such that it is impossible for man both to perceive what is of benefit to the civic life of men and, perceiving it, to be alike able and willing to practice what is best. Even if a man should fully grasp the principle that the public interest sought to prevail over private interest, should he afterwards get control of the State and become irresponsible autocrat his mortal nature will always urge him on to grasping and self interested action. It is not right for reason to be subject to anything, for no law is mightier than knowledge; but genuine reason does not exist anywhere and hence it is that we have to call on law to rule".[55] According to Aristotle, the 'Rule of law' is 'preferable to that of any individual'. The whole meaning is that one should follow the rule of law or submit oneself to it as there is no escape. This view also shows a distrust of political power which can be exploited for personal ends. 'The Rule of Law' used in the context of international society aims at settling disputes on the basis of legal rights. The order is maintained through settlement of disputes according to law. It implies, in its most general sense, the existence of public order by the authority of law. If the rule of law is to be taken in the sense of general law, most of the states are following the principle of the rule of law. But due to the rise of liberalism and the burdens of despotic rule the popular leader began to react and rebel against such regimes. The peculiar characteristic of English history is that it shows a reaction against the absolutism of Kings. At first, against the authority of King John, Barons reacted and the famous Charter was got signed into. When Barons grew weak Parliament became strong to curb the power of Kingship. In this sense, the powers of the Crown and its servants are derived 'from and limited by, either legislation, created by Parliament, or judicial decisions taken by independent courts'. It implies checks and limitations on very political authority except (perhaps), of a representative legislature. It is then an indirect expression of the principles of liberal democracy. It also implies separation of powers because merger of powers may lead to absolutism. It also implies 'equality before law', as it is assumed that 'among equals the laws should be equally administered, i.e., that like should be treated alike. "The right to sue and be sued, to prosecute and be prosecuted, for the same kind of action should be the same for all citizens for full age and understanding, and without distinction of race, religion, wealth, social status, or political influence".[56] In criminal law, together with the principle of equality before the law, the doctrine asks for limitations on the police powers of the State. The rule of law in this sense is expressed in the doctrines 'nulla poena sine lege.' It then means that categories of crimes be fixed, and punishment be given only for crimes so prefixed according to general law. The criminal be tried by ordinary legal procedure and by ordinary courts. The doctrine of the rule of law also implies the principle of liberty and Dicey formulated it on the basis of individuals and *laissez faire* ideology.

"England as most of the states in the world, travelled from the state of *laissez-faire* to collectivism and the conception of the social welfare state. With this change came the doctrine of state maternalism. The state took charge of the social welfare (education, health, employment, etc.) of the people. With the socialisation of the activities of the State and the change in its functions, the state could not but assume greater and greater power, and this naturally results in the regulation of individual liberty for social good. This development of the 20th Century entirely changed the ideological context in which Dicey had given the exposition, of the rule of law and has thereby made it inapplicable to the conditions prevailing today.''[57] The modern approach differs from Dicey's doctrine of the rule of law. Dicey's rule of law doctrine is based on the principle of separation of powers. Against this doctrine of separation of power, it is asserted that power should be considered as a means to an end and no power can be said to belong to any particular branch of Government. It may be also mentioned that the International Commission of Jurists (affiliated to UNESCO) in 1959, suggested certain meanings of the 'rule of law' which, briefly stated are:

(i) Right to representative and responsible Government and protection of civil liberties;
(ii) Adequate control of delegated legislation and remedies for individuals for wrongs committed by the state;
(iii) A fair and public trial; also presumption of innocence, right of appeal and avoidance of cruel and unusual punishment; and
(iv) Independent judiciary and organized and autonomous legal profession.

It is submitted that such a widening of the meaning of the rule of law has converted it into a moral doctrine. In its ideological sense the doctrine of the rule of law covers, the whole spectrum of ideology from that of revolutionary, to those of ultra-conservatives just as it is the case with natural-law philosophy. So, to one, it means ''the absolute integrity of private property, to another the maintenance of private enterprise free from state control and official regulation and to another the preservation of the 'right to work' against the power of the unions to determine conditions of labour. To some, the rule of law means a minimum of administrative power, even if it entails the sacrifice of good government, whereas to others it means, on the contrary, assurance of the state to all of minimum standards of living and security''.[58] In its accepted moral meaning, the rule of law puts political power at a discount and wards off the dangers which may arise out of an unscrupulous use and exploitation of political power by ambitious politicians. It will thus be seen that this doctrine which starts as a doctrine of procedure becomes a doctrine of substantive law and further extends itself to a complete legal philosophy incorporating all the moral idealism. Inspite of such interpretations and modifications as have been given to the doctrine, it has yet to succeed as an effective base to build up a just social order. It needs not much proof to show that it has failed to solve the problems faced by law viz. the problem of disharmony, mal-distribution of wealth and social justice.

Our enquiry into the main tenets of the doctrine of the rule of law was motivated to highlight the principles which, in modern democracies have taken firm roots and for reasons that have already been adduced. It was also an attempt, an humble one, to indicate that even the much praised doctrine has not succeeded to make lies of men happy and contented, nor has it succeeded in minimising conflicts, nor it has improved justice-machanism, which even today remains, dilatory, cumbersome and expensive. The humble submission of this author is that the conflicts of a materialistic civilisation are irreconcilable because they are inherent in it–they are an integral part of it. It, therefore, needs a complete reorientation of legal ideology on a different basis which as a fundamental principle may embrace not only the mere materialistic aspect of life but also emphasises the more important and vital aspect of it, namely, the spiritual and the inner cultural which form the Volksgeist of a people–a particular people.

RIGHTS AND DUTIES

No legal system can subsist without rights and duties in the sense of acts and forbearances towards others. The ancient Indian law, like any other legal systems of the ancient world, protected and recognised the interests of individuals living in the community through law. Rights and duties construed as allowances, benefits and obligations were the part of ancient Indian legal system. But the concept of rights neither developed into the concept of natural right nor did it nurture the psychology which is peculiar to the legal philosophy of the West. Modern concept of right brings with it to the owner of such rights, the sense, that he is owning these rights like property. He thinks that others owe him the duty to respect his rights. He is the owner of these rights though such ownership is called only incorporeal ownership. Such rights make men ego-centric. They only fee a concern about themselves with an unconcerned and indifference towards others and the affairs of society. This has resulted in the attitude of man to disown society and become irresponsible to its purposes. The enforcement of one's own legal rights through a legal action, which is just like a battle, is itself steeped in the idea of conflict, and quarrel of civilized combatants. To this extent the lopsided view of one's own rights generates disharmony as well as disintegration of social unity. Thus, the doctrine of natural rights seems to have given too much sanctity to the idea of individual rights.

The doctrine of natural rights 'has its birth in terminological confusion created by natural law doctrine. Robson considers that Jus Naturale produced the doctrine of natural right as a result of the ambiguity of meaning inherent in the wood 'jus'. One meaning of Jus is 'right', that which is morally binding. Jus may also be 'a right', that is, an actual and legally enforceable right. In the latter signification, jus naturale means a right of nature, a right possessing inherent validity by virtue of its own essential justice and moral force. It was from this that, the doctrine of natural rights which became the ally of freedom and a weapon of attach against tyranny was evolved.[59]

The doctrine of natural rights has arisen only due to the loosening of control in Western society at the end of the medieval age. Feudalism, a social institution waned and ethics and religion lost hold upon the lives of people and state got so pre-occupied with military expeditions that the affairs of society were neglected while individual was taxed un-necessarily. The individual had to resort to the doctrine of rights for his safeguards against growing despotism of the State. At its initial stage the doctrine of rights performed the social function by giving expression to social purposes expressed by the legal system as a whole. Economics, politics and law all worked both for the individual and the society. There was harmony between the individual ego and the social purpose. Both functioned for one another. But the degeneration set in, and process of disorganization started due to the changed circumstances. "When this process of degeneration has gone far, as in most European countries it had by the middle of the Eighteenth Century, the indispensable thing is to break the dead organisation up and to clear the ground. In the course of doing so, the individual is emancipated and his right are enlarged; but the idea of social purpose is discredited by the discredit justly attaching to the obsolete order in which it is embodied".[60]

Due to new economic relations, in the later half of the Seventeenth Century, the state itself began to be considered as a machine. Reformation had already made Church a 'department of secular' Government. Machiavelli asserted the freedom of the state to disown morality and spurn the religious yoke. In the Eighteenth Century, state and Church ceased to work for the maintenance of social ethics and for furtherance of the common ends. Now people began to consider that their economic activity was beyond the jurisdiction of morality. When the medieval democracy was shaken from its roots and the democracy of revolution was still in the womb, the Government grew indolent and aristocracy turned irresponsible, Church was now remotely concerned with the daily life of the masses, Christianity lost its great hold, God was reduced into 'frigid' categories of abstractions–and individual began to assert his independence and forged the weapon of his rights.[61]

It was said that state had no authority to infringe these rights. The existence of state is only justified in the maintenance of rights. The most important right was that of property. The whole society began to be looked upon as a joint stock company where political power and distribution of goods like dividends were to be determined on the basis of the shares of property. It was thought that no moral limitations could be imposed on the economic self-interest of the individuals. Rights then appeared as foundations of social order. The pursuit of private end began to be looked as public good. French revolutionaries held rights as absolutes of social and political order. Natural law ideology of rights was converted into utilitarian basis by Bentham and his followers. Adam Smith asserted that by economic mechanism these rights could be converted into public good. The individualists, like Turgo, Jefferson, etc. used the doctrine of individual rights to mitigate the abuses of the times–i.e., to do away with the last vestiges of feudalism which was an obstruction to free economic activity in society. Today again, due to the failure of *laissez-faire* doctrine and due to class conflicts, degeneration of society and commercialisation of human relations, this doctrine of rights has revealed its destructive visage owing to which curbs have been put on it. "In England these categories are being bent and twisted till they are no longer recognizable, and will, in time, be made harmless. In America, where necessity compelled the crystallization of principles in a constitution, they have the rigidity of an iron-jacket. The magnificent formulae in which a society of farmers, merchants and master craftsmen enshrined its philosophy of freedom are in danger of becoming fetters used by an Anglo-Saxon business aristocracy to bind insurgent movements on the part of an immigrant and semi-servile proletariat''.[62]

There has been a general reaction against the doctrine of natural rights which has become a synonym for exaggerated individualism which is unconcerned with social purposes, and is indifferent to degradation and deprivation of a great mass of humanity. It was castigated as freedom or right to exploit. It was a great obstacle for the legal science because it had extra-legal validity. Austin was of the view that rights are acts or forbearances in the context of positive law. To him the relation of right and duties only prevailed in case of relations between citizens *inter se*. Rights are legal creations. Sovereign is the creator of rights. Rights against sovereign are contradictions in themselves. Sovereign's power cannot be limited as otherwise it becomes a negation of sovereignty itself. One has no right against the sovereign. Even if it is said that sovereign has got rights, it is also a negation of sovereignty because rights can only be created by superior authority. No superior authority can be conceived of so as to grant rights to the sovereign as this will, in effect, be again the violation of the very logic of sovereignty. No one has superior power to grant rights to the sovereign. Sovereign has then neither rights nor duties. The subjects or citizens have only absolute duties towards the sovereign as he holds the power to command obedience. It is quite clear that against sovereign, which is only a personification of state, the individual can have no rights. The absolute rights are not logically admissible in the science of law as they cannot be explained in the legal relations, apart from the context of law. These rights are only relative to a particular system.

If rights are objective, i.e., if they mean allowances, benefits etc., allowed by law, one can scarcely object to the doctrine of rights. The advocates of the doctrine of rights want to subordinate the objective law to grant subjective rights as a predetermined a priori conditions of civic life. It is pre-supposed, as Kelsen observes : ''First there arise subjective rights and chief among these–property, the prototype of all subjective rights, Sand only at a later stage does there emerge the objective law as a political order, protecting and serving the independently arisen subjective right''.[63] Accordingly, the whole idea of rights is grounded in the assertion of the subjective right of property. ''The ideological function of this whole contradictory conception of subjective right is clear enough. It is intended to uphold the idea that subjective right, that is, private property, is, in respect to objective law, a transcendent, a priori category–in impassable obstacle to the construction of the content of the legal order. This conception of a subjective right different from and independent of the objective law becomes the more important when the latter is recognised to be a constantly changing order, created by men and founded neither on nature nor upon the eternal and divine will, particularly when the construction of the objective law proceeds in a democratic fashion. The conception of an independent subjective right, which is even more 'just' than the objective law, is a device to protect the institution of private property from damage at the hands of the legal order. It is not difficult to understand why the ideology of subjective right is related to the ethical values of individual freedom and autonomous personality when in this freedom property is always included''.[64] Kelsen points out that the concept of right gets undue emphasis in the legal systems of today whereas the concept of duty gets only step-motherly treatment. A legal system is, no doubt, capable and competent to confer rights on individuals but if it does not so confer them, but only imposes duties, to express legal relations, the system can successfully discharge its legitimate functions. His intention is to put the notion of duty in the forefront. Right is only a device of capitalistic legal order founded upon the concept of property to protect individual interests. In this way, the pure theory of law rejects the dualism of subjective and objective law and thereby has also removed the possibility of any ideological misuse. Legal relationships, called 'Rights' can equally be expressed in terms of duties.

The doctrine of individual right is likewise rejected by Duguit. To him the conception of subjective right is either superfluous or dangerous and he only recognize duty. According to him there is no such thing as subjective right either in the State or in the individual; the terms 'social right', and 'individual right' are meaningless. As for 'natural right', it was, like the 'general will', a term invented by the Eighteenth Century merely as a set-off against the pretensions of absolutist sovereigns.[65] Iuguit, in order to strengthen his view, quotes a passage from Comte, and recommends that it be placed in the Chamber of Deputies.

''The word *right* deserves to be banished from political terminology as much as the world *cause* from philosophical terminology. Of these two theologico-metaphysical concepts, that of *right* must hence forth be considered immoral and anarchical, that of *cause* irrational and sophistic......Right has no true meaning unless it emanates from a super human will. In its struggle against theocratical authorities, the metaphysics of the last five Centuries invented so-called human rights which at best could possess only a negative function. At the first attempt to give them a truly organic significance, they immediately betrayed their anti-social character by striving everlastingly to consecrate *individuality*. In the state of the actual world which recognises no celestial prerogative, the idea of right disappears for ever. Every man has duties towards every other man, but no man has any rights properly so called.....In other words, the only right which any man can possess is the right, always to do his duty.''[66]

According to the Scandinavian realists the metaphysique of rights is not a blessing for the real science of law. Further, the doctrine of rights does not serve the purpose of language. According to Ross, the notion that between purchase and access to recovery, something like legal right of ownership is created, is 'nonsense'. The word 'right' has got no *semantic* reference. It has originated from facts which are not remembered now. The sentences in which it occurs can be re-written without mentioning it. It only describes the legal relations of factual circumstances which entail legal consequences. The real function of rights is to describes law in force or its application in particular circumstances of the case. The concept of rights does not ''designate any phenomenon of any kind that has inserted itself between the conditioning facts and the conditioned consequences, but is solely a means by which it is possible–more or less accurately–to visualise the content of a set of legal rules, namely, those that concept a certain dijunctive plurality of conditioning facts with a certain commulative plurality of legal consequences''.[67] It appears to this humble author that the concept of 'right's has found entry into different legal systems, only to safeguard the interests of the individuals against those who are prone to disown responsibility. In order that life of the society (social, political, religious, etc.) may remain orderly and peaceful and without conflicts, the concept of right was evolved as a device to achieve these goals. Thus in Western society when social responsibility was disowned and the individual merely looked to their own interests the doctrine of natural or individual rights was formulated. It would thus seen that the doctrine of rights thrives upon distrust and dies in arrogance. It pre-supposes conflict ridden culture. It is the peculiar effect of Western culture which has started from Greece where man for the first time, was viewed a political animal. Thus begins a course of journey in conflicts, and antagonism begins, which has not ended as yet. It has its aim in harmony and co-existence, but not integration and synthesis.

The great virtue of Indian culture was that it was integrated. Therefore, no protection by way of a doctrine of rights was needed. The State, the individual, and the classes were integrated by the great concept of Dharma conceived as duty which alone was the 'Right' and the individual never thought of having the rights. Law was not the instrument of government or an agent of state nor was it an indifferent spectator to the activities of the individual. Dharma, as a law, was a total concern of Man–a complete philosophy of life and action. Man was only to do duty by which he could participate in Dharma. Right, or Dharma, like ***Brahman*** (absolute reality), is metaphysical reality, is immanent and transcendent. Every individual is the embodiment of Brahman when he identifies with it. But when he suffers from limited consciousness and thinks of himself as a limited self, he is divested of Brahmanic consciousness and considers himself separate and apart from the ultimate reality which in fact he is not. In this state of non-brahmanic consciousness he lives a miserable life. Similarly, Dharma alone is right. But when a man thinks of 'rights', he makes himself limited by his selfishness. Dharma as Right is objective but when this dharma or right is broken into rights and appropriated by people and institutions for their own interests, the sense of 'right' as good or integrating force vanishes. It results into disintegration and disorganisation. The only way to own Right is to perform one's functions well. Right can only be expressed in doing one's duty. Duty is the only passport or title of Right. The Gita rightly asks the person to do his/her duty according to dharma which is the law and according to one's station in life (Swadharma). There are no rights but only duties, what one ordinarily means by rights is what others should perform duties for him. Therefore, when one speaks of rights, he is in fact pointing towards the duties at the other side. If duty is the object of the so-called right we need not use the concept of right at all. Brahman, as has been pointed above is the metaphysical reality which is unknowable in its unmanifested form. But when it is manifested through 'lila' or 'kama' it becomes Sakriya Bralman. It is expressed in religion as Sagun Bralman or God. Its social aspect which is also the legal aspect is dharma. Which, in metaphysical aspect, is the character, function and nature of the world, the mystic force, the quality or property of all things. In order to reach Brahman one must have true knowlege. In order to reach Dharma one must have true deed or faithful performance of one's own duty. Detachment, another name of tolerance and co-operation is a *sine quo non* both for knowledge of Reality (Brahman) and enforcement of Right or Dharma. For the former, one has to de-personalise in knowledge, and for the latter, in action. Indian Ethics, Metaphysics and Jurisprudence are then variations of the same theme through different media. In the West the juristic, Summum Bonum is reached approximately through the doctrines of Natural rights, common law, public policy, equity, justice, etc. but due to their limited approaches the reach to juristic heaven is inaccessible to them. The concept of dharma includes all the Western legal ideology shorn off their antagonisms.

The doctrine of rights did not get the fruitful soil in India. In Indian language there is no appropriate word denoting only 'rights'. The Word 'Adhikar' has not the meaning of rights in Sanskrit. It is only due to the Western influence that it has taken over the meaning of rights which was necessary for the movement of freedom against British regimė. 'Adhikari' in Sanskrit is one who is fit or able or qualified for a particular task. He is not understood in the sense of a person owning power or rights. The ancient Indian is not allowed to speak as owner of the rights but he is a participant in the 'Right'. He is not in any danger of alienation of himself from society. He is not an anarchist, who distrusts state and government. To him the State is not a confiscator of rights but a follower of right. To him religion is not an institutionalised violence against other religions. Society to him is not something like a prison where there are checks or restraints on him. He never considers his civilization as a curse. The Ancient Indian lives and thinks in freshness of spirit, works for synthesis and integration through his thought and action.

The inappropriateness of the doctrine of rights is again proved by modern Indian case law and consequent amendment of the constitution several times which is nothing else but the revival of the concept of dharam which puts 'duty' on the forefront. No amount of amendment, no modification, no further borrowing from alien soils will remedy the gaps that are there until and unless were revert (making such allowances for new changes due to science and technology) to the basic Indian concept of law which is already therein in ancient concept of 'Dharma'.

Notes and References

1. The Hindu Judicial System, p. 212.
2. *Ibid.*, p. 213.
3. *Ibid.*, p. 219.
4. *Ibid.*
5. Magisterial and Police Guide by Hon'ble Justice P.N. Ramaswami, M.A., I.C.S. (1951), M.L.J., Pub., Vol. I, p. 32.
6. *Ibid.*, pp. 32-33.
7. *Ibid.*
8. Socio-Dynamics of Crime : Their cases and Cure by Prof. S.C. Thanvi, Lucknow Law Journal, 1967-68, Vol. XIII, p. 30.
9. Specific Problems of Law of Tort in India, Journal of Indian Law Institute, Vol. II, 1969, No. 4, Oct-Dec., p. 511.
10. The History of Hindu Law, T'LL-1930 by Radha Binodpal, p. 325.
11. *Ibid.*, p. 325.
12. *Ibid.*, p. 325-26.
13. Kane : History of Dharmasastras, Vol. III, p. 412.
14. Ancient Indian Political Thought and Institutions (1963), pp. 144-45, (B.A. Salatore).
15. Legal Philosophy from Plato to Hegal – By Huntington Cairns, p. 93 (Paper Back 1967).
16. *Ibid.*, pp. 256-57.
17. *Ibid.*, p. 64.
18. *Ibid.*, p. 524.
19. *Ibid.*, p. 425.
20. M. Ginsberg, On Justice in Society Pelican, 1965, pp. 147-48.
21. H.S. Maine, Ancient Law (Allen's Edition) Pub. Oxford University Press, (1959) - p. 141.
22. M. Ginsberg, On Justice in Society (Pelican Publication), 1965, p. 148.
23. The idea of La, Dennis Lloyd, Penguin Books, 1970, pp. 144-45.
24. *Ibid.*, p. 145.
25. Henry Maine – Ancient Law, Edited by Sir C.K. Allen, World Classic, Oxford, Pub. 1959 pp. 268-69.
26. The Cultural Heritage of India, Ram Krishna Mission, Vol. II, p. 514.
27. *Ibid.*, pp. 514-15.
28. Ginsberg, On Justice in Society : (Pelican Books), pp. 103-04.
29. R.H. Tawney, Acquisitive Society, p. 48 (Indian Edition), Pub – Oriental Longman, L.T.D. (Reprint 1955).
30. *Ibid.*, pp. 50-51.

31. *Ibid.,* pp. 80-81.
32. Fundamentals of Sociology, Pascual Gisbert, Pub. --Orient Longmans, Bombay, Calcutta, Madras, New Delhi, (1959), p. 142.
33. Raj Dharm, Special Number, Vedic Arth -- Vyavastha (Hindi), 15 Nov. 1970, p. 51.
34. *Ibid.,* pp. 56-57.
35. *Ibid.,* 61.
36. All men are brothers : Life and thought of Mahatma Gandhi, pp. 170-71, Navjivan Publishing House, Ahmedabad-14 (1960).
37. *Ibid.,* p. 171, Sec. 6.
38. *Ibid.,* p. 179 para 27.
39. *Ibid.,* p. 179 para 28.
40. Mahatama Gandhi : Drasta Aur Darasan (Hindi) by Dr. Badri Prashad Pancholi, Archana Prakashan, Ajmer, 1969, p. 60.
41. *Ibid.,* p. 61.
42. *Ibid.*
43. *Ibid.,* pp. 63-64.
44. Bhoodan -- Aurohana -- (Hindi) by Dana Dharma -- Adhikari, p. 70.
45. *Ibid.,* p. 75.
46. Jurisprudence -- Salmond, 11th Edition, p. 503.
47. Paton Jurisprudence ELBS, 4th Edition, 1972, p. 591.
48. The Supreme Court Speaks by Leo Pfeffer, pp. 154-55, Pub. --Indian Edition, Uni. Book House, 1967.
49. *Ibid.,* pp. 155-56.
50. (a) *Ibid.,* p. 156.
    (b) *Ibid.,* p. 159.
51. *Ibid.,* p. 160.
52. American Constitutional Law, 4th Edition by Roco. J. Tresolini, Macmillan Publishing Co. Inc., New York, p. 310.
53. *Ibid.,* p. 310.
54. *Ibid.,* pp. 313-14.
55. Legal Philosophy from Plato to Hegel -- By Hintington Cairns, John Hopkins Press, Baltimore Paper Backs, 1967, p. 112.
56. The Law and the Constitution, Ivor Jennings, 8th Edition, p. 50.
57. British Constitutional Law by Dr. Shiv Dayal, Second Edition, Pub. --All. L. Agency, pp. 73-74.
58. Law and Social Change, Friedmann-Abridged Indian Edition (1970), p. 374.
59. Robson, Civilization and the Growth of Law, p. 247.
60. The Acquisitive Society--By R.H. Tawney, Orient Longman's Ltd., Indian Edn. (Published 1955), pp. 8-9.
61. *Ibid.,* p. 11.
62. *Ibid.,* p. 19.
63. Introduction to Jurisprudence with selected texts by Dennis LLoyd, 1959, Ist Ed. p. 314 (Extract from the Pure Theory of Law by Kelsen).

64. *Ibid.*, pp. 314-15.
65. C.K. Allen, Law in the Making Edition, (1958), p. 574 (Quoted).
66. *Ibid.*, p. 576 Note I.
67. Dennis LLoyd-Introduction to Jurisprudence with Selected Texts, (1959), p. 276.

Epilogue–A Plea for Spiritual Jurisprudence

The ancient Indian legal philosophy has revealed to us its metaphysical base and spiritual character, from which ensue the concepts and theories which make it an integrated whole and a great synthesis of law, life, and experience. From its metaphysical base ensues the theory of reality as Existence pervaded by consciousness, which the Upanisads proclaim as 'Atman' or 'Brahman'. This Reality is immanent. Behind all the names and forms, facts and experiences, theories and ideas there is one which is the substratum of all and that alone lends unity inspite of diversity. The reality is not only the material essence but with its sentence, consciousness, and purposiveness, allows man, who is endowed with rational will and capacity for highest knowledge, to participate in the conscious purposes of this universe. He can identify himself with the reality itself, merge himself in it, and thereby can attain oneness and unity in the realm of actual experience which is called spiritual experience. In such experience lies man's highest realisation. But in order that a greater part of mankind can attain to such a state spiritual realisation, all our institutions, organisations, ideas, and human relations have to be oriented in such a manner as would make this realisation possible. Law is an instrument of social control and organisation and a means of human welfare and happiness. But at the same time, it is a part, nay, a vital part of the reality itself. The ancients realised this truth and were, therefore, able to formulate a legal theory which subserved the highest purposes of life. In the present age, this aspect of law which, if I were to express frankly and fearlessly, though humbly, has been totally ignored. The consequences of this lapse are disastrous for the whole human race, despite all advancement which is claimed for it. It is, therefore, humbly submitted that law must be so understood, interpreted and constructed as to perform the therapeutic function of saving us from the baneful influence of this materialistic civilization which has already de-humanised us. Law can perform this function only if the legal theory itself is to be rescued from the Octopus of Western influence and spiritualised in the light of ancient Indian legal philosophy and concepts.

The necessary consequence of a spiritual view is that all divisions, departmentalisms, water-tight compartments and reactionary views become unnecessary and our limited views are changed into a total perspective which brings integration, harmonisation, and synthesis. Spiritual jurisprudence of India does not give a distorted and broken view but a higher perspective, synthetical understanding, and an integrated study.

Law, in order to be law, must exist as a reality which manifolds itself in different forms, which manifests and grow endlessly to realise the higher purposes of life. It is not merely precept or formulation but is a living law, a working principle and an enlightened guidance which is conducive to happiness and welfare. Law partakes of the Reality, nay, it is the Reality itself. In the Vedas, law is expressed as Eternal law or Order (Rit), and is identified with Reality or God. The vision of law is not a revelation of a limited particularised truth. Jurisprudence is not a run-away attempt in solitude or Seclusion. Even the analysis of concepts has to serve as the method of understanding of the whole. When we consider law in this prospective, it appears fruitless to quarrel about theories and schools as it would then be tantamount to a negation of jurisprudence and its integrative potentiality.

To our ancients, true knowledge of science of law does not arise mere from its precept, authority, organisation, administration, enforcement. etc., but from a total concern with life and its problems. It is knowledge, practice and welfare activity. The way of study of law lies through logic, history, and ethics but does not end with them. All the particularist mainfestations cannot reveal the inexhaustible "Beyond" and the implicit "Within" or "Behind". Reason, faith, practice, experience, value, expediency, utility are means for its study and understanding and realisation without any exclusiveness, or sovereignty of any one of them. It is a healthy union of form and matter, theory and technique, interpretation and adjudication, manifest and mysterious and stability and change.

Modern antagonisms of schools and theories are nothing but the projections of our individual and social imbalances and complexes. We need an interpretative science of jurisprudence which resolves all problems, removes all confusion, reconciles all conflicts and re-channelise our energies to the task of legal development and law-reform. That is how jurisprudence can become meaningful to us. It becomes then the 'Yoga' of law, life and experiences; hence a theory of individual and social existence and an expression of progress and a project of welfare and happiness. The jurist, as logician, historian, moralist, utilitarian, pragmatist, liberalist, pacifist, engineer, solidarist, libri pens, practitioner etc. is a partner and a participant with others in the great 'Yajna' of law. Spiritual jurisprudence of ancient India looks to law as the multi-dimensional reality with all its forms, functions and meanings, law is the manifestation of One which is the True, the Good and the Beautiful which is Sat (Existence), Chit (Consciousness) and Anand (Bliss). Its knowledge lies in its realisation and by realisation alone it is known. In this knowledge lies man's real happiness. Law as part and parcel of reality has to be known from within as well as from without. The truths of Indian legal philosophy are grounded in the theory of existence and are realised through spiritual experience of our sages, seers and legal philosophers who actually said, and felt in their moments of spiritual experience the throbs of the great Existence', as an irrefutable fact. The authenticity and verifiability of this experience was so great and valuable that all their conceptions of law, prescriptions and regulations about behaviour, theorisings of man and society are founded on this truth of spiritual experience. It is due to this that it ennobles knowledge, refines sentiment, sublimates passions and inculcates the sense of service and sacrifice and thus transforms our social and political existence. By evolution of a method called 'Yoga' they have opened the doors of spiritual realisation to all those who have spiritual thirst. It is under the impact of this spiritual thirst. It is under the impact of this spiritual culture that Indian mind merges and obliterates differences and integrates all in one and seeks in them great unity in all its diversity. This is reflected in all the facts of Indian culture and law.

Today, if we want that we should live in this world in peace and harmony, with mutual concern and mutual respect; that goods of existence are apportioned and shared by all in the interest of all; that people should participate in plans, and projects of government; that the worth and significance of human life be recognised and valued; that governments be run in the interests of its people; that classes and individuals cease to exploit each other; that citizens think in terms of their duty and become responsible; that there be no distrust between the individual and the State; that resources of matter and energy and human organisation be pooled for the greater benefit of the whole;–if we aspire for all these, we should spiritualise all our jural, social, political and economic existence in all its theory and practice.

In pursuit of science the prevalent trend of the Western Culture is more towards the exploration of matter and phenomena. The dominant characteristic of materialism is that it considers atomistic plurality as final and ultimate which is disconcerting to unity and integration. As a results of this, in life, a particularist and separatist view point is asserted. In the field of law arises one-sided theories; self-interest is boosted; schism and departmentalism is justified; conflicting interests become the permanent subjects of jurisprudence which cannot be reconciled and no workable theory is put forth. 'Duty' is viewed as bondage or slavery and 'Right' is pluralized into rights to be appropriated by individuals to forge the weapon in the war against state and other individuals. Law is viewed, either as an aspect of government and the enforcement of its policies or is viewed as a mere ritual devoid of all reality and sanctity. In the absence of the master-concept the concepts of contract, property, procedure and rule of law are heightened to such an extent with their 'smuggled ideological' content that the integrated or synthetic view of law becomes impossible.

The irony and tragedy of this materialistic civilisation is that inspite of the progress of science and accrual of the greatest amount of material comforts, in it, lurk disquiet, dissatisfaction, frustration and weariness amidst all the so-called prosperity and affluence. There is a reaction against this overpowering influence of materialism. To make this thraldom more graceful and honourable, the ideas of 'self-preservation', co-existence, interdependence, social solidarity balancing, of interests, the greatest good of the greatest number, perforce are propogated and adopted, and a somewhat different and wider perspective of law is taken and its canvas is made large and a certain mystique is employed in disguise and is expressed in guarded language to bring about harmony, integration and cohesion. The natural law doctrine thrives upon this felt-insufficiency of materialistic jurisprudence. But all these devices, by which unity is sought, fail in a large measure, because they are incomplete and imperfect. If there is no conviction and faith in the spiritual reality of law or if there is no conception of law as a total human concern, all these broad and liberal approaches are liable to be in vain and are bound to be exploited by the state, society, individual or class. However, being conscious of its weakness 'Scientism' and 'Positivism' have been modified to a very large extent in such a way that ethical or other value-considerations have been introduced in one form or the other. The legal theory is taking a dangerous turns. Historicism, putting more credence on instinct and feeling, has faith in collective consciousness, general will and spirit of the people, etc., as a result of which irrationalism has begun to undermine the systematic study of law. American realism, as judicial empiricism, puts the whole theory of law in a melting pot. All these abnormal developments and juristic hostilities are due to the extra-ordinary course, which has been taken by conflict-ridden civilisation of the West. All the conflicts, between State, individual, society and church *inter se*, have been reflected in juristic, political and social theories. This is the reason why there is separation between law, morality, religion, and metaphysics. All the distractions, in the theory of law, are the progeny of materialistic approach to life which has reached its saturation point.

It seems that a counter-reaction, against mechanical uniformity and commercialisation of human relationships and erosion of human values has also started. In the field of law, jurists have begun to realize the need for a wholesome view of law. Efforts are being made for a constructive juridique which can take integrating and synthetic view of jurisprudence. But the jurists have not yet left the materialistic pretensions and are still haunted by positivistic view points. Herbert Spencer realised that unification of knowledge should be the mission of philosophy. Jerome Hall pleaded for the integrative jurisprudence and has castigated the particularist tendency in jurisprudence. "What is needed today, in the opinion of Hall, is an integration of analytical jurisprudence, realistic interpretations of social and cultural facts, and the valuable ingredients of natural law doctrine. All these divisions of jurisprudence are intimately related to, and dependent on, one another".[1] He sees integration of fact and thought in man who is 'simultaneously rational-valuing-physical animal'. In human mind there is unification of 'otherwise disparate processes'.[2] Erich Fechner finds in law a mixture of idealistic and realistic elements. He has tried to demonstrate the inter-relations and connection between these elements in a legal order. Timasheff has shown in law there is 'ethico-imperative co-ordination'. Law presents a combination of organised power and groups conviction. The power mechanism is not more important than ethical and social considerations of law. In fact, it seems that people are dismayed by the 'single track and one-dimensional theories about law'. Professor Dennis Lloyd has also realised the need of a synthetic approach to the study of jurisprudence. In our own country, as early as 1955, Dr. Sethna, M.J., has laid the foundation of the Indian School of Synthetic Jurisprudence. Sethna wants to synthesize and harmonise conflicting ideas by merely taking a mid-way view by avoiding extremes and effecting compromises.[3] He is in search of connecting links and wants to steer only a middle course. His endeavour is to bring compromises amidst rival extremes. All that he wants is to see all jurisprudential aspects at one time or at one place.[4] In view of Roscoe Pound Sethna wants to bring all the approaches to a common focus.[5] Jurisprudence is viewed as the harp that "produces the melody of law, and the legislators, judges and lawyers are musicians who play (and sing) on the strings (the fundamental principles) of this harp".[6] To him, the end of law is the greatest good of the largest number of society. The greatest value of law is love. "Love is truth, love is beauty; love is sublime".[7] Again, he wants law to represent "the general will of people, and that judges would respect reasonable traditions, customs, and usages of long standing".[8]

All these approaches to unite juristic schools, theories, attitudes and methods, without having a theory of unity of the whole Existence with law, are liable to fail. These efforts are directed, it seems to make a digest of jurisprudential theories, schools and methods which may serve as 'Reader's digest'. This is an admixture of various theories, and with due respect to the learned author, it has to be stated that it is far from being the synthetic jurisprudence. All these attempts represent a materialistic reaction against a materialistic jurisprudence. They are inspired by utilitarian motive and do not provide us with any philosophic justification. What is needed is a complete recasting and overhauling of views about jurisprudence and its problems.

Without the faith and belief in the unity of the whole existence, which is represented and reflected in law, we cannot provide rational grounds for forging the bonds of social unity through law. In absence of metaphysical and spiritual approach all the approaches to law are half-hearted and inadequate. They are also alien to us because they do not take into consideration our culture which is predominantly spiritual. As spiritualism has unravelled the mystery of life it will certainly engage in unravelling the mystery of law. Thirst for knowing what is mysterious and unknown is still in us. Law has derived its power and hold in the past from magic, myth, music, ritual and religion and is still, in a measure, assisted by them. The Indian juristic mind of the past has also cognized suprasensible world and a state of spiritual realisation which transforms man's view about man, society and universe. The enlightened one sees the whole world as ONE and the mankind as brotherhood and on this basis devotes his life in service. He has compassion for all. All the property, power, position, and authority which create legal problems, hard to solve, become irrelevant. All the differences appear unreal and with this they seem to vanish. Man, in such a state, gets the real and unadulterated knowledge. If law has to accomplish the goals set by it for the development, progress and reformation of the individual and society it must develop according to the spiritual vision of one world, one community and one law. Man's life, then, will be full of love, sacrifice and service.

We have to realise that matter divides, disintegrates, isolates and frustrates, while spirit unites and integrates. Spiritual jurisprudence gives such a unity that all the views doctrines and parts of law are 'one' from the point of view of their nature and are many only for the sake of convenience and they never cease to represent the whole. All the distinctions and divisions, then become provisional because, in essence, they represent the one. The matter of law is impregnated with spirit or reality or higher purposes of life. What is real is what is good and conducive to welfare. The real is actual as well as ideal, i.e., value. Existence itself is value; value is inherent in existence. The spiritual base of the Indian jurisprudence is quite manifest and clear. Law arises, as has been mentioned above, as an expression of this sentient universe, possessing consciousness or 'Kama'. Rit is not only the order but is said to have magical binding force. Dharma is also described as the mystic force of this world. Satya or Existence is the existence and Reality itself, which has to be realised by the truth of spiritual experience. 'Danda' is not only a raw force but is the variant of Dharma. Yajna is not mere Sacrifice or ritual but a participation in the higher purposes of the spirit; it is as good as Yoga or merger by means of action. Karma is also causative aspect of the conscious reality which becomes the principle of moral retribution. The ultimate authority of law lies in the Vedas which are said to be revealed texts and are said to be impersonal. Even Mimansa or interpretation, with its faith in Apurva, and Vyavahar as analogical extension of Yajna and Satya (inquiry for truth) are indicative of spiritual elements. Thus, ancient Indian legal philosophy can be seen as the spiritualisation of the reality of law.

The peculiar characteristic of spiritual jurisprudence of India is that all the important concepts partake of the nature of each other. Rit (or Dharma), Satya and Yajna express order, right, duty and welfare. They can be substituted for one another. They enforce each other. In them, there is interconnection, interpenetration and mutual relevance. These are the aspects of the same reality, i.e., law.

If we believe that Indian Culture is predominently a spiritual culture and the Indian bent of mind is still attuned to the spiritualistic thinking; if we realise that spiritualism unifies and dissolves all differences and merges man's interests into those of the community or society, and encourages co-operation and co-ordination, and resolves conflicts; if its cult does away with all the injuries, harms, malpractices and wrongs of human life; if it provides the outlet for the highest type of pleasure, called bliss; if law can be a doctrine as well as practice, and a way of life and living;–let there be spiritual jurisprudence to fulfil the needs of spiritual culture of India and thereby to rescue it from degeneration and degradation. Let us model our concept of law on the spiritual foundation of our culture.

It has already blessed us with legal concepts in the past which ushered in an era of peace, tranquility, harmony and good will. Let us hope that in our efforts to make this life happier now, we do not miss to build on the wisdom of the past which, if suitably and appropriately utilized will consecrate our whole legal system.

Notes and References

1. Jurisprudence, Edgar Bodenheimer, Revised Edition, (1974), p. 163; Hall, "Integrative Jurisprudence, p. 44.
2. Synthetic Jurisprudence–Edited by M.J. Sethna, Pub. –N.M. Tripathi, (1962), p. 34, Contribution of Hall.
3. *Ibid.*, Preface – p. (v).
4. *Ibid.*, p. (vii).
5. *Ibid.*, p. 8 (Contribution of R. Pound).
6. *Ibid.*, p. 12.
7. *Ibid.*
8. *Ibid.*, p. 18.

Glossary

1.	Achara	- Practice.
2.	Adharma	- Negation of Dharma.
3.	Adhikari	- Qualified.
4.	Adhyaksa	- President.
5.	Agni	- Fire.
6.	Ahimsa	- Non-Violence.
7.	Aisuarya	- Summa Potestas, Supreme Power & Authority.
8.	Anadi	- Eternal.
9.	Anand	- Bliss, Pleasure etc.
10.	Anand-Maya-Kosh	- Sheath of Pleasure.
11.	Anathan	- Orphans.
12.	An-ritti	- Acts against orderliness–Wrongs.
13.	Anuvada	- Description of facts etc.
14.	Aparadha	- Crime.
15.	Aparigrah	- Not to commit. Adultery.
16.	Aprathstha	- No fixed.
17.	Apurva	- A Theory of Mimansa–Spiritual effect created by actions.
18.	Apurva Vidhi	- Injunctions (Mandatory).
19.	Arambhak	- That which starts.
20.	Artha	- Weath, Utility, Expedience, Political Considerations.
21.	Arthashastra	- Famous work by Kautilya.
22.	Arthavada	- Explanatory Material.
23.	Asat	- Untruth.
24.	Asvami Vikray	- Sale by one who is not an Owner.
25.	Asteya	- Not to Commit Theft.

26.	Asu	-	Magic Power which binds.
27.	Atharvaveda	-	One of the Vedas.
28.	Atman Kam	-	Self Love.
29.	Bhagini	-	Sister.
30.	Bhasa Pada	-	The Plaint.
31.	Bhoodan Yajna	-	Sacrifice of Land, Land Distribution Movement started by Vinoba Bhave.
32.	Bhrhat	-	Wider.
33.	Brahman	-	Absolute Reality.
34.	Chala	-	Chicanery.
35.	Damdupat	-	Interest should not be more than double of principal.
36.	Damna	-	Restraining from wrongful action.
37.	Dana	-	Charity, Distribution.
38.	Dana	-	Force, Punishment.
39.	Danda-Dhara	-	Wielder of Danda.
40.	Dand-Niti	-	Science of Punishment.
41.	Danda Parusya	-	Assault & Battery.
42.	Devtas	-	Powers.
43.	Dharme	-	Law, Duty, Religion etc. (Chapter. 3)
44.	Dharman	-	Eternal Statute.
45.	Dhamani (Plural)	-	Eternal Statutes.
46.	Dhan	-	Wealth
47.	Dhany Purush	-	Wealthy Persons, Good Persons.
48.	Dirga-Sruta	-	Long Tradition
49.	Ghee	-	Butter Oil
50.	Havis	-	Offering.
51.	'Himsa'	-	Injury.
52.	Indra	-	War God.
53.	Ishwara	-	God.
54.	Kaivalya	-	Salvation.
55.	Kalivarjya	-	A Doctrine of 'Unsuitability due to Kali Age'.
56.	Kaliyuga	-	Age of Decline.
57.	Kama	-	Enjoyment, Joy.
58.	Kantak-Sodhana	-	Weeding out Thorns.
59.	Karma	-	Action, Law of action.
60.	Karma Kand	-	Ritualism.

61.	Karuna	- Compassion.
62.	Kriya Pada	- The Adducing of Evidence.
63.	Ksatriya	- Fighter Class-Ruling Class.
64.	Kuldharma	- Dharma of Family.
65.	Kutumba	- Family.
66.	Lakshmi	- Godess of Wealth, Wife of Vishnu.
67.	Lila	- Play, Maya, Power of God
68.	Lobha	- Greed.
69.	Lokik	- Concerned with this world.
70.	Lok Smagraha	- Welfare.
71.	Lok Vivista	- Intolerable to the public.
72.	Madhuparakor	- A Meat Preparation.
73.	Mahabharat	- Epic of Great Battle.
74.	Maitri	- Friendship, Brotherhood, Goodwill.
75.	Mandala	- Part, Group
76.	Matsya-Nayaya	- State or condition in which Bigger Fish Swallowing the Smaller.
77.	Maya or Lila	- Magic, Power of God.
78.	Mimansa	- Interpretation of law and Texts.
79.	Mimansakas	- Interpreter.
80.	Moksha	- Liberation.
81.	Mudrita	- King's, which affixes seal.
82.	Nyaya	- Logic–a system of philosophy.
83.	Niravana	- Liberation.
84.	Nirnya	- The Decision.
85.	Nisedha	- Prohibition.
86.	Niyam Vidhi	- Directory Rule.
87.	Paran Patria	- Guardian, Parental.
88.	Paripalanam	- To nourish
89.	Parmatama	- God.
90.	Pataka	- Sin, Wrong.
91.	Pradestr	- Officers of King.
92.	Pradvivaka	- Judicial Officer.
93.	Prajapati	- God.
94.	Praja-Suya-Yajan	- Yajna for the benefit of Public.
95.	Prakirnaka	- Miscellaneous.
96.	Prakriti	- Nature, Prakrit in Sankhya as one of the reality.

97. Pratijna - Plaint.
98. Pratisidha - Negative Injunction.
99. Praja Paripala - Protection of the subjects from dangers.
100. Praya Schitta - Expiation.
101. Preya - Pleasurable.
102. Puranas - Mythological Books.
103. Purusa - Primal Being; also Reality
104. Purva Pakash - Questioner, Opposite Views.
105. Purvi - Which has happened before.
106. Raj Dharma - Kings Duties.
107. Raja Sasana - Edicts of The King.
108. Rig Veda - 1st Veda.
109. RKS - Rig Ved Sahita.
110. Rishi - Sages, Seers.
111. Rit - Order.
112. Sabha - Assembly.
113. Sabhyas - Members.
114. Sachidanand - Existence, Consciousness & Bliss.
115. Sadachar - Virtuous Conduct.
116. Sam - Equal, Common.
117. Samanveya - Balancing, merging reconciliation, Harmony.
118. Sampatidan Yajna - Sacrifice of Wealth.
119. Samsiddhi - Equalisation of view or creating equal conditions.
120. Samya Charika - The rules agreed upon.
121. Samya Yoga - Having one view for all.
122. Sanatak - Student.
123. Sarvabhut - Fully made, great, completely, offered.
124. Sasan - Ordinance, Administration.
125. Sastras - Precept, Texts, Codes.
126. Sat-Chit-Anand (Sacchidanand) - Reality (Existence-Consciousness-Bliss).
127. S.B. - Sathpath Brahman
128. Satya - Truth, Reality, Truthfulness.
129. Satyayugh - Age of Purity.
130. Shakti - Power.

131.	Shanti	- Peace.
132.	Shastrakars	- Authors of Dharmasastras, Jurists, Interpreters.
133.	Shree	- Wife of Vishnu
134.	Sista	- Positive Injunction.
135.	Sistas	- Learned Virtuous.
136.	Smriti	- Remembered Text.
137.	Smritikars	- Writers of Smritis.
138.	Sresthin	- Belonging to Traders.
139.	Sreya	- What is good.
140.	Sruti	- Revealed Text.
141.	Stridhana	- Woman's separate property.
142.	Subhasadas	- Members.
143.	Sudra	- Fourth Varna.
144.	Swadha	- Potency.
145.	Swa-dharma	- One' own Dharma or Duty.
146.	Tapas	- Austerity.
147.	Tyag	- Detachment.
148.	Upedesh Sastra	- Didactic.
149.	Uttar Pada	- The Reply.
150.	Vadicrat	- Action by the Plaintiff.
151.	Varnas	- Classes.
152.	Varta	- Vow, Ordinance of Gods.
153.	Vasudeo Kutambak	- One world as one family.
154.	Veda	- Revealed Text, Sruti.
155.	Vibhag	- Division, Partition, Inheritance.
156.	Vibhutis	- Aspects, Forms.
157.	Vidhi Vakya	- Injunction, Rule.
158.	Virat	- Cosmic, Primal Being.
159.	Vishnu	One of the Gods, Collective Consciousness.
160.	Vivad Pada	- Issues, Topics.
161.	Vratam	- Command of Gods.
162.	Vridhan	- The Old.
163.	Vradhitan	- Diseased, Patient, ailing.
164.	Vyavahara	- Litigation, Law in Action.
165.	Yajna	- Sacrifice, Ritual, etc.
166.	Yajnamana	- Sacrificer.
167.	Yajnic	- Who performs Sacrifices.
168.	Yugdharma	- Law according to age.

Chronology

I. ANCIENT PERIOD (2000 B.C. TO 1200 A.D.)

Periodical Division (From Ancient to Modern)
Ancient :

(a) *Rig Vedic Period* – (4000 B.C. to 1000 B.C.)
(b) *Later Vedic Period* – (1000 B.C. to 700 B.C.)
(c) *Last Phase of Vedic Period* – (7th B.C. to 8 B.C. to 1600 B.C.).
(d) *Sutra Period* – (6th to 2nd Century B.C.)
(e) *Epic Period* – (600 B.C. to 200 B.C.)
(f) *Puranas* – (300 A.D. to 600 A.D.)
(g) *Smriti Period* – (600 A.D. to 900 A.D.)

II. MEDIEVAL PERIOD (1200 To 1700 A.D.)
–Commentators, Compilation Etc.

III. MODERN PERIOD (1700 A.D. TO ONWARDS)
– Digests etc.

Note : This is only a broad demarcation. Dates are not exact.

Kinds of Literature :

1. *Vedas* - Rig, Yajur, Sam, Atharva.
2. *Brahmanas* - Matters related to Yajna etc. in Prose.
3. *Aranyakas* - Yajna dealt in Philosophical method.
4. *Upanishads* - Last Parts of Aranya Kas – are Philosophic works.

5. *Vaidanganas*		Literature created to make Vedas intelligible – Its parts. 1. Education 2. Meter 3. Grammar 4. Nirukta. 5. Kalpa 6. Astrology.
6. *Vedanakramani*	-	List of Verses of Vedas, Names of Rishi, Kinds of Meter and Devatas addressed.
7. *Sutras*	-	Knowledge given in Aphoristric Style 1. Saur Sutras 2. Graha Sutras 3. Dharma Sutras.
8. *Epics*	-	Ramayan and Mahabharat.
9. *Smritis*	-	Remembered Texts.
10. *Puranas*	-	Mythology and History.

11. Commentaries and Compilation of Dharmasastra works.

Dharamasastra Literature related to Law :

1. Dharma Sutras.
2. Smritis.
3. Commentaries, digests and compilations – Medieval Period and Modern Period.

Chronology of Literature – Jurists and their famous works :

Writers and Important Works.

(Many Dates are Probable, some are controversial)

(4000 B.C. to 1000 B.C.)	- Vedic Sahitas - Brahmanas - Upanisadas	(Rig Veda) (Sam Veda) (Yajur Veda) (Atharva Veda.)
600 B.C. to 300 B.C.	- *Dharm Sutras of Gautam.* - Apastamba, Baudhayana, Vasistha.	
500 B.C. to 200 B.C.	- Geminis – Purva Mimansa.	
500 B.C. to 200 B.C.	- Bhagawat Gita.	
300 B.C. to 100 B.C.	- Artha Sastra of Kautilya.	
200 B.C. to 300 A.D.	- Manu Smriti.	
100 A.D. to 300 A.D.	- Yajnavalkya Smrit.	
100 A.D. to 300 A.D.	- Vishnu Dharmasutra.	

100 A.D. to 400 A.D.	-	Narada Smriti
200 A.D. to 500 A.D.	-	Vaikhanasasmatra Sutra.
200 A.D. to 500 A.D.	-	Commentator of Gemini-Sabara.
300 A.D. to 500 A.D	-	Brihaspati Smriti on Vyavahar (Still not available).
400 A.D. to 600 A.D.	-	Katyayana Smriti (Not still available).
500 A.D. to 550 A.D.	-	Varahmir author of Panchsidhantika, Brihatsahita, Brihajajatak etc.
600 A.D. (Before)	-	Harita Dharma Sutra.
650 A.D. to 700 A.D.	-	Kumaril's Tantra Varticka.
600 A.D. to 900 A.D.	-	Majority of Smritis–like Parasara, Sankha, Deval-Pitamba.

Commentators and Encyclopaedic Writers and Digests

800 A.D. to 850 A.D.	-	Visvarupa – Commentator of Yajnavalkya.
825 A.D. to 900 A.D.	-	Medhatithi–Commentator of Manu.
966 A.D.	-	Uttapal–Commentator of Varahmir.
1000 A.D. to 1050 A.D.	-	Author, Dharesvara, Boja Deva.
1080 A.D. to 1100 A.D.	-	Vijnanesvara–Commentator of Yajnavalkya–and Authority of Mitaksara School.
1100 A.D. to 1130 A.D.	-	Nibandhakar–Laxmi Dhar.
1100 A.D. to 1150 A.D.	-	Jimutavahan of Daya Bagh School.
1110 A.D. to 1130 A.D.	-	An Aparaka–Commentator of Yajnavalkya.
1150 A.D. to 1200 A.D.	-	Smrityarthsar of Shreedhar.
1150 A.D. to 1300 A.D.	-	Hardutta–Commentator of Gautam and Apastamba Sutras.
1200 A.D. to 1225 A.D.	-	Smritichandrika of Devan Bhatta.
1150 A.D. to 1300 A.D.	-	Kaluka–Commentator of Manu.
1275 A.D. to 1310 A.D.	-	Shree Dutta, author of Pitra-Bhakti, Samaya Pradeep etc.
1300 A.D. to 1380 A.D.	-	Sayan–Translator of Vedic Sahitas and Brahmans.

1300 A.D. to 1380 A.D.	- Madhavachariya–Commentator of Parasar Smriti–Parasara-Madhaviya and authorr of other works.
1375 A.D. to 1440 A.D.	- Sulapani, Commentator of Yajnavalkhya–Dipak Kalika and author of other works.
1400 A.D. to 1450 A.D.	- Vivad Chandra of Misru Misra
1425 A.D. to 1490 A.D.	- Vachaspathi–Author of Sudh Chintamani, Tirth Chintamani etc.
1500 A.D. to 1525 A.D.	- Sarsavati Vilas edited under the Patronage of Raja Pratap Dev. Rudhra.
1520 A.D. to 1575 A.D.	- Rughunandan, author of Sradh Tatva, Thirth Tatva, Suddhi Tatva, Prayaschit Tatva etc.
1590 A.D. to 1630 A.D.	- Nand Pandit–Commentator of Vishnu Dharma Sutra, Vaijayanti and author of Dattak Mimansa, Sradh Kalplata, Suddhi Chandrika.
1610 A.D. to 1640 A.D.	- Kamalakar Bhatt–author of Nirnya Sindhu and other works.
1610 A.D. to 1640 A.D.	- Virmitrodaya of Mitra Misra.
1610 A.D. to 1645 A.D.	- Nilkantha–Author Vyavahar-Mayukha and other works.
1790 A.D.	- Kashinath Upadhyaya.
1730 A.D. to 1820 A.D.	- Bala Bhatta–Bala Bhatti, His Commentary on Mitaksara.

Famous Commentators :

Sabra – Commentator of Jamini (200 A.D. to 500 A.D.)

1. *Names of Commentators of Manu :*
   (i) Medhatithi (825 A.D. to 900 A.D.)
   (ii) Govindraja (1090 A.D. to 1110 A.D.)
   (iii) Kalukas (1150 A.D. to 1300 A.D.)

Note : **Many dates are probable and some are controversial. They have been taken from Kane's Dharmasastras.**

2. *Commentator of Yajnavalkya :*
   - (i) Yijnanesvara (1080 A.D. to 1100 A.D.)
   - (ii) Aparaka (1110 A.D. to 1130 A.D.)
   - (iii) Sulapani (1375 A.D. to 1440 A.D.)

3. *Commentator of Gautam and Apastamba Sutra–Hardatta* (1150 A.D. to 1300 A.D.)
4. *Commentator of Parashar Smriti*–Medhavacharya (1300 A.D. to 1380 A.D.)
5. *Commentator of Narad Smirit.*
   Asahaya – (About 800 A.D.)

Bibliography

Adhikari Dana Dharma - Bhoodan-Aurohan.

Allen C.K. - Law in the Making Ed. 19

Altekar - The Course of Dharma.

Aristotle - Politics (Penguin Classies).

Austin - The Lectures on Element of Jurisprudence

Barker - Introduction to Natural Law and Theory of Society Vol. I, 1934.

Barker - Principle of Social & Political Theory.

Barker, Earnest - Greek Political Theory - Plato & his predecessors, Pub. Metuen London 4th Edition, 1951.

Barter - Law, its Origin, Growth and Functions.

Basham, A.L. - The Wonder, that was India, Publication - Roopa & Company, 1967.

Bentham - Limits of Jurisprudence Defined.

Bentham - Theory of Legislation.

Bentham - Principles of Morals & Legislations.

B.G. Gokhale - Indian Thought - Asian Publishing House.

Dr. Bhandarkar - Some Aspects of Ancient Hindu Polity. The Mahindra Chandra Nandy Lectures, 1925, Published by Benaras Hindu University, 1929.

Bhave - Binoba - Bhoodan Yajana (Ahmedabad Navjivan Publishing House).

Bodenhelmer- Jurisprudence.

Bose, Abinash, Chandra - The Call of the - Vedas 2nd Edition, 1960 Bhartiya Vidya Bhawan.

Bryce - Studies in History & Jurisprudence.

Buckland - Some Reflections on Jurisprudence, Law, its Origin, Growth and Functions.

Cairns - Social Philosophy from Plato to Hegel.

Cairns Hintingtoon - Legal Philosophy from Plato to Hegal - Paper Back, 1967.
Castberg - Problems of Legal Philosophy.
Cohen - A Critical Sketch of Legal Philosophy in America.
Cordozo - The Nature of Judicial Process.
Cose & Rosenberg - Sociological Theory.
Datta & Chatterjee - Introduction to Indian Philosophy.
Dennis Lloyed - Jurisprudence - Ed. 1st.
Derrett - Introduction to Modern Hindu Law.
Diamond - Primitive Law.
Dias & Hughes - Jurisprudence.
Dias R.W.M. - Jurisprudence - 3rd Ed., 1970.
Dicey - Law and Public Opinion in England.
Divakar, R.R. - Upanishad in Story & Dialogue, Bhartiya Vidya Bhawan.
Divatia, H.V. - Art of Life in Gita - 1970 Bhartiya Vidya Bhavan.
Diwan Paras - Modern Hindu Law - 1972.
Doyal, B.B. - Vedas & Allied Scriptures.
Duguit - Law in the Modern State.
Ehrlich Pride F. - Fundamental Principles of Sociology of Law.
d'Entreves, A.D. - Natural Law - Published by Hitchinson University, Library, London.
Fellex S. Cohen - Ethical Systems and Legal Ideals.
Fridrich Carl Joachim - Philosophy of Law in Historical Perspective.
Fried Mann - Legal Theory.
Friedmann - Law in Changing Society - Indian Edition.
Friedmann - Law and Social change-Abridged Indian Edition, 1970.
Friedmann - Communist Theory of Law.
Fuller - Law in Quest of Itself.
Fuller - Problems of Legal Philosophy.
Gandhi M.K. Edited by J.P. Chandra. - Gita, the Mother.
Gandhi M.K. - Hindu Swaraj or Indian Home Rule, 1944 - Navjivan Pub. House.
Ginsberg - On Justice in Society.
Ginsberg - Law & Public Opinion in England in the 20th Century.
Gisbert Pesoual - Fundamental of Sociology - Pub. Orient Longmans Bombay, Calcutta, Madras, New Delhi, 1959.
Gokhle - Indian Thought Through Age.
Good Hart - Modern Theories of Law.
Good Hart - English Law & Moral Law.

Gosh - Hindu Law.
Gray - Nature and Source of Law.
Gurvitch - Sociology of Law.
Hall Jerome - Studies in Jurisprudence Criminal Theory.
Hart - Concept of Law.
Hart H.L.A. - The Concpet of Law.
Hearn - The Theory of Legal Duties & Rights.
Hegel - Philosophy of Right.
Holland T.E., - The Elements of Jurisprudence 7th Ed.
Holmes - Common Law.
Jenks - The New Jurisprudence.
John D. Finch - Introduction to Legal Theory.
Dr. Jolly - Sacred Book of the East.
Jones J. Walter - Historical Introduction to Theory of Law.
Kelsen Hans - What is Justice.
Kelsen - Communist Theory of Law.
Kane - History of Dharmasastras.
Kautilya's - Arth-Sastra.
Kunhan Raja - Fundamentals Problems in Indian Philosophy.
Lass Well - Power & Personality.
Llewellyan - Jurisprudence.
Lloyd - Introduction to Jurisprudence.
Macmillan - Spiritual & Moral Value of Mankind.
Maine - Dissertion on Early Law & Customs.
Maine - Village Communities in the East and West.
Maine - Lectures on Early History of Institutions.
Maine, H.S. - Ancient Law.
Mazumdar (Editor) - History of Culture of Indian People Vol. I Vedic Age.
Misson Ramakrishna - The Cultural Heritage of India.
Pannikar, K.M. - The Idea of Sovereignty & State in Indian Political Thought.
Paton - Jurisprudence.
Pfeffer Leo - The Supreme Court Speaks.
Pound - The Spirit of Common Law.
Pound - Social Control Through Law.
Pound, R. - Interpretations of Legal History - 3rd Edition.
Pond Roscoe - Law & Morals.
Radhakrishna - The Bhagavadgita.
Radhakrishnan & Charles - A Source Book in Indian Philosophy.

Radha Vinod Pal - History of Hindu Law (Tagore, Law Lectures).
Hon'ble J. Ramaswami, P.N. - Magesterial & Police Guide.
Rawls John - A Theory of Justice.
Robert Lingat - The Classical Law of India.
Robson - Civilization & the Growth of Law.
Roco J Thesolini - American Constitution - Mecmillan Publishing Co., New York.
Ross - Law and Justice.
Salatore, B.A. Ancient Indian Political Thought and Institutions - 1963.
Salmond - Jurisprudence - 10th Ed.
Dr. Sampurnanand - Evolution of Hindu Pantheen.
Sarkar, U.C. - Epochs of Hindu Legal History
Savigny - On the Vocation of our Age for Legislation and Jurisprudence.
Sen Gupta - Ancient Law.
Sen Priya Nath - Hindu Jurisprudence - Tagore Law Lecture, Published by University of Calcutta -1918.
Setalvad - Common Law in India.
Sharma, C.D. - A Critical Survey of Indian Philosophy.
Dr. Shiv Dayal - British Constitutional Law 2nd Ed.
Subramania, K. Bala - Hindu Ideals - Pub. Vidhya Bhawan.
Tawney R.H. Acquisitive Society.
Prof. Thanvi S.C. - Socio-Dynamics of Crime : Their Cases & Cure - Lucknow Law Journal, 1967-1968.
Vardachariar, S. - The Hindu Judicial System, p. 82.
Vinogradoff - Lecture on Early History of Institutions.
Vinogradoff - Common Sense in Law.

Index